Anything is Possible

*The true story of the little psychic who didn't
have a clue*

Lynne McGee

Contents

First published 2024
Paperback ISBN: 978-0-6450403-9-5
Ebook ISBN: 978-0-6450403-8-8
All information correct at the date of publication.

Published by Lynne McGee
Editing and Design Laura Boon, Its All Write

About the Author

Lynne McGee. B.A., Dip Clinical Hypnotherapy, Dip Stress Management Consultancy (Counselling), Dip Life Coaching., Dip Polarity Therapy, Dip Therapeutic Massage

Born in South Wales, U.K., Lynne emigrated to Australia as a child in 1969 and received Australian citizenship in 1985. She has spent her life pursuing her love of formal learning while also pushing the boundaries of her alternative skills, dabbling in psychic and mediumistic abilities, teaching tarot and psychic development, and testing herself to see what her otherwise ordinary, human mind can achieve. She enjoys encouraging others to do the same.

You can correspond with Lynne on Facebook: https://www.facebook.com/Lynne65writes/

Acknowledgments

To the strangers I met at a Tarot Party who encouraged me to teach what I lived, and became my first students, here it is, the book you predicted I would write one day not knowing that I had always wanted to write.

To my husband of almost forty-two years, you are and always will be my rock. I couldn't have chosen a better man to do life with. I love you and our wonderful girls so much, and I thank you for putting your wholehearted support behind my little project.

To those who befriended and supported me, through all or any of my life challenges, and listened to my endless, often late-night chatter. Hugs to you. You are still my best people.

Lastly, to my editor, Laura Boon, laura@itsallwrite.com.au, big thanks for all the time, effort, and excellent advice and support that you have given to help make my dream come true. This story could never have shone without your help.

Foreword

7 years of age: I want to write a book. I want to be the next Enid Blyton. I am completely unaware that my own life is already more 'magical' than anything she had ever written.

10 years of age: I am going to write a book when I grow up. I want to teach and become an author.

18 years of age: Other people: 'You should write a book. People want to know this!' I am withdrawn and scarred, not ready to share. I have survived a severe and debilitating illness and a detailed Near-Death Experience.

24 years of age: Married and, ironically, now editing other people's books.

32 years of age: I am too tired to write that book. I have a chronic illness, and I'm a mum of two children I'd been told that I medically shouldn't have. What can I say of interest now? What matters? I write and bin poetry that no-one gets to read.

39 years of age: Other people: 'You have to write that book. It's not too late!'

41 years of age: I sit in a coffee shop for hours on end and write that book.

42 years of age: I find an agent. Start the amendments following advice. My daughter is diagnosed with stage 4 cancer. Writing is cast aside.

45 years of age: I dig out my manuscript and completely rewrite it. Submit to an agent. Computer corrupts all files. Receive an automatic rejection. Struggling with several health challenges, I give up on the idea and put goals aside. Staying upright is a struggle.

50 years of age: I retrieve smatterings of my original story from computer files and commence an unenthused rewrite simply out of fear of forgetting the order of events due to an ageing brain and chronic illness.

53 years of age: I set a timeline aside. I judge my expanded story to be unbelievable, true though it is. Illness has broken my confidence. My enthusiasm has died. I keep a copy of the timeline and outline only for personal reference. I don't want to become the old lady who 'forgets when'.

60 years of age: I am constantly fatigued due to chronic diseases, but I again think of writing 'that book' and fulfilling my childhood dream. I don't want to have 'on my deathbed' regrets. It is, after all, a completely unique story. I did, after all, want to be a writer, an author. I realise the urge is not dead yet after all.

62 years of age: I sign up for a couple of short writing courses and enjoy writing again, but I complete nothing. I get hit with illness, operations, a house move and job loss. I am locked out of my state for weeks due to Covid, my husband is diagnosed with cancer triggering unexpected PTSD on my part. This is immediately followed by the loss of both parents in a two-month period. I am broken. Barely functioning.

64 years of age: I sign up for a 'short book' writing course. I am teamed up with a random stranger to be 'Book Writing Buddies'. We both leave the course in a short period of time but meet online once every two or three weeks and get to know each other a little. It turns out that our pairing connection is far from random. The universe had plans for us to meet all along. We both continue to write. I set a goal. I will complete my manuscript before I turn 65. It's now or never!

65 years of age: The book is completed just before my birthday. I become the author of an unpublished and unpolished manuscript at last. Without that original timeline, kept from so long ago, I would have struggled to recall the order of some events. I am ageing and that's okay. I am here. The fact that I remember the story at all is a living miracle. A doctor reminded me recently that a human brain begins to melt down at a body temperature of 42C. Mine reached 47.3C and less than three months later, I started a university degree. That fact alone should convince you that **'anything is possible'**.

Author Note

To protect the privacy of individuals and to focus
more on the phenomena than the characters I have
chosen to not attribute a name to anyone
mentioned. Most I am no longer in contact with.
Some are now deceased, and I would not risk
offending any remaining family members.
Hopefully, if you have any of the skills that I
mention you will find it easier to relate to. Easier
to stand in my shoes and understand my reactions
to these events. Hopefully, this will make your own
journey easier.

Chapter 1

Birth

In the beginning there was a woman in labour lying on a bed and about to give birth. Not that I knew what she was doing. The atmosphere was cold, at least it seemed that way to me, although I had no idea why when I was feeling nothing but fear. There were two other ladies in the room, attending to the woman in pain. I had no idea where I was except for the fact that I was looking down at them from a very high and dark place. I remember feeling scared to the point of terror at the responsibility I was expected to take on, and I also remember feeling like I was running out of time. There was some kind of urgency to make the decision and jump, a move I had to make, and what I remember more than anything is I did not want to make it. I just wanted to go back, although to this day I do not know where 'back' was nor what it signified. All around me was blackness, except for the view beneath me, down there. Somewhere outside of me, in the dark space that surrounded me, a voice spoke mind to mind. No words were heard and yet words were understood. They were clear, masculine in tone, and in English. I had to make a choice. I had to go now. Right now! There was no more time. I seemed to have made a commitment, but still, I was terrified. I did not want to go. Then, as if against my better judgement, something inside of me also said I had to go. An inner voice this time. I could not fail. I could not chicken out. The next thing I heard was crying. I had arrived.

The woman I had seen in pain, was now referred to as my mother, and was handed the parcel that was me. To be clear I did not relate to myself at all. I was just all in my head, or perhaps just all brain, as I was completely unaware of my body. As my mother looked down at my form, she screwed up her face and spoke. Instantly the atmosphere in the room became frigid, and the two women attending to her seemed to harden. Their eyes met, and one of them hurriedly turned away and hastily cleaned up while the other leaned over and looked directly into my eyes. Her emotions were soft, that much I felt. However, when she looked at my mother again, she spoke to her in an icy voice. None of this I understood. I was only feelings. A small bundle barely alive, feeling. The feeling felt wrong.

Years later my mother would recount her first words upon being handed me after birth, and they were not pleasant. She had thought I was ugly. I was overdue, very wrinkled, and to her disgust I had long hair not just on my head but all over my little body. Being outspoken and blunt, she went right ahead and told me what she thought. It was probably not the best start to a relationship, but when you have the facts, the world does make a lot more sense.

I have a very vague memory of being held by my father, feeling his jumper against my cheek and even the colour of it, but my mind can no longer retrieve the details beyond the fact that unlike my mother he instantly made me feel safe and loved. As an adult I came to realise that it was my dad I bonded with first. He was my safe place. After that, I have no other clear memories until day three of my life.

The woman who was my mother was holding me at the time I became aware of my surroundings. There was a voice coming from her side, not close enough for me to see a person if I even knew what people were; certainly I had no names for them by day three. My mother was sitting in a bed and holding me when the lady to the side of her spoke again, and I found myself being passed over into this stranger's arms. I felt no fear. I didn't feel anything. I was just a package being handed around. I became aware quite quickly that this lady was more slightly built than my mother, she was gentler, and somehow, she was kinder. The lady held me and murmured something at my mother and as they conversed, she slowly looked down straight into my face, and our eyes met. In that moment I felt love pouring into me, love that I had no memory of feeling up to this point, love that was still a feeling I had no name for yet, but it was in that moment, as we gazed at each other, that I fell deeply in love with my grandmother. It was the most exquisite feeling that I remember to this day.

My grandmother murmured some words only to be spoken to in a harsh tone by my mother. I cringed. I cringed not at her words but at her tone, for words were meaningless. Then the noise started. I had no idea what the noise was, and I had no idea where it was coming from. I just remember disliking it. Without warning my mother leant from the bed and took me off my grandmother, instantly breaking that feeling of being basked in love. I remember my mother being less than gentle. Words pattered back and forth, my mother sounding snippy and hard while my grandmother was soothing. My mother's voice changed yet again as another woman appeared at the end of the bed. Instructions were given as this woman leant forward and took me from my mother. In that instant every fibre of my body dissolved, and the noise that I so disliked intensified phenomenally. I knew I needed to stay with the lady even if I didn't know who she was. I needed to stay with my mother.

As an adult this all makes a lot more sense than it did at the time. The noise I heard was me. I was crying. I was due for a feed. My mother had pressed a buzzer and a nurse had come to collect me to return me to the nursery where I would be bottle fed, a decision my mother had made before my birth. My older brother, just one year older than me, rarely slept through the night, and she was already exhausted.

That was the start of a life I did not want to live, a life I remember being afraid to take on. A life that began with a memory I cannot verify, and yet a memory that remains clear in my head to this very day. It seems to have always been there. Now, you may think this is too bizarre to be real. What child has memories of being three days old, and what fool claims to have memories of a time before they were born? Well, as I said, I cannot verify a time before I was born, possibly no-one can. However, when I was about sixteen years old, the memory of meeting my grandmother was so clear that I decided to check with my mother to find out if it could possibly be true, and if so, what her memory of the occasion was. I told her first what I recalled and then she told her side of the story.

'When you were three days old your grandmother decided to come and visit "the new baby" while I was still in hospital. You had been brought from the nursery for visiting hours as she had let the hospital know that she was coming. Well, as you know, I didn't particularly get on with your grandmother, and so when she arrived, I continued to hold you until she asked if she could hold you herself. She took you from me and looked down at your still hairy face and had the cheek to tell me how beautiful you were! You weren't at all, so I was instantly angry with her insincerity. Horrid woman. Then shortly afterwards, maybe five minutes into her holding you, you started crying. I called the nurse and gave you to her to take back to the nursery to feed because I didn't want to do it with your grandmother there. It's what they did in those days anyway, and I didn't have to feed you myself as you were on a bottle. By the time the nurse took you away you were screaming your lungs out, and I was glad to see you go.'

Thanks Mum. If the change of atmosphere in the delivery room hadn't been enough then I'd say that this 'giving me away to be fed' when I desperately wanted to be with you was the end of any hope we had of truly bonding. This action and attitude set us up for life. I was glad to have my memories confirmed, though, and my mother did at least have the grace to be utterly amazed by the accuracy of my own memory of the event. In actual fact she found our chat quite mind blowing and couldn't wait to recount what she'd been told to my father.

So that was me, 'in the beginning', so to speak. This was how I viewed my world. I was different to most babies from the start.

Within a few weeks there was huge frustration as I became stronger and fully aware that I had once been able to speak, to communicate effectively, and suddenly all I could do was cry. I recall sobbing my little heart out one day because 'they' had taken my ability to speak away, and all that I could ever get out was a cry or a gurgle, but never any words. 'They' being whosoever it was that I'd communicated with before my birth. A 'they' I was completely certain were real, even if I now couldn't recall who they were or what they looked like. I found this both infuriating and frustrating. Strangely, I felt the loss of language skills were a punishment and wondered what I had done wrong and why I was being punished this way, and that of course made me cry more.

This memory is as clear as day, as is the tightness I felt in my chest as I thought it. All crying episodes, however, ended in my falling asleep, and then waking up having put the frustration behind me until the next time. Looking back, I seem to have been mostly baby but with these almost adult, or older child, thoughts and feelings.

Six weeks after my birth I lay in my cradle and came awake to my brother's pudgy face close to mine as he leant over and rubbed my cheek while uttering words that I did not comprehend. I can safely say that at six weeks of age I did not understand the English language and that this frustrated me as much as not being able to speak it. I felt that I had spoken it before. Before when? Before what?

He blabbed on for a couple of minutes and then disappeared from my view only to appear at the kitchenette in my line of sight. Then something interesting happened; a wave of fear passed through my body and all my senses became alert. Simultaneously, my chest tightened. Within seconds he was climbing the cupboards, and as he pulled himself up, with great difficulty, from one handle to another, I became terribly afraid and my heart pounded. I struggled to focus as he reached the bench top, and, holding on to the handles still above his head, he proceeded to edge his way over to the other side of the kitchenette. All I felt was danger. I didn't know why I felt this way, and I didn't understand the situation. I can only think that this was instinctive animal behaviour because I don't even know why, at six weeks of age, what happened to him, or what might happen to him, was any of my concern. My world was tiny, and I had no experience. I did not know that if children fell from that height they didn't necessarily bounce, and yet, I was frightened.

I was six weeks old. This meant that my brother was one year and seven weeks old, plus a couple of days at the most. He should not have been climbing unaided on kitchen cabinets.

The little monkey reached the end of the kitchenette and almost fell. He regained his balance with difficulty, grabbed for another cupboard handle, and then, with only minor fumbling, he opened the cupboard door and pulled out a packet of chocolate biscuits. Realising he could not climb back across the bench, he hesitated for perhaps two minutes, frightening me when he once again almost lost his balance, and then, having decided what to do, he dropped the biscuits onto the bench below and retreated the way he had come. I lost track of him after that. I do remember my world went black for a short period of time until suddenly something very rough was being rubbed on my face around my mouth. I squirmed to get away from it and started that horrible cry that I had swapped language for.

The crying quickly woke my mother. and then all hell broke loose. My memories for some years to come went like this: my mother loudly questioning my brother as to how this mess got on my face. My mother asking him loudly and scarily where he got chocolate biscuits from? My mother finally asking how on earth he got up to get them out of the cupboard. There was no doubt he had been up there because he left the cupboard door ajar.

This was the moment I became aware of the act of lying, as my little blonde-haired, blue-eyed, gorgeously chubby brother burst into tears at the ferocity of her questioning and cried several times, 'Din did it! Din did it!'. The little love could not yet say my name and so he called me Din. My mother's voice was loud, I was afraid of her. The next minute she was standing over me with her face not far from mine, and I felt something even rougher on my face than the chocolate biscuit my brother had bitten before rubbing a piece around my mouth. My mother was scrubbing my face with a washer to remove the marks, all the time telling my brother off. She was hurting me in a way that he hadn't, but she didn't seem to care, or notice, or perhaps both. She then turned towards him, somewhere beyond my vision, and as she continued to berate my poor brother, I heard the crinkling of biscuit paper before once again my world turned black, and I was once again asleep.

I was a teenager and my older brother had gone to university in another town when one afternoon, over a cup of tea and a biscuit, I found myself telling my mother about my brother's adventurous climb to get the chocolate biscuits. Her mouth dropped open in amazement, and her eyes turned to saucers as she swore, before saying, 'All this time we had no idea how he got them out of that cupboard. It never entered our heads that he would have the dexterity to climb up and get them out without falling! Well, there you go, mystery solved after all this time!' She confirmed my story, my memories, were completely accurate, including her cleaning chocolate from around my baby mouth, and once again she marvelled over the ability of a baby's brain.

We are all so much more capable than we think we are. I am certain that within each of us these memories are tucked away somewhere just waiting to be retrieved. The problem is that most of us don't know how to access them, and while I don't think that most of us need to, I'm sure that Nature didn't intend us to keep these early memories up front. All I know for a fact is that at this tender age I didn't feel safe. I hadn't bonded with my mother and her personality was quite hard. She was both young and exhausted and consequently impatient. My father was often away from home for work for weeks or months at a time, while she tended to two little ones alone, one of whom still barely slept due to having an advanced brain that was constantly seeking stimulation. She was doing it tough and that had repercussions on both her children. The loudness? That I'm afraid was just how she was.

I was seven months of age when I had my first traumatic encounter with Spirit, not that it was in any way Spirit's fault. I had eyes only for my father and then, one day, he'd kissed me goodbye, kissed my brother, kissed my mum, and walked out the door for a sea trip that was to break my heart. At the time he was a merchant seaman, and we lived in the UK in a mobile home which my mum kept spotless along with us little ones.

When he didn't return, I recall a period of grieving, but not how long it lasted. I recall the ache in my chest and what I'd now describe as a sense of loss. As he hadn't been able to move for me wanting his attention at that stage of my development, it was like the light had gone out of my world. To make matters worse, my mother, in his absence, became very short tempered, and even though we were so small she always sounded cross with us.

I recall one day she had a photographer come to our home to take pictures of me and my brother. At six and a half months, I had low muscle tone, and my mother had already labelled me as 'lazy' because I struggled to sit up and tended to lean forward to support my weight with my arms. What I didn't know then was my mother was an obsessive perfectionist in certain areas of her life, one of which was her children and how they both appeared and behaved. When the photographer eventually became impatient about trying to keep me upright and asked for pillows to help support my weak torso, I copped her wrath. I was roughly pulled into position yet again and told I was a completely lazy girl. Now while I didn't entirely understand what she was saying, I did understand from her body language and her tone that I had failed her. When tears welled in my eyes as a sickening feeling filled my stomach, I was told not to dare cry and very bluntly to stop it, to cut it out, to behave and, of course, to sit up. I couldn't do it. She repositioned me one more time as the photographer adjusted his camera and a couple of quick snaps were taken. Immediately after he left I was put down for a sleep. Six and a half months of age, and I now felt like a failure. I was sad to my very core, and knowing I was a very naughty girl, but not knowing why, my world once again went black. Sleep was a relief.

When the pictures arrived, they were delightful, but until the day my mother died the story of my ineptitude at being able to behave perfectly in front of a photographer was told every time the family album was pulled out. To this day the pictures evoke a terrible feeling of inadequacy in me, beautiful though they are. The photos remind me of both my feelings of failure and of the longing that remained inside me for my father, ridiculous after all this time. More ridiculous because I know, as an adult, that this was not ever my mother's intention.

Then my father returned.

Late one night I was woken from a deep sleep and lifted by my mother into my father's arms. Still snoozy and not fully aware, a feeling of intense love and safety rushed through my body and my world became perfect yet again. I snuggled sleepily into his arms, and as usual his thick heavy seaman's jumper brushed my cheek. I breathed in the smell of the wool, and the smell of it and him induced a feeling of pure sleepy bliss. I don't know how long she let me stay there with him. I remember how I felt. I remember his gentleness. I remember his whispering words of love, still without understanding what he said. Perfect.

Then, not realising at all the damage that she was about to inflict, my mother insisted that he take me back to bed for fear that the next day I would be grizzly and difficult to manage. He protested, but she insisted, and it was with great reluctance that they walked to my bedside where, taking me from his arms, she laid me in my cradle.

As she took me away from him my mind screamed. A

feeling of true agony ripped through my tiny form, and I sobbed hysterically. Everything in my body protested at our separation. Even while screaming I was aware of my mother saying that I was overtired, and she should not have woken me up. He wanted to comfort me, to sit with me, but she wouldn't allow it and in the blink of an eye he was gone.

I was hysterical. I felt my brain splintering. Then a lady appeared as if through the wall of the mobile home, through the cabinets that sat by my bedside. Her form emerged lightly and then solidified, and I knew her, but I didn't know where from. I felt I had always known her, and yet I have no other memories of her being with me before this time. Now I know that this lady was not a real living human; I didn't at the time, but she was tender, and she was kind, and as I turned my face hysterically towards the wall, trying to escape the pain in my head and heart, as my mind shattered, I recall her clearly saying, 'It's alright. I am with you. I am here.' She touched me compassionately on my back. Like my father this woman emanated love, profoundly gentle love. Her presence lit up the room. Sadly, my infant mind was in overwhelm. and if she had come to save me from this pain, she arrived too late. As I turned to that wall, my mind splintered and my world went black.

What fascinates me now, as an adult, is that I understood this woman even though she did not speak. It was mind to mind communication, and it was clear. I was starting to understand some language by this stage, making sense of the sounds around me. I'd understood that my mother was telling my father to leave me be and let me cry for example. This woman was different. Words were telepathic, unspoken and yet heard. I did not fear her. I simply accepted her love.

If a baby can have a nervous breakdown, and I don't see why that isn't possible, then I suggest that is what I had that night because when I woke up the next morning, I would not let my father near me. Every time he even came close, I would begin to scream. I was traumatised. My tiny mind associated him with deep pain, and for years to come I remained frightened of him. I would see other people in the park playing with my dad; he would take my brother and a herd of other young children that all played together to find conkers in the woods, or he would play ball with them outside our home. I would watch them all walking together up the hill away from our home, off on an adventure, and I would long to be with them, but the minute he came near me, I would scream. My doting dad was heartbroken. It took about eight years for me to be able to even talk to my father without absolute fear. I was in my twenties with a child of my own before that fear faded away. Interestingly, the love between us remained hidden away, in my case in some secret part of my heart, His was always waiting for an opportunity to show itself. So many years were wasted.

The lady was my first clearly remembered encounter with a spirit. I awoke recalling everything about her except a clear vison of her face. She felt like she had always been there for me. I both knew her and knew she had always made me feel loved. She became a frequent visitor as I got older and stayed with me for many years. Unlike an imaginary childhood friend, I never played with her. I never asked her to come. I never conjured her up when I was lonely. She simply appeared as I was falling asleep or just before. I don't know what she did to me, if anything, but it was similar to hypnotism, or perhaps meditation. One moment I would be lying there distressed over injustices or punishments meted out, frequently inappropriate in their harshness, and the next moment she would be at my side.

She would always tell me what to do and explain why. Sometimes I had to pull my covers up, sometimes I had to have my arms out of the covers. I might be gently asked to stop crying and to listen to her stories. Her stories were always explanations of what I was learning and why, and unlike my mother's remonstrations, they were always backed up with reassurances of love and self-worth.

On many occasions she would talk to me, and I would remember nothing she said until it was time for her to say goodbye; it was almost as if she put me in a deep trance. At no point did she frighten, scare, or intimidate me; she was always gentle, loving, straightforward and honest about my behaviours, whether they had been appropriate or not, and what I needed to learn from them. Sometimes she taught me things about the world or how to behave in it; sometimes she showed me, somewhere in my head and through telepathy, that other children were going through similar things. I never received anything but love from her though. Occasionally she would bring someone else with her, or at least, she would arrive and tell me to prepare for their arrival, so I wasn't scared by them. When I was about six, she told me her name was Sara. It didn't take me long to look forward to her visits as they were often the highlight of my month. She was almost the gentle mother my own mother couldn't be. She was, if you like, a Spirit Guide, but we had no words for them back when I was a child. No-one talked of such things.

Sara was the one who told me I was going to get very ill quite soon, but they (whoever 'they' were) would take care of me. She said my illness was going to make my life hard but that I would be alright. I was upset by that news, but if Sara said I was going to be fine then I would be. I trusted her absolutely.

Chapter 2

Childhood

Wind the clock forward a few years, and my life was unusual, but, like all children, I did not realise that. My logical mind set in around the age of eight. I started mentioning during play things that startled my playmates, made them look at me oddly and had them tell me I was crazy, so I learned to keep quiet about my nightly visitors. When you're a child, you assume everyone lives what you live. We all grow up a little before we learn that that's far from the truth.

During play with a couple of neighbourhood children, I recall mentioning something about coming out of my body at night and sitting on the roof of my house with a male figure. I mentioned this naturally and casually, along the lines of, 'You know, when you come out of yourself with the night visitors that teach you things. Let's pretend we're doing that here.'

Apparently, they weren't doing that at all and thought I'd lost all my marbles. The initial odd looks were followed by name calling, and I was never included in their games again.

They thought I was odd and through them I was discovering the same.

I had no idea of the many changes lying ahead of me, and my strange meetings with spirits, which I thought were normal and happened to everyone, were about to hit a new level. This was the sixties, and I wouldn't hear about spiritualism until I was in my late teens. I didn't even know that the beings I was seeing and interacting with were called spirits. They were my night visitors. Spiritualism, as it is now known, existed somewhere out there but certainly not in my home and neighbourhood, possibly not even in my town!

Before my eighth birthday, I was already having strange psychic glimpses. One Christmas it came to me what my Christmas presents would be and where they were hidden. I was just a child. Naturally I had to check this information out. They were hidden where I had thought, but I wasn't brave enough, or more likely was too scared of my mother, to peek inside any of the covered parcels. I had to wait until Christmas to confirm my previous psychic insights and then wonder how my brain could have known both the hiding place and the contents without having seen them before?

By this point in my life, I had started to 'visit', after bedtime, with what I believed was a young girl who lived in an old house at the bottom of our street. The house itself had an elderly lady living in it who never spoke to us children when we walked past on our way to and from school. At night though, when I was unable to sleep, I'd find myself mentally going to her garden where the little girl called Anne played until the sun went down. I assumed she lived there but never questioned the fact that I should also have seen her at school.

One evening I was lying in bed feeling very sorry for myself. I couldn't skip or jump rope, whatever it's called these days.

Mentally I thought I'd visit with my friend because it might cheer me up. I imagined walking down the road until I saw her on the other side of her old stone brick wall. That's all it took, a short walk in my mind, and I'd be there. As always, she greeted me cheerfully and then looking me straight in the eye, she asked me what was wrong. I felt safe enough to tell her, and I spilled the beans about how I felt so useless because I could not to coordinate my arms and my feet to jump rope. She went across the grass, around the corner of the building, and returned with a rope. She told me to watch her and to feel inside my body what I needed to do to be like her. To feel my legs, my arms, my tummy and my chest. As I watched my body came alive and parts connected in a way they hadn't before. She handed me the rope over the wall and told me to just do it. I wasn't afraid. I was excited. I stumbled first and then suddenly, almost magically, I found myself skipping. She cheered and told me to just remember the feeling when I went to school the next morning. By this time the evening light was fading, and we parted company with her saying she had to get back into bed. I never questioned this and always found myself back in my own bed immediately afterwards. The following day I was excited to go to school, and sure enough the feeling of jumping rope was still with me. Without hesitation, I was able to join in a skipping game with the other girls for the first time. I still recall one of them saying, 'I thought you couldn't skip?!' How do you explain this event to a classmate? You don't. You keep quiet, and you keep skipping.

Then there were embarrassing, unplanned, but informative glimpses I had about other people, such as suddenly blurting out, without knowing what it was, that the lady complaining about her symptoms obviously had menopause. I was dragged inside by the scruff of the neck for that one and seriously told off by my mother although I think my only crime was embarrassing her. I didn't find out what menopause was for many years. I hadn't at the time even known the word. The sentence I spoke simply appeared on a screen in my head to be read and blurted out my mouth.

Another time a neighbour was telling my mother that her little boy had been diagnosed with coeliac disease, a rare occurrence back then. When she said it, and without knowing what it was, a shiver went down my spine. I thought, 'I have that.' Fortunately, I kept quiet because I'd have been in more trouble if I'd said as much. My mum would have said I was just trying to get attention. That was a diagnosis that would have to wait for later in my life as I was headed towards another diagnosis first, one that was attributed to being caused by the loss of my grandfather.

My grandfather had been unwell for as long as I could remember. What we children were not told was that he was slowly dying of cancer and was nearing the end of his life. I became quite unwell at this point, and, worried about the coldness of my bedroom, my parents moved my bed into lounge-room next to the fireplace to keep me more comfortable. I ran a high fever for several days, and they called the doctor who unfortunately was unable to come out to visit. Our regular GP was on holidays, and his replacement was fully booked. My parents were told to take me to the hospital if I got any worse or stopped drinking.

As I lay there, possibly delirious, Sara appeared at my side. She told me very gently I was very ill and that my grandfather was coming to visit me. She informed me that he was going to take me on a little trip and that she wouldn't be able to come along for the whole journey but reassured me I would be well looked after, and she had just come to prepare me for the journey.

I don't know what she used because there was no bowl of water in the room and no clothes, but white cloths appeared from nowhere, and she wiped down my face and went through the motions of straightening my hair. She smoothed the bedclothes and then she stood back and a white light like a little tunnel appeared to come down through the ceiling. The white light turned into my grandfather. I had a special relationship with him as we had previously bonded during a time when he seemed to read my mind across the room, and, strangely, I seemed to read his. Our eyes had literally just twinkled, child to adult, adult to child, and we had both understood. I had broken the rule to stay in my chair as ordered by my grandmother and moved across to sit at his feet, and he had begun a conversation with me when both she and my mother had returned and shooed me back to my chair, telling me off for disobeying them.

Once across the room, I had looked at my grandfather, and again, silently, words had passed between us. We both empathised with each other's situation. I didn't know this was possible between two humans. It was my first experience of mind-to-mind communication with another person, but my grandfather seemed to know that this would be easy for me.

When I was very small my grandfather had already lost half his arm, which was removed to try to save him from cancer. When he appeared at my bedside, ready to take me wherever we were going, both his arms were intact. Later this fact would strike me as important, for there is something about that white light that changes the frequency of the brain and what is important to you changes with it. My grandfather spoke to me and told me he was going to take me on a little trip and then he was going to say goodbye because he was unable to return with me. He assured me I would be safe, and that Sara would be there to see me safely back into my bed.

He held out his hand, and I took it without even a thought. Then came the most amazing sensation of being lifted, up and out of my bed, and going higher and higher very quickly, very gently, with just a soft breeze against my skin. I had no feeling of illness now, nothing at all. We arrived at a wooden doorway after travelling through a thick white mist, and, as the door opened to us, I distinctly remember my grandfather saying that he would tell them he just needed a little more time.

The figure he spoke to was cloaked head to toe in whitish-grey garb, but strangely I was unable to see its face. There was some interaction mentally between him and my grandfather, then the door slowly closed, and my grandfather and I turned around to see a bench behind us in the middle of the mist. We were alone. My grandfather, leading me by the hand, took me to it, and we sat down. He proceeded to deliver information about my future, a lot of information, so much so that he told me I would not remember it all when I returned home but that he wanted me to know because I had a job to do, and he would be unable to help me, so telling me was the best that he could do. He told me again that he couldn't come back with me and that he had to say goodbye, I wouldn't see him again. That made me feel very sad, and I started to choke up.

As I did so the cloaked person came out from behind the door and stood almost politely a few feet away from us. My grandfather said, 'One more minute, and I'll come. We are nearly done.' He told me that I was not to worry about my parents and that I was part of a bigger universe and didn't belong to them; that I was loaned to them for my life lessons, and they would never own me.

I did not have a clue what he was talking about. What did he mean I wasn't my mother's daughter? What did he mean I wasn't my father's daughter? What did he mean I wasn't their child? Panic welled up inside me.

He gave me a hug. I choked up, the tears were coming. The cloaked being told him to hurry and said that the others were coming. There was a sense of urgency. My grandfather turned to look at me and spoke, 'Don't forget, you will be a healer. That is what you came to do.' Without another word he stood up, and as two more figures came to the doorway, he walked quickly towards it, escorted by the original being I had seen.

Within a split second I found myself back in my bed with Sara at my side. I was bawling my eyes out. What did he mean and what was a healer? Between my tears and my questions, I became aware that there were noises from the kitchen and footsteps in the hallway. Sara told me hurriedly that I was fine and that I was safe, that it would all be okay and that I would understand when I was older, and then in the blink of an eye, she was gone.

I turned my head to the wall and contemplated what I recalled hearing, knowing that somehow in the short space of time since my grandfather spoke to me, some of the information had already gone. The tears kept coming, and they were followed closely by panic as I tried to figure out what my parents would do if I didn't really belong to them. I was genuinely scared and afraid of them coming in to see that I wasn't theirs. I was so sad too for my brother. How would he feel if he realised that I wasn't his sister? This was all far too much for my child's brain to process. With a head full of questions and a heart full of mixed emotions, my tired mind buckled, and I fell asleep.

I awoke with a clear mind and no fever for the first time in ten days and shook my head as I tried to recall what my grandfather had said I was going to be. I couldn't remember the word I didn't know the meaning of, but it had sounded like teacher. After about ten minutes of struggle, I decided 'teacher' must have been what he said. It was many years before I heard the word healer again.

About ten minutes later my parents entered the room, and my mother exclaimed delightedly, 'Her fever's broken!' as she rushed to my side and placed her hand on my forehead. Instead of being shocked and horrified that I wasn't their daughter or sister, both my parents and my brother showed nothing but kindness and care along with delight to find me finally on the mend. From that time on, whenever I was asked what I wanted to be when I grew up, I would say, 'A teacher.' In my mind, though, I didn't see how that was possible given the other information I was given.

Just three months later I was in hospital diagnosed with type 1 diabetes. Sara's words were proven correct. I was ill. It was the mid-sixties and longevity certainly was not an expected outcome for Type 1 diabetics. At seven years of age, I learned to inject thick needles attached to heavy glass syringes into oranges and then into my own thighs. The insulin was thick like glue, and the injections hurt, causing swollen red lumps under my skin. I was taught to test my own urine with tablets that stank like sulphur and burnt me if they fizzled too far up the test tube and spat on my skin.

This diagnosis set me apart. When I returned to normal routines after four weeks in hospital, I discovered I was the odd kid in the class. People worried about inviting me to a birthday party. Could I even eat the supplied school dinners? Life was never going to be the same. What did they do if I had low blood sugar and fell into a coma? Would I die before an ambulance could arrive? I was now a concern to the adults in my world.

There are moments in any childhood that stand out. There are moments you love and moments you hate. There are moments that change completely how you see your world. My eighth birthday was one of these for me.

My last birthday party as a child was on the day I turned eight. I didn't appreciate the party, to be honest, as my mother simply bypassed me with most of the yummy food laid out on the table and bluntly said, 'You can't have it,' using the same voice she used for telling me off. The other kids enjoyed themselves, but I was miserable. I still appreciated that she'd gone to the effort to host a party as these were the days when mums made all the food from scratch, and you'd have been hard pressed to find any packets to open. She had worked hard, but although it was my birthday party, very few of the treats on offer were made for me. It made me sad. I was young enough to be self-oriented, but not old enough to know better. Instead of feeling special, I felt unvalued. I thought that the party was my mother's attempt to be the centre of attention in the neighbourhood for some reason. Looking back, I realise it might have been her way of saying thank you to the neighbours for their support throughout the month I was in hospital after my diabetes diagnosis. It may even have been her way of trying to convince herself I was still normal, and all was okay, as a diabetes diagnosis back then was still ominous and worrying to any parent. Whatever the reason, I was never to have another party.

The following day my mother collected up 'all the messy birthday cards' and gave them to me to keep to either draw or colour on for a short time. I knew it would only be a couple of days before she whisked them into the garbage bin, deeming them clutter, so I quietly looked at the pictures and read what people had written as I lay in bed that evening, once again unable to sleep while the sun poured through the unbacked curtains.

One card stood out for me. I loved it. It was of a young teenage girl dancing to a record on her portable record player. She wore a straight pastel-coloured dress with a skirt that flared just below the dropped waist. I was imagining myself when I reached her age and wondering how old she was, when as clear as anything, a voice in my head said, 'You won't grow up. You won't be her age. You are going to die before then.'

It hit me for six. It was a voice, but it was in my head. It wasn't my voice, but I'd heard it clearly, and I was both awake and alone. My mind reeled both from the shock of that realisation and from the instant conviction that it was correct. I began to cry, very quietly, but with a deep sadness that came from somewhere even deeper within. These days I call this 'The Knowing'. I don't know how I know, but I know when I feel this way that what the voice said will happen.

I cried myself to sleep, and for once, when my mother threw my cards into the rubbish bin, I was relieved. The information about dying bothered me for months. It would bother me intermittently for years to come, but soon a visit from Sara brought new and exciting information to focus on.

Chapter 3

Predictions

I was asleep the next time Sara came to visit me. I felt as if a bright light shone in my eyes and disturbed me. I rolled over to see what it was, and as I did so, I heard her voice telling me to hurry and tidy myself up. For the only time I can clearly recall, she leant over me, smoothed down my messy hair and then straightened my covers, telling me to prepare for the arrival of a very special visitor. At no point was he ever called anything but a visitor, but her behaviour was much like she was announcing the Queen was coming to tea, and consequently I became somewhat overwhelmed.

I snapped out of my sleepiness fully when she told me not to be afraid and warned that not only was he very important, but he was also very big and that he was coming to tell me some very important news before it was too late. Being so sleepy, it hadn't crossed my mind to be afraid until that point, but the thought of a big man coming into my room in the middle of the night was frightening. Did my mother know there was a strange man coming to visit me? Was she all right with it? I was about nine by this stage and had shifted into a more logical way of processing, normal for my age. Real life checks were now automatically part of my thinking.

Before fear could completely overtake me, however, Sara stepped back from the bed and said she had to leave and quickly. As she spoke, the room lit up with this extraordinary light, something I hadn't previously experienced and find hard to describe even today. Then she kind of just dissolved or disintegrated, as the light became a huge intense ball and a figure looking exactly like a Native American chief appeared at the foot of my bed as if he'd stepped out of the light.

These days, with the rise in New Age Spiritualism, this symbol is quite common in relation to spirits, but this was the sixties, and we lived in South Wales, and the only Native Americans I'd ever seen were those in movies on television, and they were, sadly, depicted as the bad guys in the television western's my father frequently watched. I had no positive image of Native Americans at that point of my life, and absolutely no reason to 'conjure' one up in my imagination. This was scary. The whole event was scary. I almost panicked and called my mother. I even opened my mouth to do so, but by then he had solidified in my vision, and my voice simply disappeared. I registered in almost the same moment that although I was still intimidated, my fear was rapidly easing. I presume this was because of my implicit trust in Sara as well as the energy he exuded. He was certainly an impressive and powerful figure but definitely not frightening. Sara told me not to talk but to listen, and I was ready to do just that. A sense of absolute awe seeped through me. At one point during his speech, though, I once again had a huge spark of fear and thought again of calling my mother. Before I could, the fear again backed off almost as soon as it started.

He was telling me the most amazing information about my future, and just as when Sara gave me information, I was far more believing than disbelieving. I don't think I doubted him at all!

According to him, we were going to leave Wales and emigrate to Australia where my life would improve. At the time we were viewing advertisements on the television trying to encourage British people to move to Australia. It looked magical to me, but I hadn't ever thought of living there. I was in Wales living through another very cold winter with minimal heating in our uninsulated home, but on the television I saw beautiful sunshine and beaches. Wales had marvellous beaches, and sometimes sunshine, but it came with bitter cold and an awful lot of rain too. In Australia there were miles and miles of wheat fields and kangaroos and koalas, magical animals in my mind. It looked like a really exciting place to a nearly nine-year-old.

He followed this with perhaps the most exciting information I had ever been told by anyone. My mother was going to have another baby when we were in Australia, and it would be a surprise, so I wasn't to say anything. It would be a little boy, and he would be born on my birthday. I didn't quite understand but it seemed he was going to be some sort of reward and that he would bring a lot of joy into my life. I didn't know what the reward was for. I really didn't understand what this was about other than that I was going to get a baby brother. Don't get me wrong. I would have been happy with a sister. I had wanted a baby brother or sister for years and had always thought that my parents would have another child. Mentioning babies would have been a huge 'no' to my mother though, who when asked if she was going to have another baby always replied that there wasn't any point as she already had one of each. It would no doubt have got me a mouthful about how rude or forward I was, so it was perfectly safe for him to tell me to tell no-one, as I wasn't going to open my mouth. I was also not allowed to talk about going to Australia.

They were the only two secrets I recall being asked to keep. He told me more, much more, all about my life, small details and bigger ones, but there was one that I didn't want to hear. I was told I was going to die. I would live to see my brother and we would have a few years together, but when I turned sixteen, I would become seriously ill and I would die. For some reason, baffling to me, this was apparently necessary and something I appeared to have signed on for. I really did not understand this. I was still a child, and it didn't make sense to tell me that I wouldn't become an adult. It was emotionally too much to deal with. I was filled with terror and sadness at once after again being told that I wouldn't grow up.

Looking back, I find it interesting that it wasn't the dying that bothered me; it was the not actually growing up and getting older that was worrisome and scary. Now of course I can wonder why that was, but at the time that didn't even register.

During his chat, he also told me some of my abilities and skills, my more unusual ones, were going to be taken away, and they wouldn't be returned to me until I was much older. This upset me. I felt almost punished by this, and just like the idea of not growing up, it added to the well of sadness inside me. I'd been slowly developing or discovering various psychic tricks such as moving objects with only my mind and a little telepathy. The moving objects skill got me a telling off for not keeping my room tidy.

I had a display of foreign dolls on my dresser. Each one had its place, chosen as always by my mother. After discovering one night when the sun lingered endlessly above the horizon that I could, if I concentrated, make one doll turn around into a new position, I practiced the skill while bored at school. It worked, but unfortunately my mother entered my room before I returned home to check out whether my experiment had worked. Seeing the dolls facing the back wall, she was annoyed, and I copped a telling off when I returned home. The telling off didn't do much good because it was offset by my excitement at the experiment being successful. I hadn't expected it to work and was thrilled that it had. I continued to practice turning the dolls at night but made sure they were facing the correct direction before leaving for school each day. This was one of the skills that disappeared shortly after the Native American male appeared to me and losing it both frustrated and angered me as I thought it wasn't fair to take this away. It had been so much fun!

After delivering his news this Native American chief, complete with headdress, simply said it was time for him to go, made me promise to keep my secrets, and then, along with the bright light, he simply shrank and became smaller and smaller until he faded away into the light, and then the light too disappeared. Sara came forward almost immediately, from my left side, stepping out of the dark and remaining in a much duller pool of light. She quickly tucked me in again, told me to sleep, and then receded into the light surrounding her, leaving me in darkness.

I cried. It was pitch black and absolutely freezing in my room. I hunched down under the blankets as far as I could get. Without either of these spirits in the room, it felt empty, abandoned. I used logic against the fear of dying, deciding that sixteen was still years away and anything could happen by then. Maybe they would come back and tell me everything had changed? I briefly wondered if I could change it, but that seemed way beyond my ability and did my head in a little, so I turned my focus to the good news. We were going to Australia, and I was going to have a little brother! I was delighted, and I fell asleep with a smile on my face imagining Australia and a new little boy running around. 'My birthday present' was the last thing I remember thinking before I fell into a deep and comfortable sleep.

When I awoke in the morning, I was aware that there were many details of the man's visit I had already forgotten. I recalled Australia and I recalled the news about dying, but most of all I recalled the fact that I would have a baby brother, and with that on my mind, I happily went to school imagining this future where I wasn't always cold and where my parents were happier. I wondered if my parents knew we were going to Australia but remembering I'd promised not to tell anyone about this, I couldn't ask them.

Six months later it turned out the Native American Indian was correct. One afternoon, my parents sat my brother and me down for a chat and asked us how we would feel about going to live in Australia. Like all parents who intended to get their own way and had already made up their minds, they fed us all the good lines, all the fun lines, the things I have already mentioned such as the beaches and the sunshine. We were children, so let's be honest and say they probably didn't need to. I'm fairly certain we both would have said 'yes' to the adventure anyway. The following day the wheels were put in motion, and my parents applied to emigrate to Australia.

Before we emigrated I was to have another unusual experience. On the way home from school a few months later I saw the old lady standing in her garden at the bottom of the hill. She was standing right where I met Anne at night. She was talking to an elderly man and didn't notice me. I crossed the road to walk up the hill to my home and as I walked, I got the deepest saddest feeling that the old lady was about to die. I hadn't seen her in the garden for several months, and she did look frail, but I had no real idea about whether she was about to die or not. I turned and looked back at her, flooded with sadness, and, as I did so, she turned her head from her companion and looked me directly in the eye. Immediately I felt feelings I simply had no words for deep inside me. There was a sense of inevitability, and at the same time a sense of knowing. I didn't know what to do with it, so I turned and trudged up the hill with her on my mind.

Two nights later, unable to sleep, I went down the hill via my thoughts to speak with Anne. To my surprise Anne seemed to want to avoid me. She stayed back in the garden not coming to the wall until I became upset and asked what I had done wrong. There would be no skipping and no playing and no laughter tonight. Seeing my distress she left the side of the house and came to the middle of the garden looking terribly sad. She told me she was going to have to go away, and that we wouldn't be able to play anymore. My heart sank, as you can imagine. She was so special to me. Who else would I visit?

I asked her where she was going, and she simply replied that she had to leave, and she wouldn't be coming back. As she spoke, she looked up to what I had always presumed was the old woman's bedroom window. The curtains were already drawn, even though it was still early for an adult. My gaze followed hers, and this strange deep sadness I'd felt on the way home from school filled me from my stomach through my chest and up my throat into my head. I looked at her and told her I would miss her, and then she said something incredible. She told me we would meet again a long time in the future and that I would recognise her even though she would not look like her current self. She told me that I would know her by her eyes and that I didn't need to be sad because although we couldn't play together now, I would at least see her in the future. She said that our future meeting would let me know that I was on the right path and was just a reminder. I was about to ask her what she meant when she suddenly looked up at the window above us and quickly told me she had to go inside. She spoke with urgency as she looked up quickly to the window again, then back at me, said a quick 'Goodbye', and ran around the back of the house as if her parent had just called her indoors for being naughty. If they did, I hadn't heard them.

In a blink I found myself at home crying my eyes out, sitting upright in my bed, and feeling immensely sad and incredibly lonely as if I had lost my best friend. I snuggled down for comfort pulling the covers right up to my chin even though it was a warm evening, and I thought of her words, 'You will know me by my eyes,' and 'We will meet again.' I really hoped we would.

The next morning I was miserable and had the strangest feeling that my brain had been changed for ever, but at just nine years of age, and with limited understanding, dealing with this type of thing was very difficult, even more so because I didn't have a trusted adult I could talk through my emotions with.

A week later as I walked home from school, I checked out the house once again. It looked and felt empty. All the curtains were closed. I presumed that Anne had moved away with her family, but the feeling I got was that the old lady had died. No-one in our street had previously died as we lived in a newly built housing estate, so I had no reason to think the lady had died or that was what the closed curtains symbolised, but still, I felt sad, for both reasons. As I continued up the hill to home, I noticed my mother and a neighbour having a chat outside our home. I shook back my sadness and prepared to be polite to the neighbour. In my mother's eyes, it was unforgiveable to allow moods to influence public behaviour.

Like the good daughter I tried hard to be, for fear of repercussions if I failed, I politely waited for my mother to finish speaking when I arrived, and then I said a quick 'Hello'. My neighbour acknowledged me with a smile, and continued chatting, asking my mother if she'd heard that the old lady at the end of the street had passed away the week before? As she spoke, the lady's eyes looking into mine flashed before my face, and I saw, for the first time, the resemblance to Anne. They seemed to be the same person. I felt suddenly nauseous, confused by my own thinking. Surely that couldn't be correct. I was being silly. Suddenly I was simply overwhelmed with sadness. Inside, something told me this was true. Logic told me loudly it couldn't be. Regardless, the lady had died.

I was glad when they stopped chatting, and Mum and I finally went inside, but that night, as I lay in bed waiting for the sun to go down and my room to finally darken, a space opened in my mind. Could Anne and the Old Lady really be the same person, and if so, how was that possible? I wracked my brain trying to remember if I'd ever seen them together. I hadn't. I thought of the times Anne would suddenly say she had to go inside because she was being called, and how she would then quickly turn around and run around the corner of the house. I thought about the one time I asked her why her front door was never open and how she'd looked uncomfortable for a minute, until her face cleared, and she told me she wasn't allowed to bring dirt in from the garden so always used the back entrance. I recalled too how she had immediately relaxed when I accepted her answer.

I still couldn't work out how they could both be the same person. Not once did it enter my head that if my body was actually lying in my bed, it shouldn't be possible for me to also be down the street playing with Anne, albeit always on the other side of the gate.

I was quite a few years older before it all clicked into place that the Old Lady was lying in bed asleep and coming to meet me in Spirit, often giving me simple advice and lifting my mood. When Anne was suddenly called by the voice I never heard, her body was beginning to lift out of sleep and her spirit needed to return. The Old Lady had known she was dying; in the form of Anne, she was able to warn me that she had to go away and wouldn't be returning. To this day my mind boggles over this and while I may never have proof that this is indeed what was occurring, the experience has remained with me as the most logical answer, based on future learning and experiences that I have since lived through.

Anne was right. I was to see her again, but much would change for me before then.

We received our flight tickets to Australia in August 1969. I was ten, almost eleven, when we headed to Sydney. The process of leaving friends and relatives was tumultuous and gut wrenching. My mother, true to her nature, brooked absolutely no tears from either of her children. We were not allowed to express our natural feelings of sadness at leaving the only home and people that we had ever known, but we were allowed to show excitement about the upcoming adventure.

On the train trip to the airport, my mother's workmates, who worked in a factory café along the route, had gathered to wave her on her way. As the train slid past, they wildly waved tea towels to farewell her, making sure the train passengers saw them. My mother waved back, and then began to cry, and my father hugged her.

Nothing sets a child off more than the sight of their mother crying and tears slid down my face as I literally felt her sadness pass through me. Instantly cross, she jumped on me. 'Don't you dare cry! Stop that nonsense!' Her voice was harsh and commanding. I choked my tears down with a struggle, but due to her initial sadness rushing through me, I had a deeper understanding of the enormity of her own feelings and was aware that for her this was no adventure and was actually very hard. I was to remember this in the months to come as I cried silently at night in the Immigration Hostel. I knew that behind her tough exterior my mother probably cried too.

Being a child, the fascination of our new country and its different ways were both scary and educational. Unfortunately, I didn't like either my teacher or my new school, which compared to the one I'd been to in Wales was massive. I found the change emotionally difficult. There were a few other immigrant children there, but instead of bonding as a group, there was some sort of competition to be the best, the strongest, the smartest. I presume they felt a need to prove themselves in their new environment, but I just felt like I was drowning, to the point where I dreaded going to school each day, something I'd formerly loved. I was delighted when a couple of months later our mother told us that we were going to join our father in an inland mining town that was much smaller than Sydney. I hoped that the school would be as well. Naturally we were all very excited at the thought of joining my father after so much time apart. My brother and I were excited, as this time we felt that we were heading off on a real adventure. My mother, who knowing more about the place, was feeling very wary of her upcoming new home, and it showed.

Chapter 4

Spiritual Warnings

A bout a month later I started school 'Out West' as people referred to it. Initially I wasn't keen on it either, mainly because it was so different to anything I'd ever experienced, but it was much smaller and the teachers were a lot less formal than in Sydney, and I soon settled in, even though other students made it obvious they thought I was 'odd'.

Children will always point out your oddities, and Out West they wasted no time doing so. My crimes were apparently twofold: having a Welsh accent, which they struggled to understand even though I spoke only English and wearing white ankle socks with Clarks sandals. Many of the children didn't even wear shoes! This was indeed a whole new world.

What they didn't know was that I too thought it was odd to wear white socks in a place where gutters and playgrounds were piled high with red dust. Dust that was added to and subtracted from on an almost daily basis by dust storms that blew in seemingly from nowhere and headed out in a similar direction. The classrooms had louvred windows, and the dust blew through the gaps even when they were closed and blanketed all within in red grit. My socks didn't have a hope of staying white, but my 'You will be pristine!' mother insisted both my brother and I wear them, not realising this made us stand out as odd in our new environment and made us the target of many jokes and insults for the first couple of months. We were saved when we went to high school because there the white socks, hilariously to us all by then, were compulsory.

In just one term I had mostly adjusted to our new life, helped I think by the fact many of my classmates were also imports from different places and various countries. We at least had that in common and were able to relate by talking about what our other country or town had been like. By the time the school year ended a few months later, I was looking forward to returning the following year. I had no idea my 'weird' would kick in again by then in a far more significant way.

When the new year started there were more new faces, not unusual for a mining town. One of the older schools had closed and some of the pupils had been allocated places at our school. Amongst them was one little girl that I took a shine to and fortunately she felt the same way about me, so we became good friends. She was my first friend in Australia. We started walking home together and would separate at her gate while I continued walking onwards to my own home.

A few months into our friendship, after a class in which we discussed World War 2, we found ourselves in a conversation about our feelings on both war and soldiers as we trudged home through the heat and dust piles that filled the gutters. She was not normally an intense person, but suddenly and unexpectedly, her eyes filled with tears, and she blurted out that she was scared that her dad, who had been a soldier in the early part of World War 2, had killed people. Having spoken the words aloud, for the first time in her life, she began sobbing. What happened next was beyond anything I had so far experienced.

As the tears rolled down her cheeks, I felt my spine fizzle as something passed through me from the top of my head to my feet. A whiteness filled my brain, and I started to speak, reassuring her, explaining that soldiers rarely have a choice in war and that if he had shot someone then it was to save the lives of others or his own, which didn't make her father a bad person as she feared. He was simply, awful as it was, doing his job. I had never thought of this before. I had no idea where the words were coming from. I hugged her and kept talking and explaining until the light cleared and the fizzing in my spine stopped.

She stepped back and said that she'd never thought of war like that and thanked me for making her feel better. Meanwhile my own logical mind was going over the words I'd spoken with something bordering on amazement, because they were completely new to me too and showed a perspective which I'd never had cause to think about. My own grandparents spoke often about the war as their home had been bombed several times, and I knew all about rations and blackouts. I had heard stories of my grandfather doing both blackout patrols and digging people out of the rubble of their bombed homes, of my nan and my mum running through their burning home town as it was blitzed. These deeper thoughts about a soldier's choices were, however, completely new to me.

I told her she should just think about her future because we couldn't change anything that had already happened, after which she quickly became animated and told me of her plans for her future. I had only vague ideas about my future at that young age, so I was very surprised when she said confidently that she would be getting a job as a secretary at the mine, work for two years and then go to London. As she elaborated, I broke down inside, and I can only describe what I felt as 'internal weeping'.

I became a bit harsh, choked up, and told her she was young and should maybe change her plan. The fizzing feeling in my spine had returned in full force, and all I knew was that she must not follow her plan to go overseas. Every time she said the word London, I felt utterly nauseous. In the end I spoke bluntly; she still had time to change her mind but that she shouldn't go to London. She was shocked both by my voice and my words and tried to convince me that what she believed was an excellent plan. I wasn't buying it. Everything in my body screamed 'No!' as soon as she mentioned London. When I asked her 'Why London and not somewhere else?', she said that of course she would go to other places too but that she really wanted to go to London. We ended up having our first argument as she was understandably hurt that I didn't like her life plan and was almost nasty in the way I was talking. I remember telling her I was happy she wanted to be a secretary, and that was great, but she shouldn't go overseas, but I didn't know why, and then, just like it had started, the fizzing in my spine stopped.

At this point she looked at me like I had two heads, and then stormed off to her front gate with a look of thunder. I watched her greet her mum who was in the garden, and then without a goodbye I walked off and burst into tears. I cried all the way home. I didn't understand what had happened. I didn't know why her trip overseas to fulfil a dream was an issue, but I knew beyond anything in this world that my friend should not go to London and somehow she had to be persuaded to change her plan. I prayed she would forget this goal by the time we grew up.

I was upset for weeks after our talk. Our friendship continued, a little tentatively initially but grew stronger as the year progressed. I slowly put what had happened behind me, but I did remain convinced that my friend must never go overseas and fulfil her aim of going to London. Then, once again, life distracted me with the news that the Native American chief's words had come true. My mother was pregnant.

Not that I knew it at the time, but the pregnancy was supposed to have been impossible as my mother had had her womb scraped just four weeks before and the pregnancy was at least six weeks along. Miracles happen, but so does incompetence; perhaps the scrape wasn't done correctly. Twins ran in her family, so later it was conjectured that our new sibling may have been one of twins initially and that his tiny little embryo was missed during the procedure. No matter, with her rushing to the bathroom to be sick every single morning, it was real. She had been told not to have more children as she had major thyroid issues and a large permanent embolism in her leg blocking the main vein, yet here she was, pregnant.

Never has a baby been more wanted. Once the initial shock passed for my parents, we were all over the moon about this 'accident'. We were all 'accidents', and we were all much loved and wanted babies, but this one, coming later in her life was the most unexpected of the three of us. No matter, he was to be adored. Many months were spent joking over names but strangely we all agreed on one thing from the start. The baby was a boy.

I lay in bed at night thinking about the chief's words and hugged them to myself. Australia had happened and now the baby. My trust in spirits, or 'night visitors' as I called them, strengthened. The months flew past in no time, and then, on my birthday, just as I'd been promised, a baby boy joined our family, and all our hearts were captured. In my eyes he was the best present a girl could ever receive, and I adored him from day one.

Chapter 5

Out of Control and Saying Goodbye

I was in high school, nearing the end of year 10 and fifteen years of age. To one side of me was a demountable metal building used for a classroom. I was on my way to my next class further along. The students inside, dismissed, erupted onto the veranda, grabbed bags from the racks outside and rushed to their next class. This was a large high school, the only one in the town, and I had taken an academic program hoping to go to university. My primary school friend had followed her choice to take a secretarial stream and so our paths barely ever crossed. I only occasionally saw her from a distance. I'd not actually spoken to her for over a year.

Suddenly she was running down the few steps towards me, her best friend in tow, shaking a piece of paper in front of her and squealing with excitement. She had been accepted by the mine to join the secretarial pool, her first job! She explained, smiling broadly, that now she would be able to go overseas in two years and that her plan was coming together. She was beside herself with excitement.

I can't say how long it took me to react but as she reached

me, her dear excited face talking into mine, I lost it. There was this tremendous vibration that went through me from head to toe and instantly I was shaking her violently by her shoulders and shouting into her face at the top of my lungs, 'You can't go! You can't go! Please don't go!' Over and over again, I shouted the same words. I was so violent her head was swinging all over the place, her face turning white with shock. At some point, I realised that two girls, one her best friend, were doing their best to pull her away from me. Just as quickly as I'd started, I let go and burst into tears. As they herded her away from me to safety, I heard myself saying over and over, 'I'm sorry. I'm so sorry.'

It took a couple of minutes and the ringing of the class bell for me to pull myself together and register that a crowd had gathered around us. People had seen this awful thing that I had done. I was shocked at my behaviour. I had no understanding of what had happened but as I hurried to class my mind was working on two different levels. On one there was a certain and absolute knowing that my friend must not go overseas, and on the other I was one terrified high school girl expecting to be reported for my violence and for all hell to break loose. I was concerned for my friend, hoping that she was going to be alright after how I had treated her, and scared by my own behaviour. These were the things that dominated my thinking for the rest of that day.

I didn't get into trouble. Not a word was said to my teachers. No report was made to the principal. I spent a week living in fear of punishment and then gradually relaxed, at least about that part of the event. I didn't cross paths with my old friend again and life gradually returned to normal. This speaks volumes about who she was as a person as most people would have made a complaint to the school principal. Their parents would have wanted me disciplined, which would have been completely fair.

My friend changed her plan. She delayed her trip by two years, saved more money and expanded the number of countries she was going to visit. When I heard that she'd delayed for two years, I was ecstatic. I was still hoping that life would get in the way of her leaving at all. I was sad when I bumped into her in a club one night almost two years later and she excitedly shared that she and her friend now had their tickets and that they were leaving in a few weeks. I couldn't help myself and once again I asked her not to go. She looked at me, straight in the eyes, and without skipping a beat, she said, 'I have to. I'm going.' I teared up and walked away.

I saw her one more time before she left. It was in the same club, and it was crowded. The bar was busy. I went to join the queue for drinks hoping I wouldn't have to wait long as it was already too hot in there for me. When I reached the bar, I ordered a drink and as I did so the crowd emptied away and there, at the other end, perched on a stool, was my old friend. She looked down the bar at me and without smiling she said, 'We are leaving tomorrow. This is my last night.'

I remember my head going spacey and odd as I stared at her and forced myself to smile. 'I suppose it's too late to tell you "Don't" now?'

She nodded gently with a strange look on her face that I couldn't interpret. Then, with a very direct and serious look, she said gently, 'I guess this is goodbye.'

Trying hard not to cry, I replied seriously, 'It is.'

It felt what it was. Final. The barman popped my drink down on the bar, and I turned to pay him. When I turned back towards her, she was nowhere to be seen. As I quickly scanned the room in search of her, the space around me filled once again with people clamouring for drinks.

Chapter 6

Impending Death and Spirit Visitors

Close to my fifteenth birthday I was lying in bed and about to drop off to sleep when a thought about dying passed through my head. I shot upright. I realised that if 'they' were right, then I was going to die in just over a year. The reality of that thought was shocking. This fear that I felt was nothing like what I'd felt as a child of eight. I was running out of years! This was too close. It was real. I wondered about the details. Would I die at sixteen, on my birthday, or would it be a few months into that year? How would I die? Would it be an accident like being hit by a car or falling off my pushbike and injuring my head? How bad would it be?

These thoughts were followed by inevitable wondering about how my parents and my brothers would feel. I decided, rightly or wrongly, that my parents would be very sad, but that my older brother, who could barely bring himself to say a civil word to me and whom I hid from in my room every time my parents left the house, would possibly be relieved that I was gone. My younger brother, however, was a completely different story. I spent the majority of my home time, and much of my going out time, with this about to be three-year-old.

Weekend ventures to the shops or to visit girlfriends usually included him 'to give my mother a break', and because I genuinely enjoyed his company. His little life had somehow given me a focus and a feeling of being loved that was missing until he came along, and as much as I could, I spoilt him. I imagined my parents trying to explain to him I had died and was never coming back, and how that would completely mess with his mind. In my head I could see his face, and my heart crumbled. I was more bothered by this than I was by the thought of my own death!! As fatigue took over, I lay back down thinking seriously of my own demise. I eventually went to sleep in tears. If I was hoping for reassurance from the night visitors, it didn't come.

The following day the thoughts of death were deliberately pushed back into their file box in my brain. The good thing about being a teenager rather than a young child is that the logical mind dominates, even if it isn't always sensible. It becomes easier to dismiss the world in your head. I didn't know that it would happen to me. I had no answers for the strange world that existed in my head but in some ways was more real than life. Therefore, I adopted my mother's attitude to life and just got on with living.

Two or three weeks before my sixteenth birthday though, I was woken by Sara standing by my bed. For the second time she told me that the Chief was coming to talk to me. Now I was older, I was more curious than fearful of all of this. These 'people' couldn't be real and yet the information they had given me had, so far, come true. I'd not seen Sara for a long time, so it was delightful to know she was still around and that being in a different country hadn't stopped her from coming to me. She was different, vaguer, misty, but the feeling of her was the same.

What happened next was immeasurably joyous. The Chief came along with his change of light and change of energy, not nearly as dramatic as when he appeared to me in Wales, but the darkness had been darker there, and the summer nights Out West are lighter, so perhaps that's why. He told me that because of my love and care for my younger brother I was being granted another two years of life. This development was unexpected, and the two years were my reward, but after that I would die and return to them.

I came out of what I would now call a trance feeling utterly elated. I wasn't going to die! I had two more years! I was unbelievably relieved and excited by this reprieve even though, consciously, I hadn't been aware of worrying about my demise.

My mother had snapped at me the day before that she hoped I wasn't expecting a party because I wasn't getting one, and I'd spent half an hour wondering what had brought on her outburst since we hadn't had birthday parties since I was little, except of course for my younger brother as he was still small. Why had she said that, and why did she sound so nasty when she did? Like most teens I dismissed it and her attitude quickly. Parents were beyond me. Perhaps they were beyond any of us?

I was excited to turn sixteen and felt like I was having the biggest party ever. Not dying was the best present! I was unconcerned that I was still destined to die at eighteen, merely ecstatic that I was not going to die in the immediate future! It was a high that lasted some days until eventually, the chores, the homework and the almost constant remonstrations from my mother wore me down again.

Over the next two years I slowly became isolated from most of my peers. I went to a few parties, where I was generally bored, and gradually realised I was the odd one out and didn't mix well with my peers. Drugs and alcohol appeared on the scene during my second year of senior high, and I, determined to maintain control and not end up in a diabetic coma, refused to indulge. I wasn't outspoken about what others did as I didn't much care as long as they left me alone and didn't try to force me to participate. In the end though, it became easier to just stay home and away from partying, so most weekends were spent in my room avoiding both my peers and my heavily smoking parents. A room full of cigarette smoke quickly made me feel unwell and still does.

My mother decided I enjoyed being alone. My father didn't think about it at all. My older brother was glad to have me out of the way. Occasionally I would spend time with one or two friends who also didn't participate in the more normal teen activities. Sometimes I'd take my younger brother along, sometimes not, depending on what he wanted to do with his day and what, if anything, my parents had planned.

By the time my eighteenth birthday was near, I didn't care about life anymore. By now I was depressed and emotionally if not physically isolated. My home life wasn't too bad as my older brother had left home to attend university down south, and so I'd stopped needing to hide in my room for fear of physical and verbal abuse from him. My mother and I had at last developed a level of rapport. Things were easier in some ways, but I knew there was something wrong with me.

My legs hurt all the time, no matter how much exercise I did or didn't do. My arms and back ached, and I physically struggled through each day. The walk to school and home left me in tears as my legs ached so badly, and I was sleeping only a couple of hours or so a night. It was my job to wake my parents each morning for my father's shift and to have their coffee on the table by the time they arose. I'd been stressing over this for a few years, but now, when I did drop off to sleep, I'd wake with a start, frightened I'd slept in and fearful of my mother's wrath if

I did. I would keep checking the clock into the wee hours, and my sleep cycle was shattered.

I was struggling with my homework, my head always seemed fuzzy, and I was extraordinarily forgetful. I dropped from an A grade student in some subjects to a C, and instead of stressing, I couldn't feel anything. Occasionally I worried about getting my end of year report and the trouble I would be in if I failed, but it was only a momentary fear, and it didn't motivate me to try harder. I stayed up until midnight working on assignments and homework after doing the dishes and making the next day's lunches, and then I had seriously broken nights. It was a recipe for disaster. I wasn't coping. The only reason I kept going at all was a deep determination to leave the country for the city by getting a university placement in the new year. Freedom depended on my academic results. I had to pass. I had to get away from this town and my home. I couldn't breathe. I was barely functioning.

I didn't think about dying at all in the week before my eighteenth birthday. Sometime between sixteen and eighteen years of age, I either forgot all about what I'd been told, or decided it was a load of nonsense and that something was obviously wrong with my mind. I no longer had Spirit visitors to my room and was very uncomfortable with the idea of them. Instead, I had started dreaming information, having premonitions during the little sleep time that I had. I had had no premonitions in the months leading up to my eighteenth. My mind went quiet. I had a couple of foot-in-mouth moments when I unwittingly told people something that I had never actually been told, such as secrets I wasn't supposed to know about parties I'd never been to, but I had no night-time visitors and no premonitions. I was depressed and struggling to exist.

It came as a surprise therefore when I woke up a few days before my eighteenth birthday feeling very unwell. My arms and legs didn't want to move, and they felt incredibly heavy. The day before, a small blister had appeared near my wrist. It was incredibly itchy, so my father looked at it but dismissed it as a midge or mossie bite. It was accompanied by a strange lethargy. All I wanted to do was sleep. This day was worse. As I struggled to get myself ready for school, I noticed that there were more of these watery looking blisters across my chest and on one arm. I'd had chicken pox a few months before and wondered if you could get it twice.

Briefly the Chief's previous warnings of getting very ill and dying at eighteen flew through my mind, and I felt a spark of momentary fear that I didn't have the energy to maintain. Heavy voiced, I called out to my mother, 'Can you come here please. I think I have chicken pox again.' I recall she chuckled, but as she came into the room telling me that that wasn't possible, she saw my face and paled. Something was very wrong with me. I looked terrible. She examined the blisters, asked about other symptoms and then went straight to make a doctor's appointment.

By the time I got to a doctor, I was fighting to stay upright. After a quick examination I was sent to hospital and admitted. By then, I couldn't sit up unaided, and the blisters were multiplying rapidly. Within a few hours my temperature was out of control and blisters covered my body. Within days they would merge in many places, some swelling to almost the size of a grapefruit as I lay strapped to a bed with drips in my arms and feet. Two amazing, newly graduated English doctors, who were doing their 'bush time' in Australia, fought both to identify my illness and to save my life. They were wonderful young men who accurately gauged the seriousness of my condition and were determined to do their best for me.

Blisters continued to form anywhere there was skin. My teeth lifted from my gums as the blisters emerged in my mouth and throat and enveloped my teeth, which, in turn, stuck to them and moved as the blisters grew larger. I was blinded as my eyes blistered over. Every part of my body was itching and in severe pain as the blisters stretched my skin, and then stretched it further as they filled and expanded with liquid, much of which became infected, and in some cases burst, causing excruciating pain as they grew too large and my skin gave way to the pressure.

This was a country hospital. They wouldn't have me in intensive care because they didn't know what was wrong with me and were afraid I might infect the other patients. They couldn't put me on a ward for the same reason. They had nowhere to put me.

Eventually, after some discussion, they had the cleaner empty a room used for storing cleaning goods. It was a narrow room with a small basin and just enough room to fit a bed with a chair right next to it. The room, which still held some floor mops and buckets inside the door, became my isolation room. Not knowing this, I thought I was delirious when I kept seeing cleaners pop into the room with dirty buckets of water and plonk them just inside the door, all the while looking very confused to see me in a bed inside the room. On one occasion, as I lay only partially covered by a sheet, most of my body exposed to the air, one lady stood in the doorway and stared at the mess I was. By then I was too weak to protest her staring at my nakedness, but not too weak to feel humiliated by it. Even a dying girl can still feel that.

Behind the scenes my mother was running a different battle for my life. The hospital director, was advised of my condition, and my mother, strongly supported by my attending doctors, requested that I be flown to a city hospital. The director refused to authorise the request, but the fight continued. A week later, he told my parents that I was dying and could die just as easily where I was and didn't need care elsewhere. My parents, determined to get me the best help possible and advised by the attending doctors that they didn't have sufficient equipment at this country hospital, went to the bank and asked for a loan to privately fly me to the city. One of the English doctors, working hard to save my life, was incensed by my treatment, and so supportive he offered to lend my parents the money himself if the bank refused the loan. The kindness of some people is astonishing, and I am still touched by his generosity to this day. They got their loan though, the bank was a little kinder, and the Director reluctantly signed off on the paperwork necessary to equip and transport a patient on a Qantas flight to Brisbane. I knew nothing about this. I was just trying to survive.

My mother arrived at my bedside the morning after the loan was granted, and basically bullied me into 'staying with it and coughing my heart up.' I was semi-delirious for most of this time and have only vague memories of her sounding really cross with me and automatically obeying her out of fear. She just kept waking me up and yelling, 'Cough! Harder! Harder!' I couldn't tell whether this went on for a short or a long time; all I knew was I wanted her to stop, but she wouldn't let up, and eventually I floated into oblivion, her voice becoming indistinguishable from the sound of my breath. I was to find out later she had spent approximately four hours getting me to clear my lungs as I was drowning in my own fluids. She carried out two large basins of infected fluids I coughed up before she gave in and let me rest.

The day before I had refused, by violently shaking my head, to have a tube put in to drain the fluid. Because I was now eighteen years old, they legally weren't allowed to override my wishes unless I wasn't able to tell them otherwise. My mother tried to convince me to have the tube inserted up my nose, but I wasn't having a bar of it. I was lucid at the time, and I still remember this voice speaking inside me when the nursing staff, and then my mother, asked if I would allow them to insert the tube. The voice just kept saying 'No!' in a commanding tone, and my gut began screaming not to do it. Even in that condition I followed my intuition.

I think I knew I was dying when I desperately tried to get through to my mother that I wanted to see my father. He'd not been to the hospital at all due to his shift work and minding my brother while he was home so my mother could be at my bedside. I'd asked for him a few times in my garbled way, but this day I was adamant. The trouble was making myself understood with a mouthful of large blisters now starting to bind together and pulling my teeth from their gums, and a head full of nonsense from the pain medication and antibiotics they'd filled me with to try to keep me alive. Eventually I got my message through, and my father arrived. I couldn't see him at the end of the bed, my vision didn't extend that far anymore, but I could hear his voice and made some noise. The blisters had clouded and distorted my vision like a fish-eye lens, and my world was closing in. Intuitively my mother realised what was wrong and got him to move closer. Once I saw him lean over me, I was happy. Everything was alright. I'd heard his voice. I'd seen his face. He cared enough to visit me. He left after what seemed like a short time, and I felt this incredible sadness that I couldn't identify. I didn't want him to leave. I really didn't want him to leave and there was some type of desperation attached to this feeling. I was to feel this same unidentified feeling again, only this time accompanied by a deeper fear, the following day.

My mother sat by my bedside, chatted to the nurses in a serious tone as they came and went, disappeared for intervals and returned. She always returned. In my consciousness I was aware of this just as I was aware of the group of trainee doctors who came in to visit when she was absent, pulled back the sheet leaving me naked and stood around talking about my condition as if I was just a piece of meat on a slab.

I couldn't talk, I couldn't form words at that point, but the humiliation I felt as they stood there with the door to the room wide open to all who walked past was phenomenal. My brain told me that between the cleaners, one or two random others that had come to stand and stare at me from the doorway and these doctors I had no value. I was not important, worthless. I did not matter. Mortified I felt like a piece of meat, an object to be viewed, no longer a person, no longer of any worth. My mind crawled into itself to escape the total humiliation I felt.

At some point a nurse who had attended to me for the first two days of my admittance came back on shift and burst into tears at the sight of me saying, more to herself than to me, 'What have they done to you! Oh, darling what has happened?'. She gently fussed around me for about five minutes, lifted a cool cup of water to my blistered lips and made me feel like I mattered. She genuinely cared, a very special lady indeed. My mind rebalanced itself a little through her care. I did matter. I mattered to my family. I mattered to this nurse. I wasn't worthless. I had to remember that I mattered!

The next day my mother arrived a bit later than was her norm. The doctors had gone, the door remained open, my almost nakedness remained on view. She told me that she would be leaving early as she had to go home to pack her bag and sort things at home for my brother and father. I was to be flown to Brisbane the following day, and she would accompany me. I tried to tell her that I didn't need to go, that I didn't need a plane. I didn't know why I didn't, I just knew I didn't. Apparently, nothing I said made sense at that point though; my words were far too garbled.

I did realise, briefly, that things were very bad if I was being flown somewhere, but consciousness escaped me and my mind drifted. It was just something that was going to happen. Another thing I had no say in, no control over. I was emotionally disconnected from events outside of my circle of illness now, not able to communicate this didn't really matter anymore. It would just happen regardless. Inevitability is a state, I discovered, where the mind takes a step back and just rides the wave.

The day wound on, and I came in and out of consciousness. It was one of the calmest days I had had. I was running very low on energy and the ability to fight this illness. I was exhausted. I slept.

For the first time, I objected to my mother leaving me. I didn't know what was happening, but I didn't want her to go home. I made my feelings clear even though I had little ability to talk. She stayed longer, and then longer, but finally, she went, and I dissolved. I felt unbelievably scared, abandoned, bereft; something I'd not felt on other evenings when she'd often left much earlier for a variety of reasons. Previously I had been accepting but not tonight. I remember thinking quite clearly in my distress that she must not go 'now'. Not Now. Not when I was going. How could she leave me at this point. Did she not know? I felt completely abandoned and, grieving, I slipped into unconsciousness yet again.

Somewhere deep inside me, I knew that I was dying, and that death was close. I now believe that all animals have this sense of knowing when death is approaching. I have seen the changes in behaviour in aged pets. I have heard it from my own father who expressed it clearly as, 'I am not sure how much longer I can last now.' We know, and just like I was back then, many of us are very afraid.

What I didn't know was that when my mother left me my body temperature was soaring beyond 47C, and that, medically, I should already have died. I had lost 97% of my skin which was now severely damaged by massive and infected blisters, and I looked very similar to a severe burns victim. I was unrecognizable as the girl that had stumbled into the hospital almost two weeks before. My parents were told to expect the worst, and my mother advised that if by some medical miracle I survived, I would be forever both blind and disfigured. Such was their love they were still going into debt to pay a very large bill to fly me to a major city hospital on the slim chance that they would be able to do something more for me.

Chapter 7

Dying

I looked down at the body on the bed, my body. 'Poor kid. She didn't need that, but at least it doesn't hurt now,' I thought. I didn't relate directly to myself anymore. I looked around. It was the first time I'd clearly seen the room they had placed me in. I was offended. It was nothing but a large cupboard. Was this all they thought that I was worth? People looked after their pets better than this. I felt worthless and humiliated.

Suddenly I forgot to be offended. After all it didn't matter now, did it? I looked back at the body on the bed. It seemed further away than before. Where was I? I did a check. I was looking down from the rear of the body on the bed from the top right-hand corner of the room. What was I doing there? I didn't really care. It felt good to be away from the pain. I stayed there calmly looking around for some time. 'Where do I go now?' I thought. 'Do I just stay here?' I looked down at the body again. I was glad to have left it. I was more than 'glad'. You have no idea how wonderful it felt to be free of that body. My body. I finally felt like myself again after many years of not knowing who I was.

Then, instantly, I was on a train. I didn't know how I had got there. The train kept going faster and faster. It wasn't scary; it was comforting, soothing. Through the window the country-side was pretty, green like it had been in Wales when I was growing up. I recalled my childhood. Absurdly I could see it both in front of me and inside of me at the same time, every tiny detail. I found myself crying for small lies I had told as a little one that had caused pain to my brother, his friends, children at school. Nothing serious, kid stuff, but I felt the distress they had felt. Not good. There were happy times too: the snowman we had all built one winter in our back garden. The Christmas my dad played Lego with us. The trips to the beach in the heat of summer and then the cold winds of winter. I saw flowers; blue-bells in the woods from our country walks and daffodils on St David's day. There were happy memories of when my parents had praised a poem I had written, and my joy from the day my younger brother was born. We were all so excited!

Suddenly I panicked. A massive panic attack. No! I couldn't go on this trip. I had to get off. Stop the train. I wasn't supposed to be here. I couldn't do this. My little brother would cry. I couldn't leave! I saw a coffin. My mother had her head down. My father stood frozen, his arm around her. Then I was back in our home, my brother looking up at them and asking, 'When is Ninno coming home?' (As a toddler he'd been unable to say my name, and so I became Ninno). 'I want Ninno!' I heard him exclaim. Explanations. Tears. Feelings of abandon-ment. I couldn't let him feel like that. I knew how it felt. I had to make sure that didn't happen to him. Then his tear-stained face turned upwards and looked directly at me. I felt immense panic. I had to stop this train. I had to get off. Things turned black.

Just as quickly I was calm. I wasn't on the train anymore. They were going to make me better. I was going to a special operating theatre. I could see the doors a long way away down the end of a very long corridor. Everything was peaceful now. The corridor was white and grey. That was okay, wasn't it? Was it? Weren't hospitals always dull colours? Deep inside, I registered alarm. Something was wrong here, but what was it? The theatre doors were coming closer. That was okay. I was going for an operation, wasn't I? That's what the nurse had said from behind me when she started pushing my bed along. I was going for an operation. But...something wasn't right.

I registered alarm. The hospital wasn't a hospital, was it? My mind struggled to make sense of this journey. Something WAS wrong! It wasn't painted white and grey; it was colour-less. I panicked as fear erupted from deep inside me. I didn't want to enter that theatre. It wasn't an operating theatre at all, was it? It was...? I couldn't place it. I 'knew' but couldn't 'recall'. I felt an urgent need to speak to the nurses pushing the trolley I was on. I had to tell them that I didn't want to go in there, that I didn't have to. Couldn't I choose to have operations? What operation was I having anyway? I had to cancel this one. Stat. I could not go!

'Please Stop!' I pleaded with the nurses, 'I don't want to do this. I don't need to.' There was no reply. Had they heard me? 'Please,' I begged them, 'I've changed my mind.' No reply.

The trolley continued to move closer to the doors. Why didn't they answer? Couldn't they hear me? They were supposed to be looking after me. What was wrong with them? They weren't even comforting me, telling me not to be afraid. That's what nurses did, didn't they? Why weren't they at least saying something? They weren't even chatting to each other. Why weren't they talking? Suddenly I had an overwhelming urge to see them and to tell them that I didn't want to go with them. To tell them they were scaring me.

I twisted my head to look at them. I simply had to see their faces! The theatre door was now right in front of the trolley. I didn't want to go through it. My body felt pinned down and immoveable. Panicking I frantically twisted my head from side to side to try to see these silent and uncaring nurses, and as I did, I experienced fear like I never had before, alongside a sudden acknowledgement that I no longer had any choice nor any power.

There were no nurses pushing the trolley. Instead, there were beings, light-grey in colour, and immensely tall. Their heads were hooded and faceless. Not good nor bad. Not anything. They were faceless, calm, and completely unresponsive. As I registered this, I felt rather than saw the foot of the trolly open the theatre doors and an inexplicable surge of terror ran through me.

What was I afraid of? As the trolley glided through the doors, hooded people came out of a white mist to help me. It was not dissimilar to the mist I'd experienced when I'd travelled out of my bed with my grandfather the last time I'd seen him, although I didn't make the connection in that moment. Words were spoken, only not spoken, and I became enveloped in the brightest, whitest light that I have ever experienced. There was no terror now, no fear. It had simply gone, dissipated with the closing of the doors.

There were lot of people in the light. They talked, mind to mind, moving silently and touching my body gently. It was a very peaceful place. I would love to recall exactly what happened there, but I can't. All I can say honestly is that what I felt was like a gentle washing and with it came the sensation of being healed. As quickly as they came, they dispersed, until there came a point where I became fully aware that I no longer had a body. I was a voice without vocal cords, a being totally relieved of pain and weight. I felt a sense of exhilarating freedom.

I phased in and out for some time until they finished their work with me. One figure came up to me and then another was called to my side. I was declared ready, and with mind communication only, they guided me towards an exit point. At no point did I question what I was ready for nor what came next. They guided me towards yet another set of doors which swung open as I glided towards them. Glided, not walked; there was nothing cumbersome or clunky, no weight nor footsteps, just a sensation of only being a brain and gliding effortlessly.

I moved through the white light as if being pulled along a predetermined pathway. The white light of the theatre room had been exchanged for a mist, and I continued forward, drawn by some invisible energy, as the mist gradually cleared, and I found myself in bright sunshine. Before me, some distance away, was a softly rolling green hill. I moved towards it swiftly and easily. It was as if I knew both where I was going and why, and I was pleased and excited at the same time. I was aware that I was completing my journey as I passed over open meadows where children were playing happily in small groups. The sound of their laughter and singing carried to me on a slight breeze. There were houses sprinkled throughout the greenery, all at a distance, but it was the children and the greenery I focused on.

I saw so much more than I can accurately recall, and now I believe that those details were of minor importance. What was important is I felt overriding happiness, love, and satisfaction all around me to a depth I had never experienced.

I reached the hilltop that had compelled me forward and gazed down onto a small but beautiful distant garden. That was where I was to go. From my height, I couldn't now hear the children I had passed. There was no music, no bird sounds you would expect to hear in the countryside. Nothing, and yet I cannot recall ever feeling so happy and so at one with myself. It was beautiful, but apparently not beautiful enough to make me stay. My mind, alert now, wondered where I was and questioned whether I really wanted to go forward to the garden below, or whether I should turn back to the houses and the children where I had felt happiness and love surrounding everything.

With a shock, I was instantly back in the white mist that I had been in with my grandfather many years before. It is hard to describe, but it had a different consistency to the mist I'd been in previously, different in the same way two rooms can have light blue walls yet be in different shades. There were people there, kind, gentle and somehow holding me. As I was trying to come to terms with the change, I heard these people 'talking' to me but couldn't seem to grasp what it was they were saying. I was confused for what seemed like minutes but was likely only seconds and then I was listening to myself saying that I couldn't go on; I simply couldn't do it! I was distressed and very tired. My mind was reeling, and I wanted to go back to the hill, to the peace, to the sunshine. I didn't want to be here in this mist with these strange people. Regardless, while emanating great kindness, they somehow gently manoeuvred me over to a screen which in my memory was on a grey slender stand. Today I would automatically describe a common computer screen, but this was happening to me in 1976, when I was just eighteen years old, a long time before home computers and laptops were even dreamed of. Back then, a single computer took up a whole building, and I'd never heard anyone talk about one let alone had an opportunity to see one. I had never seen anything like what was before me.

The screen lit up, and they showed me the years that lay

ahead of me in life. They weren't easy, and I remember thinking clearly, 'Oh it never ends; even when I grow up the struggle never ends.' My difficult teenage years continued into a difficult adult life. There was no escape. The pictures continued, and they had reached a point where I was now married and had two small children whom I loved absolutely. I would get what I wanted if I just hung in there through the difficult times. My heart melted and joy flooded through me, but the movie continued and what came next threw me into a state of hysteria.

I pulled away from their invisible hold screaming, 'How could you do this to me? How could you give me what I want so much and then tear it away? How could you do that to me?' I was sobbing, distraught beyond belief. I felt like I couldn't go on any longer. I knew now that I couldn't do what they expected of me. I wasn't that strong.

Somehow, and with much reassurance, they calmed me down enough to manoeuvre me back to the screen. From memory there were at least four of these beings, possibly six. The beings surrounded me now, seemingly pouring calmness into me and love around me at the same time. The movie continued. It wasn't to be as bad as I thought; please, I had to trust them. They were working hard to convince me. Through my tears and devastation, I continued to watch. Yes, things did improve, but still I sobbed with the pain of what I had seen. I was beyond tired now. I was utterly exhausted. I felt that I couldn't live the life they expected of me. I just didn't have what it would take as it was so hard and so painful. To be honest what I'd seen seemed utterly cruel. As the thoughts raced through my mind, they seemed to read every single one. Again, they reassured me that this was alright with them. I didn't have to do this. This was my choice. Then a male, much taller than the others and seemingly older, took me to one side.

He explained my choices. I could stay there with them if I wished. If I did stay, I would eventually be returned to complete another life. The new life would be harder in different ways. I was reminded that it had been my choice to choose this path in the first place, and then I was shown some of what would happen to me in each of my possible new lives.

Forgive me. I am essentially a coward. The little I saw of each potential life to come scared me half to death, if indeed I wasn't already! Vague visions of poverty, physical and sexual abuse haunt me to this day. I must have been quite broken though because I still protested that I couldn't do what they wanted me to do. I simply couldn't return to my old life.

There was an air of sadness as I announced this, but, yet again, I was reassured that the choice was mine to make and that it was alright to make this choice. Ridiculous as it was, I felt disappointed in myself, but again they reassured me that it was my choice to make, and suddenly I was back on the hilltop looking down at the beautiful garden below. The mist had gone, and once again I was filled with peace.

Once again all my feelings of trauma disappeared, and I was completely at peace with myself, my choice, and my surroundings. Looking down from my position on the hill I could see a small island in the centre of a beautiful garden that was surrounded by an even smaller stream just a way off in the distance. There was a male figure standing on the island just as calmly watching me, waiting. I couldn't take my eyes of this figure, and as I stared, I seemed to float down the hill towards him as if drawn by some invisible thread.

As I got closer to the stream, watching him standing on the island across from me, his arms slowly lifted and opened to welcome me with the same warmth that a mother opens her arms to her child. I was home. I remember thinking the words with a sudden clarity and acknowledgement that was almost startling. The pain, the anguish, the life that I had never felt that I belonged in was over to me in that moment, and finally, after so much time, I felt the peace of belonging. It was as if this was where I had needed to be all along. The little Welsh girl who hadn't wanted to be born had finally returned home.

Our eyes locked together, and I felt as if I became one with this almost Christ-like figure. Feeling great love and joy, I continued to move silently towards the hands that were held out towards me. As my feet reached the edge of the shallow stream, I lifted my hands towards his.

Instantly, a fear struck hard and fast at the very heart of my being. I knew that I couldn't cross the water. A huge sense of failure swept over and through me. There were no second chances. Crossing the stream meant that I would have failed! I could not do it. I must not. I stood there and battled the desire to be back, enfolded in the love, the painlessness that would be mine and the awful guilt sweeping over me in waves.

I never doubted for a second that crossing that stream was a far better choice than staying where I was. Nor did I doubt that if I were to cross it I would have failed myself in a significantly important way. I felt strongly that I had made a commitment and that crossing the stream was to opt out of that commitment, which I knew in my core was the wrong thing to do. I froze. I looked into the eyes of the figure and felt enormous sadness, overwhelming in its intensity, run through my body. Over the stream was the centre of all love to which I could return at any time. No fear, no judgement, no pain, and yet, now was not the time. I must not, could not, return. I had made my choice.

The being on the island smiled gently and communicated in the strange mind talk that I could still come to him. It was indeed my choice. If returned now, I would simply need to repeat my lesson at some future time. I have memories, vaguer ones, about what I would have to do, and what I still had to do.

In my mind, however, it was clear that there really was no choice other than to follow an already agreed plan. I desperately wanted to be back with this being. The love that emanated from him was so superb and encompassing that I have difficulty finding the words to describe it even now, as an educated and more worldly-wise adult. My inner battle continued, guilt vying desperately with the need for love and healing. Guilt won. I had made a commitment. I must stay and fulfil it. I found myself gazing into his amazingly kind and magnificent eyes and promising through heart-wrenching sobs that I would go back. I would do it.

I cried because I so wanted to be with him and because, somewhere deep inside me, I had discovered a greater need to go back and complete my life, to fulfil the promises that I had made. He spoke to me then, mind to mind. 'I will do it,' I told him, 'I promise I will do it.'

Chapter 8

Survival

An enormous electric shock passed through me. A massive bang and I found myself back in my body and in the hospital bed. I was sitting bolt upright with both arms still strapped to boards to keep the drips that extended from them in place. They were extended out in front of me, still wanting to join the figure on the island. Still reaching out for the love he offered. Tears were streaming down my face and my broken, swollen, damaged voice croaked out, "I promise. I'll do it. I promise!" I was instantly aware that I could now clearly see every detail of the room. My vision was back.

Then the pain hit, coursing through my body and tearing it apart piece by piece. I shrank inside myself from the force of it and recalled everything that I had seen, everything that I'd been shown. I felt a swift sense of relief that I had been allowed to come back. I would do it. I would be strong. The weight of the boards was too much for my weakened arms, and I sank back into my pillows and the continuing pain. I was resolute. I would do this. I could do this.

If I'd had my way, my story would be just like an Enid

Blyton book and 'the toys' would all settle back into their places in the toy room while the little Welsh girl fell asleep and all would have been well when she awoke in the morning. Real life, as I discovered, was nothing like that, however, and what occurred next stays with me as one of the most shocking acts of cruelty I have personally endured.

My shouting was heard by a nurse, and she'd come to see what was going on. This lady was heavy set and breathing angrily as she stormed towards me. 'Why don't you shut up. You'll wake the whole bloody ward. You've been screaming for about ten minutes!'

Shock coursed through me. This couldn't be happening. I was hallucinating. I must be. I had just promised to do what the beings wanted. Why were they punishing me more? Confused, I gasped out, 'Pain.'

As the nurse roughly adjusted the boards under my arms and did something to the sheet tangled around me, she sneered, 'Bitch, you're disturbing my TV show! I'll get you your pain meds just to shut you up. Won't help. You're going to die soon anyway!' She turned her back and stormed out.

My mind screamed at the injustice. I didn't deserve this. I'd promised. Wasn't that enough? She was back almost as soon as she'd left. 'Hurts does it?' she spat out, and with that she raised her closed fist and smashed it into the top of my blistered thigh, following it with the needle and pressing the plunger hard. 'I hope that shuts you up! I want to watch the rest of my show.' She stomped out, and I dissolved into floods of tears.

The contrast between the place of bliss and my painful reawakening was too much for me. I went into shock at this violent treatment. I was ice cold and shaking from head to toe as my jaw clenched and then unclenched beyond my control. My leg throbbed, aching and painful, a different pain to the rest of my body. Broken by my experience I began to feel sorry for myself. What had I done to deserve this? I cried and cried.

Somewhere in the midst of all the tears and pain, my clear memories of what I had been shown on the screen faded. As I very slowly calmed down, I became aware of this. Realisation brought panic. If I couldn't recall what I'd promised to do, and I couldn't recall the pictures they had shown me, how was I ever to fulfil my promise? Distressed again by my thoughts, I fell into an exhausted sleep.

While I slept there was a change of shift. A kind and gentle nurse came and checked on me. She took my pulse and then my temperature. She gave me yet another needle for the pain. I barely felt it. She commented on the large dark bruise that had formed on my thigh and wondered aloud what had caused it. I didn't speak. I couldn't. The event had traumatised me, and I was still searching for answers to what I had done wrong when I woke up. The nurse left me to my thoughts, and I wished that she hadn't because the confused loops just started circling again. If I had forgotten my promise, then how could I ever keep it? Did it matter that I had forgotten it? Would it happen anyway? I wracked my mind, played and replayed what I remembered of the event without luck. My brain refused to give up its secrets, and exhausted I fell into a deep sleep.

In later years I was to say, 'Thank God, I couldn't remember what lay ahead of me,' but that time was still a long way off.

One of my teachers, whom I was never to see again, arrived just as I was being wheeled out of the ward to the ambulance to commence my journey to the airport. She took one look at me and burst into tears. Sobbing her heart out at the sight of me, I have no memory of her words after the first outburst of 'Oh my God!' I wanted to tell her that I was going to be fine which is what I truly believed from the moment I had woken up that morning. I still couldn't speak properly though as my mouth was filled with blisters, my gums had turned to jelly, my lips were swollen and distorted, and some of my teeth were stuck to the insides of my cheeks and the roof of my mouth, having been completely displaced. I was a mess.

A bed was on the regular flight to the city down south, and a curtain placed around it provided a level of privacy. I was somehow manoeuvred by stretcher into it, and I lay at head height while the curtain was closed around me. A nurse had been assigned to accompany me as this was a legal requirement. The other passengers, who fortunately never saw me, consisted mostly of the local football team, and I found their noisy excitement extremely distressing. Neither my mother, nor the nurse, were seated nearby. My arms, chest, and legs were securely strapped to the bed for my own safety, rendering me immobile other than being able to turn my head and wiggle my fingers and toes.

About an hour into the trip, while I was mentally begging the men having a good time around me to please, please settle down and be quiet, blistered skin peeled off the inside back of my throat, and I began to choke. I tried to swallow, but it seemed that it was still attached at some point because it wouldn't move. I made as much noise as I could, trying to get the attention of someone, anyone. The noise was just a gurgle, not strong enough to compete with the voices around me. I wondered where the nurse was that was supposed to be checking on me. She hadn't been near me so far. I mentally screamed for her, and then tiring, I concentrated on trying to swallow the mess. I couldn't. I simply couldn't. I was choking, and I was already so tired. I didn't know how long I could keep this up for. I started to become frantic and pleaded mentally not for the nurse, but now for my mother, to come and rescue me.

I realised that one foot and two of my fingers on my left hand could just make contact with the curtain around the bed. Choking, I flapped them as vigorously as I could, gargling and gagging on the rising fluid in my throat. I heard the deafening noise of the footballers. I fought to breathe. I tired. I stopped flapping. It was too hard, and I couldn't maintain it. The noise of the footballers was disappearing into the background and disappeared entirely as I became desperate for air. I was going to die! It all seemed so futile and stupid. Why was this happening after all I had already lived through? Where was my mother? Where was the nurse? I couldn't die! I had things to do! This couldn't be happening to me now. It couldn't. It shouldn't. Tears filled my eyes as I mustered the last of my strength and flapped weakly, one last time, at the curtain. I felt faint. I could feel myself slipping. I couldn't do this anymore. I didn't want to die! Suddenly I was filled with both terror and anger. I couldn't die. Even if I didn't remember what it was, I had made a promise!

Fortunately, a stewardess had seen me tapping the curtain and gone to tell my mother. 'There appears to be a lot of move-ment behind the curtain, is your daughter alright?' My mother launched herself out of her seat to check on me, quickly unbuckled the tie across my chest, and then helped me to lift my head and clear my airway. She once again made me cough. Once again saved me. The relief was enormous.

As I began to breathe more easily, I recall seeing one of the footballers through the gap in the curtain. As I looked at him, his face paled, and he looked away quickly. I wondered what he thought. The sight must have bothered him for after my mother had made sure I was safe and returned to her seat and his team-mates' noise increased, he made several attempts to get them to quieten down. It worked for a short while, and I was grateful. The nurse came and looked at me only after my mother had gone to her and complained. Would she have checked on me at all? I don't think that she had any intention of doing so as the flight was almost over. Had I died on that flight she wouldn't have been blamed. The illness would have been deemed the cause, and my mother would have known no different.

Sometimes I think that when you are very unwell it is better to be unconscious. The ambulance trip was excruciating, and the hospital admission seemed to take for ever. The only thing that really remained clear apart from the pain was an argument between my mother and the admitting nurse. The nurse was telling my mother that my body temperature could never have been as high as it was recorded (47.3C) or I would have been dead. She accused the previous hospital staff of having made some serious mistakes. My mother was arguing back and telling her that the staff themselves had been so disbelieving that they had gone and got a handful of thermometers and taken my temperature with all of them, and they had shown them to her to confirm the results. They had never seen anything like it before. My mother sounded like ice, her anger tight and controlled and completely unflinching in my defence. The nurse backed down. My mother gently touched the top of my head at this point, her hand shaking badly.

I was placed in a small ward with three other women and a curtain pulled around me. Again, the noise of their chatter bothered me, and I mentally begged for silence. My fever had broken, and I was completely lucid but still unable to communicate clearly, and I was exceptionally weak. My wish for peace was granted the following morning when I was deemed too fragile to share a room and moved into a twin room without another occupant.

My eyesight and my mind were now crystal clear. From the window of my new room, I could see one other building and the sky. I gazed at the sunshine reflecting off the window of the opposite building. It looked bright and warm. I felt, what? Warm, happy? Contented? Something else far deeper. A sparrow landed on a window ledge and hopped back and forth, its head turning from side to side. My heart and body filled suddenly with tears of happiness as, at eighteen years of age, with my face swollen and forever disfigured, my body blistered and raw, my teeth hanging by shreds from their gums, I finally welcomed life. The sheer joy of being here filled me completely. It was intense. It was pure. I felt alive in a way I had never experienced before, and it was very special indeed. Bliss.

People came and took blood. A skin sample was taken from my blistered and still bruised thigh. The technician apologising as she searched for a spot not too badly damaged. More pain, tears in my eyes. I looked up, my sparrow was back. This was minor. I brushed the tears aside, and as I continued to watch him, my heart sang.

That morning, as you can imagine, my mother was thrilled to see the huge improvement I had made and after greeting me and chatting for a very short time she rushed off to phone my father to let him know I was now on the mend. I had survived. I wished he was there. I missed him. Later that day I asked for my brother whom I had vague memories of seeing by a fence at the airport while they loaded me into the ambulance. My mother said she had told him not to come to the hospital as he had exams shortly, and she didn't want him to become upset by my condition. I felt hurt by this. He'd seen me carried off a plane on a stretcher; how upset could he be by seeing me now? I would return home a couple of weeks later without seeing him though. My mother always got her way.

Getting better meant getting out of bed and going for a walk. It had to happen and a few days later, aided by my mother and two nurses, I shuffled trembling but determined up a corridor. I knew I was winning the battle and to be up and about felt tremendous, in spite of the pain standing caused in my now weakened shins. As I shuffled, I became aware that all the people in the corridor, which included an abnormal number of nurses, were watching me very closely, standing aside to let me pass. Nurses were making encouraging statements, although the patients were openly staring. I just kept going. Then we came to a mirror, and everyone froze. I wouldn't have noticed the mirror if they hadn't all suddenly stilled. I glanced from face to face to see what had gone wrong. What was up with them? I saw the mirror, and as I saw the mirror, I registered the worried look on the face of the nurse standing near it, and I understood. They were afraid. I stood and looked at the girl in the mirror. I was awed. Stricken. Who was she, this poor thing? I stared. Realisation seeped through me. This was me. The person inside me, who recognised herself as physically weakened but mentally stronger and more alive than she had ever been, did not relate to the child in the mirror.

The child in the mirror had lost more than half her hair and half her body weight. One side of her face was grotesquely swollen which made her eyes look displaced. The face itself, and what could be seen of the neck, was covered in raw and inflamed patches of skin, purple and scarlet, covered in huge scabs and wet, puss-filled, yellow blisters. The lips were swollen and distorted, and also covered by these blisters. The body itself was thin to the point of breaking. It wasn't me. I knew that. This was my shell; what I would have to work with. I was aware now of the difference between the body and the soul. The body may have taken a battering, but the soul wasn't going to let the sight of it hold it back. My soul was soaring. The body would heal.

I turned my head from the mirror and a visible sigh of relief passed through the staff. Everyone went back to normal, people moved on. Someone stated that that was enough of a walk for one day and turned me back towards my room. I replayed in my head the sight of myself in the mirror. It dawned on me that the nurses had forgotten there was a mirror in the hallway and had expected me to have a meltdown when I saw my reflection. I felt sorry for them. How awful to have to deal with that. How would you reassure someone who placed their value in how they looked? What a nightmare. Then, I wondered why I didn't. I was a teenage girl. Why didn't I care?

I had a lot of time to think while I was recuperating in hospital. Although I spent much of my time dozing, I was content to listen to the world go by and just think for increasingly greater and greater periods. I didn't doubt that my experiences were 'real'. Of course, this made no sense at all from an everyday point of view, and it made even less sense from my limited experience of life, but, and I knew this beyond all doubt, it was as real as the painful mouthwashes that I had to do several times a day in order to heal my blistered gums. I also knew that if I told anyone what I'd seen and done they would think that I was unhinged.

It bothered me immensely that I couldn't recall what I'd promised to do, and I constantly puzzled over the whole experience. My thoughts were continuously repeating what I could recall as if I was watching a movie on continuous loop. It was unsettling.

I found it frightening to acknowledge that if I had stepped into that stream and crossed to the man then I would no longer exist. Dead. I'd be dead! As for the screen with the 'Life Movies', as I labelled them, what was that about? That was more than a bit beyond my ability to grasp, as I'd seen so much but remembered so little. It was as if that cruel nurse had with one punch wiped out a whole section of my future life that seemed so vital to remember. In some sense, at a deeper level, I did remember, but as I searched inside for what it was, I felt only a heavy sense of responsibility and sadness for there remained a blank spot inside my mind, and no matter how hard I tried, I could not open the door to whatever had disappeared inside it. Whenever I did get close to reliving the weighty responsibility, my mind would just phase out of memory, and I would become aware of my surroundings again, and then I would feel incredible delight and joy at still being here and still being me.

Two weeks later, a bit stronger, with my body beginning to shed the awful scabs of a thousand blisters, I was deemed well enough to go home. My face was badly marked, still swollen and lopsided, and my body was covered in pink patches of healing and sensitive new skin. My mother didn't pack any clothes for me, a fact which led me to question whether she had really expected me to survive. She purchased a loose summer dress with a low neckline and loose frills for sleeves to hold it up for my trip home. Much of my scarring and scabbing was exposed but as material hurt when it came into contact with my skin, it was the best she could find.

Battered and still weak, I was determined to get out there to live my life. I thought that I was ready to take on the world again. I was pumped up just to have survived. If I had remembered then what I had promised during my near-death experience, I think I'd have set out immediately to change my future, but I didn't remember, so I had no way to prevent myself from living the life I was meant to live. Sometimes ignorance really is bliss. If you don't know about your tomorrows, you live fully in today, and today I was going home.

Chapter 9

The Journey Home

The airport seemed huge. I struggled along, always slightly behind my mother, to the waiting lounge and readily collapsed into a chair. Everything was too hard for my wasted muscles, and I was pushing myself to my limits to keep up with her. It never entered her mind that I would need any support, and I didn't ask because she had on what I called her fierce face. Knowing how much she hated flying, I wasn't surprised. The few words she spoke were clipped and hard. She was dealing with her fear as best she could. I recall becoming very thirsty but not being game to ask her to get me a drink, afraid that she would make me go and get it and that my legs would give way beneath me.

So, there I was, feeling excited and as if everything around me was new but struggling with the muscular effort of having walked too far on weak legs and being required to sit up and sit still. I was reflecting on the whole 'back to babyhood' thing, having to learn to do those same simple things again, and wondering if it was this hard when you were in a much smaller body. I became aware of a mother and her toddler sitting on the seats opposite us. There was a decent gap between our row of chairs and theirs, and I'd been too absorbed in my thoughts to notice them before. The mum was reading a book and glancing occasionally at her little one, keeping her safe without seeming to.

Eventually I caught the child's eye and managed a crooked smile at her. My mother launched herself out of her seat at this point and said she was going to get us a cold drink. Relief flooded through me. As she left, the little one wiggled out of her seat and stood on the carpet. I smiled at her again and wiggled my eyebrows to make her laugh. She beamed and put her hands out towards me and wiggled her fingers. In response I wobbled my eyes again. We kept up this new game for some minutes. Slowly she began to move closer and closer to me, seemingly oblivious to my disfigurement. She babbled up at me, gurgling cheerfully about a metre from my knees. Then she let out one particularly loud squeal of laughter that caught her mother's attention, and she looked up from her magazine with a ready smile for her daughter. It took less than a second for that smile to disappear, replaced by complete shock and horror. Eyes wide, she launched herself across the aisle and none too gently dragged the little girl away from me. Then she proceeded to quickly move chairs, so they sat with their backs to me. She couldn't bear to look in my direction. She possibly thought that I was contagious.

Her reaction was a slap in the face to me, an awakening to what was going to come my way now that my face and skin were ugly. Not only was my face scarred badly, but it drooped on the righthand side. I had always loved children and enjoyed playing with them, making them laugh and seeing their little faces light up. I wasn't different, but now others would think I was. Adults would only see my damage not who I was behind it. Tears stung my eyes as I realised this must be how a physically handicapped person felt. If you didn't look right, then you didn't fit in. The open rejection of my looks was both rude and hurtful, but at the same time I knew where the mother was coming from. She had a strong need to protect her child. Simple really. I now looked 'wrong' and therefore I could be a danger. She wasn't to know. She was naturally protecting her child.

Slowly my initial hurt receded, and I became more fascinated by the events that had played out before the mother took her child away. The little girl had read my eyes and my body language. In her innocence she hadn't questioned whether I was disfigured or ugly, short or tall, fat or thin. She hadn't learnt to judge by such superficial means. Still innocent, she knew intuitively who I really was. I wondered why we lost this ability to see the soul of the person not its container as we became adults. Other than keeping us safe in some circumstances, did it serve any useful purpose?

I realised that everything that I had experienced in the past few weeks had changed me enormously. I was essentially a new person. I had undergone life and death experiences that had left me with a positive attitude but had also left me vulnerable and brittle. I decided to take the lesson and be more understanding of people's reactions to me. They were scared. I got it. I could be into drugs, or have a contagious disease, or a dozen other possibilities. I doubted that their first thought would be that if I was contagious then I'd not be flying on a plane with them!

At some point during this thought process I realised that I genuinely couldn't worry about this. It was too trivial, unimportant in the scheme of things. Does it matter how you look? Does it matter how you dress? Why worry about such things when your life can be extinguished so quickly? They paled rapidly in importance at the thought of death. It trivialised them to the point of ridiculousness. I was, I realised, a very new version of me with a whole lot of ideas to think through. However, if I thought that the new me meant that the little Welsh girl, with all her strange night visitors and unusual knowledge had been left behind, I was to find out sooner than expected that she was alive and well.

I was so exhausted as I boarded the plane that each step was hard work. My weakened legs threatened to give way at any moment. It was sheer determination that got me up those steps and on board, coupled with the excitement of seeing my father and younger brother again. Inside I was terrified that my still blistered and raw inner ears would hurt from the change in air pressure, and I was bracing myself for that to happen. A blister in my ear had burst one night in the hospital and was so painful that I had screamed and then cried for over an hour until the pain of the newly exposed raw skin settled down to bearable once more. I told myself I must not lose control here no matter how much it hurt, but I was still terrified of what might happen. Over the years I had learnt not to share my fears and to internalise my emotions—very strict and controlling parenting will do that to a child—and the walls that I had built took some time to crumble after my illness. I was trying to keep up as my mother manoeuvred herself down the busy aisle ahead of me. I was my sole focus, talking my way through it. 'One more step, one more step. That's it, and another step. Good girl. Balance, just balance. One more step, and one more. Just one more, nearly there.'

The person behind me bumped me with their onboard baggage, and I stumbled. Swaying and struggling to maintain my balance, I looked up and made accidental eye contact with a stranger, a male with very curly hair. A shock fizzed through me. I suddenly 'knew' things about this man. I knew he was a liar and a thief and in some way dangerous. He was the sort of person that I had been brought up to steer clear of. I also knew beyond all doubt that I would see him again. These thoughts were so awful and intense that I thought I might pass out. I glanced back again and took in the man next to him as well, and I knew instantly that they came as a pair. They were both bad. It was my turn to move again, so I looked away and concentrated on moving forward until, finally, I stumbled into my seat. I was shaking badly, not only from the physical effort required just to walk but from the shock I had received on seeing those men. I crumbled in quite a different way. I didn't know this man. We had never met, and yet I was certain that the information that I had picked up was completely correct. He scared me in such a way that I felt physically threatened. I hoped that I would never get to meet him as I really didn't want to find out if my feelings were correct.

For most of the trip home my mind reeled. Never had my senses told me so much in an instant. I was incredulous and amazed, certainly, but the shock of realising the strength of my intuitive power, not to mention the awful impressions themselves, left me more than a little stunned. Who was I now and was this to be a normal occurrence in my everyday life?

As if I didn't have enough on my plate just coping with my current physical disability, now I was getting random insights that I neither wanted nor needed. I was so naïve about this intuition game and how it was to affect my future. With experience I would come to learn that such encounters are warnings of what is inevitable. From now on my psychic intuition would be used more and more in my real world rather than my dream world, for the illness had changed me in invisible ways I had yet to discover. I would meet this man and his mate, that was the whole point of me knowing about them, but for now, in my innocence, I could still hope that I wouldn't.

To my horror it wasn't too long before the two men came

into my circle, and we were introduced by mutual friends, albeit they were new to my friends. Once they were there, however, I avoided them as if they had the plague. This was quite easy as for some time I hardly went anywhere due to my need to heal, but even if I saw either of them at a distance, my stomach would knot up with fear. If and when our eyes did meet across a street, I felt physically ill.

Meanwhile when I did mix, it was with a very small circle, and I trusted my intuition absolutely. Members of the group fell in love with this charming and fun-loving pair of males. They came to trust them and seemed to get hooked on their company. Every time they spoke about either of them my mind would throw up a flash of the men on the plane. I felt I was correct. They were trouble. I tried several times to warn one friend whom I thought was getting too involved with the man I had first made eye contact with on the plane. I believed she was in danger and that he wasn't who she thought he was. Neither of her new friends should be trusted. She didn't want to know. She was smitten. No-one wanted to hear what I had to say. They didn't want anyone to disapprove and spoil their fun. I must have sounded like a highly disapproving mum figure. To make matters worse there was nothing to go on, nothing to back up my feelings, so I couldn't explain how I felt without looking like an idiot. I should have learned earlier to keep quiet, but it was too late. I'd made my disapproval obvious and soon found myself on the outside looking in.

I watched, worried, and waited. Things started to go sour. Cars were borrowed, advantage taken, drugs introduced, rent not paid. Instead of gloating when my intuition proved correct, I felt sick to my stomach and very sad for my friends and everyone else that they duped, but also sad for myself. I realised that my 'knowing' about stuff kept interfering with my life. I couldn't get out there and have fun. I always seemed able to see the outcome, the danger. I seemed to be three steps ahead of my peers, worrying about something that was going to happen six months or more later.

This knowing weighed me down. I didn't want to be like this. I wanted to be ordinary, able to mingle, be part of the crowd without being popular. I wanted to be included. I wanted to fit in with my peers. I didn't see any point to this 'knowing' if I couldn't use it to any advantage either. What was the point of knowing that someone was a danger, or that someone was going to do something stupid, if you couldn't get anyone to listen to you? Sure, it protected me. I wasn't naïve enough not to realise the advantage in that, but most of the detailed information that I just knew had nothing to do with me, such as knowing as soon as someone invited these men to stay at their home that they would steal from them or that lending them their car was something they should not do. I knew that trusting them was their first mistake but that it would get much worse. Each new experience had me worrying and puzzling over how to use this extra sense that had awakened, but it was made much worse by the deepening belief that I was odd. Very odd.

Still, all that was ahead of me at this point, for now I was on a plane, and I was nearly home. As the plane landed and the very painful pressure in my damaged ears eased, I had eyes only for my father. He was waiting at the gate. With my mother following, I walked shakily across the tarmac, and, sensing my strength giving out, he came out from behind the gate to catch me. I weakly fell into his open arms. It was over. I was home. I had survived. I was eighteen. My fear of my father had long given way to the love between us, and, over the years, he had once again become my safe place to land.

For the next few years, I was emotionally and physically shattered but, just eight weeks after returning from the hospital, still weak when I walked, and with bright-red, brown and white scarring covering my now healed skin sores, I went to work. I was determined to earn the money required to head off to university in the new year. I was still very weak, but I had a quiet job in a local company that required minimum effort and allowed me to sit down for most of the day.

I had graduated school during my hospital stay but missed the graduation dance and all the fuss that went with it. However, I had also received an offer of a place at university not long after returning home. Looking back, I realised that I'd known somewhere deep inside me that I wasn't going to the formal graduation as I'd not even organised a dress for the event, and although tickets were on sale a week before my illness, I never thought about buying one. In my head, I wasn't going. In my heart, I wouldn't be there.

I survived the job placement by the skin of my teeth as I experienced unrelenting fatigue. With grim determination I headed off to university in another town three months later, still exhausted, but contemplating only how lucky I was. While I was ill, the doctors had told my parents, that, should I survive, I would probably be blind and that my face would require plastic surgery. Neither was necessary. From things that were said to me, I realise that others thought I was courageous taking my severely scarred face out into the world. It wasn't courage. It was bloody minded determination and an exceptionally strong belief in something intangible inside me. Externally I might look a mess, but internally I was stronger than ever, and I knew I must not stay in this town. Whatever I was going to do in the future, I would not find it here. To go forward I needed to get away.

Chapter 10

University Days

Finally I was away from home and free to be myself. My self was tired, still weak and badly scarred. One side of my face still drooped slightly, and I couldn't carry my own suitcase more than a few feet, so I was very glad that the college I was going to live at sent someone to meet every new student. A tutor arrived and took care of my suitcase. I would have seemed hostile to him as I was fighting to stay upright and could barely hold a conversation so was almost monosyllabic for most of the journey to the college, but I was very grateful. I don't know why I felt I had to put on an act that I was stronger than I was, but I guess that was part of my upbringing and so my mask was in place from the first moment I arrived. It was unbelievably hard to pretend that I was just fine when in fact I was far from it, but I was determined not to have to return home.

Spiritually I was changed. Prior to my bout of Stephen Johnson's Syndrome which had morphed into the more severe form called Toxic Epidermal Necrolysis, my knowledge about the future had involved only myself and close friends. Now I knew things about strangers. They might be trivial, or they might be major, but I seemed to have no filter. As it was all new and strange, I also seemed to have no filter on my mouth. I would make comments that were true, but tactless and undiplomatic, so they were not always well received. A few predicted events from my childhood unfolded over the next couple of years, confusing and startling me further, causing either fascination or trauma and leaving me wondering how the human brain could possibly know this information in advance.

I woke up one night crying my eyes out, incredibly shocked and sickened to my core. I had just dreamt about my school friend dying, hit by a car in London. I had been dreaming of walking through a city street late at night, hearing conversations between one couple and then another. Suddenly I was way above them looking down. I felt tense, nervous. I scanned the area and looked back down at two specific couples, realising that I knew the two girls. My mind screamed at them to get off the street, but they kept walking and chatting. They seemed oblivious to the danger and yet I felt it coursing through my body, becoming more terrified by the moment. Then I was looking down from a really high vantage point, seeking out the danger, trying to find what or who would cause it. I saw a car approaching from several blocks away and instantly knew that that car was the source. In my mind I rushed back towards my friends and screamed down at them. They didn't hear me, and yet I was right there, close to them now, shouting at them to go into one of the brightly lit buildings on their left. To get off the footpath. To run.

Greater shock coursed through me as my logical mind kicked in. It was about to happen. My illogical fears were about to become a reality. I screamed at them again, as hard as I could, willing them all to move off the street, but they just kept talking. Then the sound of the car's engine, going much too fast, was upon us, upon them, and in the blink of an eye the car mounted the kerb, and I was back up high, watching as bodies were knocked sideways or flung up into the air and my school-friend became a broken ragdoll on the pavement. Screams came from all directions. I watched as ambulance, police and fire sirens became mixed, and I screamed with them. A cacophony of noise and faces jangled in my brain and my thoughts jumped from one individual to another, momentarily absorbing their feelings before finally becoming numb.

Next moment I jumped forward in time and I saw my friend's best friend, the girl who had helped pull us apart at school, in a hospital room, screaming violently, out of her mind with grief and shock, her eyes wide and vacant, her voice screaming as loud as her lungs would let her. As a nurse tried to hold her and another approached her with a syringe, this gentle girl punched her so hard that she flew across the room and rebounded with a massive crack off the window. I recall regis-tering not only her feelings but also my horror at what she had just done to the nurse. Quickly I started mentally going back and forth between her and the accident site, refusing to accept that my friend had died, seeking to find her somewhere, anywhere, broken and in severe pain. I found her on a trolley. A paramedic was speaking as her damaged face was covered. She was dead. It was only at that point that I woke up sobbing and shaking, wanting to vomit. I was in shock from a nightmare. I was ice-cold and shaking even though it was a warm tropical night. I stayed awake for hours, unable to shake off the visions that I had seen, attempting but failing to convince myself that it was a horrific nightmare. Finally, just after dawn broke, exhausted, I slept.

I expected to hear very soon that my dear friend had been killed in an accident, but I didn't find out for a couple of months as my mother chose not to tell me until I had completed my semester exams and returned home for the holidays. I remained on edge and scared. I was in awe and now terrified of the human mind, my mind. It didn't seem to belong to me. How could I have been so certain that this was going to happen to her when we were just little girls in primary school? How could I have known that she must never go to London? Where did this information come from?

At no point in the weeks ahead did I ever think that her death hadn't occurred that night while I was asleep. Eventually the nightmare passed from the front to the back of my mind, and so it came as a shock all over again when, a couple of days after my return home, my mother produced the copy of the local paper with the news of her death and told me other details that had been passed around the town. I felt sick, but in front of my mother I did not, would not, show any grief. I had learned that showing vulnerability in front of her would somehow be used against me in the future. The grief came out later than night in the privacy of my own room, as my mind replayed my past nightmare on repeat, and the original pain and confusion resurfaced. How could I have known?

The grief of my friend's passing has never really left me. She was my first friend in my new country, the kindest and sweetest person I ever knew. I never heard a cross word from her lips. To me, hers was a death that never needed to occur, and yet, it did in spite of me trying to prevent it. Why?

That Christmas break I dated a local boy from a large family. My mother didn't like him. She struggled with his strong Australian accent and the fact that he chewed gum a lot of the time. I think some of the attraction was that my mother didn't approve, but he was a gentleman around me and very kind. One evening he took me to his home as they were having a party in their shed. It was large and set up as a family room for the ten children, and it had a pool table in one corner. It wasn't long before I was invited to play. I was bent over the table, about to take my first shot, when the door opened in front of me and a cold blast of air blew in catching my attention.

I looked up and came face to face with 'Anne'. Our eyes met and neither of us could look away. The noisy room dwindled to silence and eyes became focused on the pair of us. I began to feel uncomfortable, then very uncomfortable, but still, I couldn't look away. One of the brother's broke the silence with the words, 'Do you two know each other?' We both looked down at our feet and then at him, and Anne, with a puzzled look on her face, moved across the room to take a seat.

My boyfriend moved to my side and repeated his brother's words, 'Do you know each other? Do you?'

I said shakily, 'No I don't know her. What is her name?'

His reply froze me to the spot once again. 'That's Anne,' he said, 'One of my younger sisters.'

He looked at me strangely as the brother who had broken the spell between us came over and said, 'What the hell just happened there?'

I had nothing to say. I was in shock. My boyfriend shrugged and replied, 'No idea!' as he gave me a puzzled look.

We moved silently back into our game and in moments the tension eased. Meanwhile my brain was racing. My stomach was knotted. My heart pounded. My mind raced at a hundred miles an hour. I had just met Anne. Not Anne my current boyfriend's sister, but Anne, *the* Anne, my helpful advisor and friend from my out of body visits as a child. Only, I was nineteen and she was now several years younger than me! She had the same face, colouring, build, everything, but she was too young. In my dreams, she was always older than me. Now she was younger.

My thoughts raced realising that what had occurred wasn't just in my head as others had felt it too. She had felt it. What was going on? What did it mean? With my mind racing and focused on this, I missed my shot, and I don't recall a great deal about the rest of the party after that other than that I deliberately went to introduce myself to this version of Anne later in the evening and found out that she was about to fly out of town to start studying to become a nurse. She seemed like a nice girl albeit a little hesitant to chat with me. I went home wondering how she could possibly be the same person, now younger than me, on the other side of the world and nearly half my lifetime later!

The apparent insanity of this meeting sent me spinning for days afterwards, and off and on for a few years to come. My questioning mind couldn't let this one go. I hashed and rehashed the incident and my childhood memories. I never found a logical answer. Of course, there was an answer, but it wasn't logical. Despite all that I had already experienced, I was still seeking explanations for everything from a logical viewpoint. A form of self- harassment that I was to torture myself with for some years to come.

Several weeks later I returned to university, still wondering, still puzzled. I had relived all that I could remember of my last conversation with Anne as a little girl. If she was to be a reminder that I was on my path, then that itself was unnerving. What path was I on? I felt that I had done nothing to fulfil the promise that I had made. Had I wasted the last year? As I had so many times before, I tried desperately to recall the promise, but every time I drew a blank, a void through which I could recall nothing.

Perhaps Anne was a wakeup call, a warning that things were about to change? Perhaps, she was just a milestone along a long, life path because now the dreams started in earnest. I began to have frequent premonitions during my sleep. I called them the 'dreams' and wondered what they were all about as they often didn't make sense at the time. Soon, within a couple of months, I began to live them out in real life and although they were mostly unimportant and harmless, they worried me a great deal as I seemed to be living life as an action replay much of the time.

When I dreamt a whole conversation only to have the exact conversation with a friend two weeks later, my mind would go into a spin. Dreaming of two other people having a conversation in a specific placed at a specific time, triggered by something that just immediately happened, and then living it out in real life three weeks later, made my mind spin off its orbit. This was my life, a new world that I'd been thrown into. I didn't like it, but I didn't seem to have much choice in the matter.

As a coping mechanism I stopped watching the evening news because it was almost all *deja vue*. For a whole term I isolated myself from current affairs only to find that the first time I ventured back to the TV room, I had not only experienced premonitions of the news itself but could recite whole lines of the report before it came over the air. On one occasion I was standing in the doorway, too nervous to venture inside for fear of what I might hear. I recall the girl who stood next to me as I spoke and her look of utter shock as the newsreader echoed my exact sentence.

'How did you know that?' she asked.

'Err, it was on before,' I bluffed.

'No, It wasn't!' spoke another girl, 'I've been watching all afternoon!'

I fled, and I never went back.

For all my early childhood spiritual teaching through my night-time teachers, the more adult me had no means of coping with what was now becoming an almost daily event. I was often frightened and scared by my ability. I alternated between feeling perfectly normal for hours at a time and then doing a complete about face and feeling I was going completely crazy.

By now my skin had repaired as much as it was going to, my face barely drooped at all, and my physical energy had levelled out at around thirty-five percent of my pre-illness days. I was adapting to this. I had a lovely small group of friends that I valued deeply and had shared my near-death experience with, and they accepted both me and my story, warts and all. What I couldn't and didn't share with them was the fear I was losing my mind. I became more gregarious, more insecure. I laughed louder and more often, and the mask I lived behind grew stronger. Because of the fatigue I played no sport and as my finances were critically low, I had no hobbies. I went nowhere, rarely leaving campus. I lived in my dorm and almost all my entertainment revolved around having coffee with friends in their rooms. I was one of many students in this situation. I certainly wasn't alone.

On another level, though, things had changed. I began to attract people who had very real, worldly problems. They were all males who, far from being interested in me as a female, wouldn't normally be seen dead in my company. I also had little time for them. However, the universe had different plans that were contrary to ours.

The first time it happened, I was particularly intrigued to find myself deep in conversation with someone I found mildly irritating. He obviously wasn't happy and felt very sorry for himself although I had no idea why as we hadn't mixed up to this point. He was someone I saw and heard mainly in the communal dining room. He was in the year below me. This day he was sitting on a stairwell and as I passed him, I felt a bolt of electricity rush through my body from head to toe. I stopped and heard myself ask him what was wrong even as my logical mind told me to keep going.

Completely unexpectedly, perhaps for both of us, he poured his heart out. I stood there, took it all in and just as unexpectedly heard myself tell him off in no uncertain terms and giving him advice I had no right to give. My voice came out deeper than I had ever heard it as the electric feeling continued to rush through me passing from head to toe. I honestly don't know who was the more shocked as I heard myself sternly telling him finally that if he wasn't happy at university he should go home and get a job, and maybe come back in two years when he had sorted out his family situation and was financially independent, because, in my opinion, his family life was more important right now. I told him, 'Stop wasting your life worrying about them and taking up someone else's place here. Just go home and be with them. You can come back next year or in five years if that's what you want then.'

He looked up with tears in his eyes, stunned at my stern lecture. He looked me straight in the eye and replied, 'You're right. You are, absolutely, right. You sure know how to hit where it hurts don't you!'

'Think about it,' I spat out, as the electricity surge drained from my body leaving me shocked. Shaking violently, I walked away from him and continued climbing the stairs.

The event left me feeling shattered, as the withdrawing of the electrical flow left me feeling very weak and unwell. I had become myself again in those last draining moments and now I was afraid of what I had done and said. I whispered to myself that I had no right, no right at all, to talk to someone like that. I had verbally smacked the poor boy. What did I know of his private circumstances other than what he'd said, which was not a lot. He needed help, and I had been cruel. Where had my words come from? How could I give him advice anyway? What did I know living here in my little room keeping my own company?

Distressed at what I had done, I sat in my room and cried like a baby. I replayed our conversation repeatedly in my mind, recalling his face and his incredulous tone as he asked several times, 'How do you know that about me?' How indeed did I, and what had I said that I shouldn't have known?

I was so distressed I skipped dinner, but the next day a trip to the communal dining room completely shattered any sense of calmness I had achieved. I walked in to see a group of his friends sitting around talking. All eyes turned to stare at me, and then one of them asked, 'What did you say to him? He's gone home. He's chucked in his course. He said he was leaving because of something you said to him!'

I felt instantly ill. I was responsible. I had been influential in changing the course of a stranger's life without thought or consideration, and without any factual knowledge of who they were or why they felt the way they did. Even though I acknowledged that something very strong and overwhelming, something out of my control, had occurred the previous day, I felt guilty, responsible for a potential disaster that I may have caused. I didn't understand why I had stopped to talk to him in the first place. I had no defence. I had learned from him why he was miserable, and I was absolutely positive he needed to be at home with his family, but at the same time I couldn't explain the conviction I held about the direction he should take nor the strength of my words.

His friends treated me like the enemy, as if I had committed the most awful crime. Was leaving university because you were unhappy there a crime? I didn't think so. I retreated into myself for a few weeks because of this. It wasn't the first time and wouldn't be the last. I was beginning to think that I was an out-of-control cannon ball. I tried to console myself with the fact that previous convictions and dramatic behaviours of mine had been proven correct, so, realistically, there was a glimmer of hope this one would work out too.

The young man remained on my mind throughout the year. I heard he got a job and was happier, but when he didn't return the following year, I worried again that I'd done the wrong thing. That worry continued for the next few years as thoughts of him intermittently popped into my mind, and I remained concerned about my place in his life, and the damage I may have caused.

This wasn't to be the end of the story. Five years later, I received a phone call from a friend telling me she had someone at her house who would love to see me. She was highly cryptic and refused to give any clue as to who it was. I went to her house with my then fiancé. I was quite anxious as just because someone wanted to see me didn't mean that I would necessarily be happy to see them, and as an introvert the fact that I didn't know who I was about to see caused me stress.

The mystery person was the young male from five years before. He had returned home to support his brother and father after the death of his mother. He had taken a job with a local bank, and he was now holding down a very successful position. He loved both his job and his life.

I was stunned both to see him and to hear him thank me for what I had done. He told me that he believed that but for my 'kick in the butt' conversation he would never have been brave enough to walk away from university and do what he really needed to do. I replied that he'd made his choice, and I was just the catalyst.

He laughingly told me that I was really much more than that, and then warned my fiancé never to argue with me. 'She knows how to pack a punch,' he said, grinning from ear to ear. We had a lovely time catching up, and I went home enormously relieved and cried with both relief and pleasure. For five years I had carried the guilt of possibly ruining this man's life, and now I had found out the opposite was true. As was my norm, my mind relived the incident, and I realised that I still had no answers for what had happened and how I had changed into 'message delivery mode' that day on the stairs. There were never satisfactory answers.

That moment of gratitude and thankfulness was still ahead of me, though, as I emotionally struggled my way through these years, and this young man wasn't to be my only confrontation out of 'nowhere'.

The standout events were two separate incidents with males of suicidal intent and a run-in with a group of drug-takers/growers. Both males had girl trouble. In both confrontations someone else seemed to step inside my body. The deep voice and the infinite wisdom took over the scared young woman I really was.

One memory makes me chuckle to this day. I spent four hours patiently, and then not so patiently, pointing out to him that he was just attention seeking and didn't really want to die. A discussion about death ensued. I explained that death itself wasn't scary; there just wasn't a lot of point to it.

'Life is the scary thing,' I heard myself say, 'you're just being a wimp!' I spoke with confidence and related my own near-death experience. Somehow, he forgot his worry, drowned his own self- pity and walked away. I saw him whenever our paths crossed for a few years. Last I heard he was doing well.

Just like the man on the staircase, the second potential suicide had no intention of speaking to me nor anyone else. He was just in the wrong place at the wrong time, although I now believe he was exactly where he needed to be to get help. I didn't even know his name. I knew him by sight, and he was a year or two below me. I was walking back to my dorm room after a late lecture and had almost reached the door when I noticed an unusual shape off to one side in the dark. I stopped, nervous, and identified that it was most likely a human huddled over, sitting on the ground.

I approached tentatively, drawn by the feeling of utter misery emanating from the shape. As I came closer, I recognised the hooded face.. He was one of the younger students, a relatively new boy. Normally, I would have just rushed inside and left him there to do whatever it was he was doing in the near dark, but his sad energy drew me over. Suddenly the familiar bolt of energy shot through me yet again. Something was seriously wrong. I could smell it in the air. I moved to sit on the path in the dimness just a few feet from him. This encounter was different. When I spoke my voice was soft and gentle. We sat there for a very long time and while I was bitten from head to toe by mosquitoes, I heard my voice cajole and coerce. It was hypnotic even to me.

We talked about death and dying. Its full implications. What he wouldn't become, and what he might become if he stayed and worked through his current problem. I gave him every ounce of compassion I had to give, every grain of empathy and understanding. I had no awareness of the ongoing electricity pulsing through my body, until slowly, and ever so gently, it came to a halt.

I heard later that he stayed up all night. I went to bed but didn't sleep. The next time I saw him he looked shocking, obviously depressed and very sallow skinned. He continued to look awful for a couple of weeks. When we passed each other, he avoided my eyes and ignored my quietly offered, 'Hello.' I didn't stop offering it. He was embarrassed that he had bared his soul to a stranger, and it showed. He never spoke to me nor looked directly at me again. It didn't matter. I knew somehow that he would be alright. He was, and a few months later he was an obviously thriving and happy young man.

My penchant for attracting disturbed minds was becoming more obvious, even to myself. I sometimes thought that perhaps it was a case of 'like attracts like' as I was often depressed behind my cheerful mask. My life was confusing, having a foot in one world and a foot in another every day. My body still ached all over, and the constant pain wore me down. Some would say that as a Scorpio I attract people who need help. Some would say that it's to do with a person's personality. Some would say that this was all just a part of my destiny.

Looking back from the latter part of my life, I think this is normal for quite a few people. I am not the only one. Regardless, more and more often people came to my room, just to talk, to offload. I found it so strange to find them sitting in my room. Having walked past to find the door open and made some excuse to enter, they would suddenly confess their innermost secrets, plans, desires or less memorable moments. They were rarely people that I socialised with; more usually people that barely spoke to me as we passed in the dining room every day. They came and they sat, they talked, confided in me, and then they went away. We didn't bond. Once they left, our brief relationship ended. I was often left wondering why. What had their visit been about? I still don't know. I can only assume that something drew them to me in their time of need. I certainly wasn't reaching out now; if anything I was becoming more withdrawn.

Then I made a mistake. It was personal, and it was huge and proved beyond all doubt that having extremely good intuition didn't always stop me from behaving like the young human being I was. In fact, I made one of the least sensible choices of my life by choosing to ignore my intuition and renew a relationship with a young man that I had ended a couple of weeks prior. I gave in to the intense persuasion of a close friend, who made me feel cruel and then incredibly guilty for being so.

My upbringing won out, the belief constantly drummed into me that I was not a nice person, and she got her way. I backtracked and made up with my ex. A couple of months later I became engaged to this man that I'd initially run from. I couldn't ignore my intuition for ever though, and as it grew louder, I knew what I had to do. When I broke off the relationship for the second time, I learnt what it was like to be stalked and, eventually, I suffered violence at his hands. This was a lesson I learned the hard way, and one I was determined never to repeat.

In my defence there was never any sign of this man becoming violent. He was soft, gentle, kind and intelligent— and then he wasn't. It was that simple. At the end of the relationship, when things got heated between us, we both blurted out the same thing, that we had ignored our intuition at the beginning of the relationship. We froze and stared at each other. It was bound to end in disaster; we had made the same mistake. Our relationship was meant to be a lesson in life. I never made the same mistake again, and I sincerely hope that he can say the same. What I learned was to trust my intuition 100 percent. Nobody knows you like you know yourself. Listen to that inner voice.

Eventually I had to move to another city to escape him. I lived with a constant sense of *deja vue*. I presumed this was because I was running on heightened adrenalin. Living in fear does that to you. It heightens all your abilities, but it is simultaneously exhausting.

Chapter 11

Psychically Linked

I settled into a mundane life in my new city, moving house a few times as you do when you rent, and watched as my closest friends transitioned to married lives. I never thought about getting married I was twenty-three, had experienced violence and thrown away the chance to marry. I had no interest in finding the man of my dreams. After all, the first one had gone pear shaped in a big way, so why risk a second? My dreams were far more involved with world issues and disasters that I remembered when I woke up each morning. Boyfriends weren't part of it. Husbands weren't even in my imagination.

My leisure time was mostly spent with my head in a book, and I was invited to more parties than I ever attended. Did I get lonely? Yes, sometimes, however, I was naturally a loner who could come to life in front of people as required but was happy to return to my own private cave as soon as possible. I still didn't have much in common with my peers. For one thing, I was quite conservative for the time. I was not into sexual dalliances and discovering earlier in life that I was highly sensitive to alcohol, I'd chosen to not drink at all. 'Book Nerd and Boring' was how I described myself.

I often spent time on the weekend putting pen to paper, filling the garbage with pages of self-rejected manuscript. I was my own worst critic. I enjoyed writing for writing's sake, and I occasionally thought back to a childhood dream I'd held for a few months of becoming 'like Enid Blyton' and wondered what would have happened, how life might have been different if I'd followed that path. I toyed with the idea of writing a romance novel, but I never really took myself seriously.

For a short period of time, I even toyed with the idea of putting my own strange experiences to paper, but to be honest, when I tried, I found them too freaky. Even at this stage of my life, my 'near death experience was still too raw to rehash in my mind, let alone commit to paper. I knew that if I did write it down, I would be announcing to the world that I was 'weird'. I couldn't handle that possibility. I felt odd enough as it was.

'One day I will write the whole story.' I told myself, 'One day!' I felt deep inside that this was a definite 'have to do' thing in my life, but I also knew that at this time it was beyond me. It hurt too much. There was far too much emotional turmoil surrounding the whole event.

So, instead, I wrote poetry, expressing my innermost feelings, losing myself in my words, healing any pain that rose to the front of my mind. Mostly, this alone time was comfortable. It fitted me well. I didn't need a social mask until Monday, and on Monday's I would pop it on like a second skin, ready to play out the other part of my life.

I was not expecting it when my future husband came on the scene. All my premonitions about things that would happen in my life at first appeared not to have prepared me for this one. Funny how that works.

I was at a party one night, mostly against my wishes, having been dragged along by a friend and her housemate. I'd been spending the weekend at her place and had brought no party clothes with me, and I was feeling very uncomfortable dressed in her appropriated outfit and makeup. I had come at her and her flatmate's insistence only because, in the end, I was too polite to refuse. While everyone else danced or chatted with each other, I quietly positioned myself by the fireplace where I was thankfully left to myself. Slowly I relaxed from the stress of my social anxiety. With the warmth from the fire seeping through me, I started to trance in and out of a daydream when, very slowly, I became aware of a slight feeling of *deja vue*. Nothing immediately clear, just a curious 'been there, done that' kind of drifting sensation. Certainly not enough to warn me of what was about to happen.

An icy draught fluttered the flames and broke my meditational stare. I glanced up and slightly behind myself towards the door where I saw two men standing. One was tall, dark, and casually dressed. He was facing my way, and he loomed over a shorter figure whose face I couldn't see as his back was towards me. Instantly I felt...anticipation? Nervousness? Something indefinable. I quickly and uncomfortably looked away and stared back at the fire, mulling over my strange reaction to the two men.

The shorter male had very red hair. In the darker male, I sensed an arrogant self-assurance, an attribute I had taken, without realising it, an immediate dislike to. While I gazed and thought, the two men continued their conversation, and the door, letting in the cold breeze, remained open.

My eyes flickered backwards and forwards between the men and the fire, and as they did, so my nervousness rapidly increased. I felt that something was about to happen. Something important. I wasn't sure that I wanted it to even though at that point I couldn't identify exactly what it was. I wondered what on earth was wrong with me as panic rose in my chest and up into my throat, and a strong desire to just get up and run took over. I searched the group of dancers for my friend, hoping that she was ready to leave. I wanted to go home. Now!

A movement in the doorway captured my attention again. The males had changed position, and the redhead was now facing inwards, surveying the room as he talked. He had a dreadful handlebar moustache that was far too large and bulky to look attractive on such a medium build. The sense of wanting to run away intensified, and I looked away, seeking relief from my panicky feelings, but once again, I felt compelled to look back. I was confronted by a bright pair of blue eyes that seemed to have little to do with the facial hair. Shock waves passed through my body and my mind screamed as if in pain, 'No, not now. I'm not ready.' Shaking, I tore my eyes away and glared at the fire. I could not marry this man!

Perspiration broke out on my forehead. I felt physically ill. I knew beyond all doubt that this was the man I would spend the rest of my life with. Instead of cupids and violins I was instilled with a deep, nervous, fear. I had only had my comfortable life up and running the way I liked it for about six months at this point. I wasn't ready to have that changed in any way. It seemed though that I wasn't going to have much choice in the matter.

Of course, as in every Mills and Boon love story, he eventually approached me and of course we chatted, also like in every Mills and Boon. I was as cold towards him as I had been to every male who had shown any interest in my life since my previous break up. My problem was this one simply didn't go away.

This kind and gentle man was to insinuate himself beneath my armour as he pursued me with dogged, stubborn determination. My barriers stayed strongly in place, and I went to great lengths to not be involved again. I didn't share my contact details, and l even changed address, but still he found me. To be clear, it was never about whether I liked him or not, for something in his eyes got to me that very first night. No, it wasn't about him at all; it was entirely about my own fears caused by past trauma and the enormity of what I somehow 'knew' was to come. I had no doubt in my mind that this man was destined to become part of my future, part of my growth.

I was to teach him about my emerging spirituality and guide him to look beyond the man that life had convinced him he was. In return I would learn about the depth of myself and through living and loving along with him, I was going to come face to face with my 'promise'.

I somehow knew and yet struggled to understand what that meant. I found myself thinking on two completely different levels, once again reinforcing that I had a foot here on the ground and another in the future. The difference this time was there were no clear pictures to explain my knowing and my fear of what lay ahead. The years ahead of us turned out to be challenging to say the least, but regardless, we were destined to love. Over the next twelve months, in spite of my first months of iciness, we both fell deeply.

When we married in 1982, I was no happy-ever-after bride. My heightened intuition told me clearly that both this man and his life were going to be challenging. I had by now had some glimpses, mini movies, snippets of recalled dreams, and I knew that the future would not to be an easy road. Why then did I marry him? Well, for me it was simple. I knew beyond all doubt that this was where I was meant to be and this was who I was meant to be with, so, tough premonitions or not, I believed that I, we, would make it work.

Being in love enhanced and increased both my clairvoyant and psychic senses, and this became obvious while we were dating. At a Christmas party the night before my then boyfriend was to head over to New Zealand for a mountain climbing holiday with a group of friends, I found myself alone at a table with one of those friends, a lovely, intelligent young man who was somewhat eccentric compared to his mates. Around us, at other tables in the outdoor setting, were many other people all laughing and chatting and generally enjoying themselves. Within minutes of my partner's departure to the bathroom, I found myself in a conversation about the impending trip, something the boys were excited about. As often happened when something important and psychic was about to happen, I felt myself begin to buzz as if an electric current was passing through my body. Within minutes I figured out that this young man didn't really want to go climbing but was using the trip to avoid a commitment to spend time with his casual girlfriend during the holidays.

I also rapidly reached the conclusion that if he went mountaineering, he wouldn't come home. I felt sickened by this thought, and, shaken, I tried to convince him that running away to the mountains wasn't the only option that he had this Christmas. We discussed why he was reluctant to go mountaineering, why he was reluctant to commit to the girlfriend, and eventually why he felt that he couldn't just return home and visit his parents. His reasoning for the latter wasn't clear, but he was definitely reluctant to both stay and commit and to set off on his planned adventure. We talked for ages, and my need to convince him to not go to New Zealand became overpowering.

During this time no-one ventured near our table although I did look around and notice some people looking our way now and again. We were a quiet, still spot in a noisy party, and my boyfriend had disappeared, so I wasn't entirely surprised by this. We must have talked for over half an hour before finally my words became more forthright, and I told him that he shouldn't go to New Zealand and that it wasn't too late to cancel the flight. It was at that point that his normally vibrating high energy body stilled completely, and he looked me directly in the eyes and said, 'I have to go.'

My world turned over. There it was. That same feeling I'd had with my school friend a few years ago. The knowing. He wasn't coming home. I tried again. 'You don't have to go. That's your perception and it's not accurate. You can make another choice. You have options. You can even stay here and see no-one if you choose.'

He looked at me and then sadly shook his head. 'I have to go.' He was almost whispering now. This loud and active man was still. Still and sad.

I wanted to cry. In my heart I knew I'd been in this space before. With that he got up and wandered off into the crowd, and I never got to speak to him again.

I was at work when the phone call came from a girlfriend telling me that one of the mountaineers in the group had been killed while climbing. At that point no-one knew who, and she was letting me know, warning me, because my boyfriend was in the climbing party.

The human brain is astonishing and complex and while in my head I knew who was gone, a part of me was naturally scared that I'd also lost the man I was falling in love with. I was still shocked by the death, frightened, sickened, and worried, despite the premonitions that I'd had. Again my mind seemed to operate on two separate levels, and the psychic me and the human me ran simultaneously alongside each other. My mind bounced back and forth between my expectations and possibilities, although it did err more on the side of expectations. I had learned something from my previous experiences.

When the announcement of the young man's death came through, I cried. I relived every moment of that last conversation, every feeling that had passed between us and once again I hated the futility of this knowing. I had to know and yet not be able to alter the course of someone's life? I felt confused, responsible, distressed, but at the same time I knew that he had somehow, on some level, known what lay ahead and chosen that route. Why would someone choose that? This made no sense to me. It still doesn't. To this day I wonder what kind of man he would have had the chance to become if he'd listened to his inner self and been brave enough to stay and face whatever responsibility he was running away from that day.

Later, my partner, traumatised by the accident and death of his friend, would tell me that the young man had behaved completely differently to his normal self from the moment they had arrived. Instead of leading the expedition he had hung back. Instead of racing ahead to arrive at the climbing site, he'd lagged, slowing the group. 'It was almost as if he didn't want to be there. He was behaving strangely for him,' was my boyfriend's comment He passed away when a very large boulder dislodged and fell from right above him. I pondered on this for a very long time. What are the chances that on that minute, on that day, that boulder came loose over a man who somehow knew he shouldn't be on that expedition?

A few months later my boyfriend set out to climb Mt McKinley in Alaska, and if I had queried my level of involvement and feeling for him before he left, then his absence was to make me do so in a most unusual way as my psychic senses took over and changed my life.

While continuing my office job in Australia by day, my body clock went haywire. As his body adjusted to international time zones, so did mine! I prowled the floor at night and fought to stay awake during the day. My brain became rattled, and I became severely accident prone. I became so numb from lack of sleep that I was afraid to drive my car. My powers of concentration slipped drastically, and I felt that I was slowly going crazy. Friends that I mentioned this to teased me and said that I was just pining for him. They called me lovesick! How do you explain to people who haven't felt this range of bizarre behaviours that are completely contradictory to your norm that this is not a case of sad to be separated but something phenomenally different, something that is so intense that it's scary. My boyfriend had previously been away for extended periods of time with his work, for stints as long as three months, Of course I'd missed him, but this had never happened to me. It proceeded to become scarier with each passing day.

Over a period of two days I began to hallucinate. I wasn't seeing in the spiritual or psychic way. I was genuinely hallucinating. Creatures came at me out of walls causing me to jump in fright. My head gradually felt fuzzy and became fuzzier, then pressured until it was so painful it felt like it might explode. My body became heavy like lead, and my legs and feet became so painful I could barely walk. I needed to wear woolly slippers and socks just to be able to put my feet on the floor, but even the act of putting the socks on was exceedingly painful. I couldn't work and phoned in sick saying that I had the flu as that was the closest thing I'd experienced, and I did ache all over. I lay in bed watching pink elephants coming towards me out of the snow. 'What snow?' I asked myself. 'What snow?!' I sat up, stunned. An hour later, it all stopped. I was left feeling teary and completely exhausted. I knew that I hadn't had the flu, but what had I had? What had been wrong with me?

It was only on my partner's return that we both realised that I had been living his symptoms and seeing inside his head. He had suffered severe high-altitude sickness and been forced to retreat alone down the mountain. He had even seen the pink elephants as part of his hallucinations. He developed bad frostbite on his feet, which were very tender, swollen and in parts completely black; dead skin that would fall off in clumps in the coming weeks.

On the other side of the globe, I had mysteriously suffered with him. My painful symptoms disappeared only when he returned to the safety of base camp. We were both incredulous. We were just two ordinary young people with no understanding at this point in our lives of how this was even possible. It was an awesome, if not horrendously disconcerting, experience to share with someone, but it was beyond explanation. Between ourselves we felt that we shared one incredibly unusual bond. No surprises then that a few months later we married.

Chapter 12

Anything IS Possible

From the day we married my psychic experiences grew stronger. I naturally wanted to share the stuff that happened to me with somebody, and who better than the man that I loved. Uh huh! Not likely! While we were dating, he had mostly laughed at or overlooked my psychic comments, but now my darling new husband disliked hearing my remarks about events that were going to happen as they were threatening his view of the world. He would show irritation or anger depending on how blatant my comments were. Watching television an actor might pop up on the screen, and I'd casually say something like, 'That man is going to die soon,' or 'That woman is going to be involved in a serious accident.' Initially he would look at me and say nothing or ask how I knew. When the predictions came true, he became nervous and asked me not to tell him in future. I promised to try.

I remember getting very angry one day after I had thoughtlessly spoken aloud once again without checking the content of what I was saying. He got very cross this time, and he told me bluntly that he didn't want to hear any more about it. Nothing! At my core I objected and, angry at once again not being allowed to be myself, I found myself thinking that there was no way this marriage would work if I had to pretend to be someone I wasn't. I wasn't going to keep it to myself for the rest of my life, and he wasn't going to win this battle. I needed to feel free to speak, and I needed him to at least accept my reality; he didn't have to join me in it. I would try harder to filter my information, but he was also going to have to learn to deal with it!

By our second year together I started to really receive clear and detailed premonitions, and, after several events I spoke aloud about eventuated, he became very annoyed by my excited waffling. I was excited by this ability now as finally quite a few of my premonitions were just ordinary rather than dramatic or life altering. With no fear or pain involved I was fascinated and enjoying them. My husband couldn't handle being told that if he did A then C would happen. In his logical mind B always came after C, but when I kept being proved correct and his actions kept getting unwanted results, he was ready to shove my advice and my premonitions down my throat.

One evening after yet another spat about the subject, we retired to bed in silence. He slept. I tossed and turned. Eventually I sat up in bed and said aloud, 'If you want me to do this, then you've got to give me some help.' I felt foolish. Who or what was I talking to? I wasn't sure I knew but after the foolishness came a feeling of complete calm. This difficult situation between us would be fixed. I suddenly knew that with certainty. I slept like a baby and awoke the next morning feeling better than I had for weeks.

A day later, the subject still unmentioned between us, the spat ignored completely, my husband donned his leathers to ride his BMW to work. A familiar electric feeling flooded through me. My psychic spark! 'Okay, you asked for practical, here it is. Don't speed on the road to the Army Base this morning. There will be a speed trap there.' He looked startled, and so did I. I hadn't exactly planned for that to come out of my mouth. I didn't even know where the information had come from.

I don't speed,' he growled, 'and there are never any police on that road anyway. It's straight. You'd see them.'

I let the subject drop as my nerves got the better of me. I didn't want another fight. How could I have been so sure? Where had the information come from anyway?

That evening, I was greeted with, 'You were right! Have you been talking to the bloke next door?' Our neighbour, who we rarely saw, was a police officer. I hadn't seen nor spoken to him for weeks and promptly said as much. 'Fluke,' he growled.

'Was it though?' I had to wonder.

Over the next three weeks I was able to accurately predict each time the police would be on that road with a speed gun. I didn't ask for confirmation. I just kept announcing if they were going to be there each day. At the end of the two weeks my husband informed me that they were blitzing that strip of road. I quietly smiled but said nothing. At the end of week three I woke up with a definite feeling of completion. 'It's over,' I told him, 'no more police.'

It was another week, after plenty of time to think, before he confessed. Not only had I been correct every time that I had informed him the police presence would be there, but prior to my warnings he had indeed sped many times on that strip of road. 'It's great for a bike, dead straight.' He went on to sheepishly admit that whatever I had, wherever the information came from, it scared him, but that it was not something to be sneered at. He would listen to me in future, but he didn't want to be involved. I took that for the rather large apology it was, and the tension that remained between us subsided at last. Looking back now, I know that incident really saved our marriage. I could never have been anything but myself, which meant a slowly widening rift would have developed given time.

I continued to want to fulfil my promise, but it still evaded me, and the following year we moved to Adelaide with his work. I took an admin position in a local hospital where, in the first three months, I heard myself laughingly tell my new boss that I was only going to be there for three months. I recall being dreadfully embarrassed at the time. You just didn't say stuff like that to your new boss! I had no idea where the comment had come from, and I certainly didn't plan to leave in three months. Jobs were simply too hard to come by!

You can imagine my surprise then when three months later I handed in my notice. My boss looked at me strangely as I explained that I had to leave for medical reasons. 'You said you'd be leaving in three months. Did you know about your illness when you started?' he queried.

We looked at each other for a minute. 'Sometimes I say stuff like that without knowing why. It's always right though,' I replied, a bit sheepishly.

'I think you might be a bit psychic,' he said and smiled at me. 'Well, we will be sorry to lose you.'

I walked away feeling stunned, which makes me chuckle now because how did I not know that I was psychic by that time? Was it because I had never talked to anyone about it? I'd certainly not had anyone say that to my face before. A small window opened in my mind, a light that would soon widen and be acknowledged in a much stronger way. I was leaving because I had been diagnosed with endometriosis and considering my age, my husband and I had decided to follow medical advice, control my diabetes as tightly as possible, and try to start a family before it was too late. We had been given twelve months. Twelve months is a very small amount of time when you consider a lifetime, and the news had been unexpected, but we really wanted children and were willing to go without financially to achieve our dream. Unbeknown to us, this change was to make for an interesting year.

At home for hours at a time and knowing no-one but my husband, I soon became bitterly lonely. My continuing exhaustion and pain seemed worse than ever. I'd thought that once I gave up work it would ease, but no, it continued as it had throughout my university days with no improvement despite the amount of rest I was getting. My body made no sense to me at all. I reminded myself that I likely had a level of depression from being alone and isolated and that it might be all in my mind. To distract myself I read a lot and taught myself to knit and make bread dough jewellery but having few relatives to gift it to and no friends, I soon stopped.

My husband worked very long hours and when he was at home, he seemed only interested in talking about his work. Gone was the gentle and attentive man who appeared with flowers on occasion and organised date nights at random moments between his busy periods. He seemed to have been replaced with an obsessed workaholic. We didn't talk much at all. We didn't play. When he did have down time, he would mow the lawn and then compulsively polish his BMW motorbike that he'd owned when we married.

I knew no-one other than him. I still had too little physical energy to join a gym although I had tried for a short time when we were first married, and as there was no internet back then I had no way other than the local newspapers to find ways to meet people my own age. My peers were at work during the week or were mothers going to mothers' groups for their weekly entertainment. I started to feel like a drudge who just took care of the house, cooked and paid the bills while my husband enjoyed his career. I was becoming openly resentful.

What I really needed, more than even company, was something to do with my mind. I didn't think of myself as intelligent or clever, I just needed to be learning to be happy and to balance my moods. I was bored and physically isolated. In a fit of disgust at letting myself live this way, I decided that I would do something for myself, even if it made us broke!

Common sense prevailed as it always has with me, and I gradually honed down my interests and found a course that we could afford to pay for. I signed up for a Diploma of Massage. This was still quite a controversial thing to do in the eighties in Australia as massage was still heavily associated with brothels, and its image was a long way from today's image of being good for your health and wellbeing. It makes me laugh now, but it shocked my parents who took some convincing that it was indeed therapeutic in the true sense of the word. I had no idea when I started just how much this course would affect me and open my mind to my psychic gifts. Surprises lay ahead.

For the first time in an age, I was happy. This proved to be a very rewarding time of rapid and deep spiritual growth for me. Not only did I discover my gift of hands-on healing but working with my hands also brought my psychic and clairvoyant abilities to the fore. In class we teamed up with partners, and it wasn't very long before I was asking my new massage partner about people, both dead and alive, that I felt and sensed around her as my hands massaged out her knots and eased her tension. We became good friends, and we remain so today. Through her I also discovered that I had the ability to 'read' photographs. The whole experience of opening this way both intrigued and exhilarated me. I completed the course and I signed on with the same teacher, and the same friend, to learn Polarity Healing (hands on healing working with the energy flows and blockages in the body) and, by the end of this course, I had two new and unusual to me experiences.

The first experience was brought about by another student in the class. We had had our test papers returned to us and were all idly chatting when she suddenly turned to me and said, 'Lynne would you hold my wallet and tell me what comes into your head?' This was random and not part of our course work; we had done nothing like it at all.

Stunned I looked at her, trying to digest her words and make sense of them. 'Why?' I eventually asked, as those who had heard her request stopped and stared at me. As the group stilled, she simply smiled and said, 'Because you can.'

To this day I don't know why I complied other than that I have always liked a challenge and that this seemed an utterly bizarre thing to do. I had never heard of reading objects and didn't associate it at all with the photograph reading I had done for my friend, so what happened next surprised me as much as it did many of the others in the room who also hadn't witnessed this skill.

Slowly at first and then quite quickly, I began to rattle off men's names. All men, no women. The poor woman. Her eyes opened wider with every name that I spoke. After blurting out several names, I stopped and looked at her hesitantly, concerned that I was doing something wrong and sensing that this wasn't what she'd wanted me to do. I wondered briefly if they meant anything, or if I was just making them up as I went along. As she remained silent, staring at me, my discomfort grew. I apologised, 'I'm sorry, all I can pick up are names. It's not making any sense, is it?' With that she threw back her head and laughed loudly.

This lady was older than me and far more worldly, having

travelled widely and had experiences I was yet even to dream of, so I felt very naïve and young sitting with her.

She reined in her laughter, tears running down her cheeks and explained, 'You have just listed, in order, every single boyfriend I have ever had, except for the one who gave me the wallet.'

I looked at her seriously for a minute while the others gasped and then I said, 'His name is (for the sake of the story) George, and he's not going anywhere. He's sticking around.'

She replied, 'Oh, you are absolutely correct about the name. Let's hope you are right about the rest.'

This event really made me think. I went home on a high, and that night I acknowledged that the psychic field was where I got my real buzz out of life. I didn't understand how it worked, but I loved it.

The second unusual thing that happened on this course also occurred near the end. We had all done our healing course working on a partner. The teacher now decided that we should do an experimental group session where everyone worked simultaneously on the same person. He decided that I was to be the body on the table. No discussion time was offered, no volunteers requested. I was 'it' for the night. I struggled to refuse as my weakness from being ordered around as a child came to the fore. I knew somewhere inside me that I should have been asked but even as my mind fought against it, I complied. I got onto the table with rising nervousness. Why I should be nervous about what had already proven to be the most soothing and wonderful therapy I didn't know, and so I remained the silent guinea pig for an experiment that went out of control.

Within minutes of everyone placing their hands on the various healing points on my body that are used in Polarity Therapy, positives to negatives, I was completely relaxed and unexpectedly travelling backwards through my life. I was with my guide from babyhood, holding her hand and skipping along a pathway. She just glided along, and I was aware of somehow travelling at her pace. Then suddenly I was following her and couldn't keep up. I was getting smaller, physically shrinking from inside myself. It was the most bizarre of feelings. The light which had been bright and sunny became a deep red and continued deepening until it became black and then blacker still. The space around me became tight and then tighter until I felt like I couldn't breathe, and then, the blackness. There was no breath! There was also no nervousness. No fear. Only a deeply calm sense of peace. They came to me, and I saw.

What did I see? I opened my mouth and gasped aloud and at that exact moment the teacher made a dreadful misjudgement. He indicated for all students to remove their hands simultaneously. Locked into my inner world I did not hear nor see that this was about to happen. My inner sight was focused entirely on what was before it. Consequently, when the hands lifted and shock ripped through my body, I felt like I was being torn apart, completely and utterly abandoned, and my grief at this abandonment was utterly horrific. In pain, my body launched itself upright and with no controls of any sort, I screamed at the top of my lungs.

We all went into shock. Everyone present was deeply upset. We were a group of empathic energy healers there to help not to hurt, and this was absolutely the opposite of what we were supposed to be experiencing. It took about fifteen minutes before I was able, in a very broken and shaky voice, to describe what I had experienced. It was mutually agreed that I appeared to have regressed to the birth canal memory and beyond. I don't know if they were correct for there are no answers, but it certainly resonated deep within my psyche. I did know that this was a journey I didn't want to end. Once the nervousness had passed, I had moved into a state of bliss from which I did not want to return. The journey itself was a complete contrast to the sudden thrust back into reality. If the students had not withdrawn their hands from my body, then who knows where their channelling would have taken me. I certainly have no intentions of repeating the exercise to find out, however, as the return was awful. I never want to experience anything like that again. What has puzzled me and will continue to puzzle me, I suspect until the day I die, was who were 'they' and what did I 'see'? This became another mystery to stand side by side with my promise.

It was around the time of the massage course when I was inspired to learn more about my unusual mind or skills, or both, that I bought my first pack of tarot cards. I felt that I needed a channel for my premonitions and knowing. I needed an outlet and thought perhaps that this would help me understand and make use of my skills. It was to become a relationship that has lasted until this day. Perhaps it shouldn't have surprised me, but it did, that within a couple of weeks I felt completely at home with them. I used to practice by reading my husband's work life, using it as a tool to try and draw him out of himself and his obsession with work. I would pick up on problems he was experiencing and confront him with the information, at first hesitantly and soon with absolute conviction. Interestingly, the shock of me seeing into his world, when he knew he had not confided in me, worked as nothing previously had, and slowly he began to communicate with me more openly again, gradually moving back from his work obsession.

To be fair to my husband, I have seen many men display similar if not the exact same behaviour over my lifetime. It is a weakness that robs them and their loved ones of so much that it makes me sad every time I encounter it. People are what is important. Careers put food on the table but who are you feeding if your family or relationships disintegrate from lack of attention? Seek balance if you want to be happy now as well as when you are older!

Life was never meant to stand still, and the lady whose wallet I had read decided to move my life along its unchosen path. Out of the blue I received a phone call from a young girl whom she had referred for 'one of my beautiful massages'. Her words not mine. The courses were complete, and I was missing the time spent with the lovely group we had become, so I agreed to give her a massage, and we set a date.

It turned out that she had been sent for more than a massage and that my course mate had known exactly what she was doing. The trouble was, did I? My new client had been raped while alone in her apartment. A stranger had entered during the night while she slept and attacked her. She had received extensive counselling which she still attended as the need took her. On the first visit, knowing nothing of this, I gave her a massage and tried hard to block the messages I was feeling through my hands and the pictures that formed in my brain. Massage completed, she thanked me profusely and then went home. Job done.

She left me deeply troubled. While working on her body I'd been unable to stop the pictures flooding through my mind and feeling all sorts of grief and trouble from her. I had picked up on problems which I believed had their roots way back in childhood. Not knowing a thing about her history, I cautiously talked my concerns over with my husband.

When she returned for a follow up session the next week, she stayed chatting for some time and spilled her basic traumas with surprising ease. She had an abusive father and had gone on to have abusive friends, relationships with married men that had always brought her grief, and finally, she had been attacked and raped. It was quite a horrendous history, and I had been right to be so concerned about what I had seen. I now felt completely out of my depth. I was only young, about twenty-six, and I had had quite a narrow and protected upbringing. I had little life experience, and I was still naïve about many aspects of the world. What did I know of helping people with problems like this? It scared me that she wanted me to help her, so, in my usual blunt style I told her so in no uncertain terms. Strangely, she implicitly believed in me in a way that I had never believed in myself. She believed in my ability to help her that had nothing to do with my training.

For the next couple of months, she returned regularly and underwent what I now know to be a form of regression therapy along with her regular massage. She had high hopes that releasing her pain would heal a serious skin disorder that she suffered. It didn't, at least not in the time I worked with her, but the positive change in her attitude to the world around her over those months was huge, and she couldn't thank me enough. I, being me, was embarrassed by her effusiveness. I had been clear from the start that I was no counsellor or therapist and that I had no real experience in working with my psychic abilities. She didn't care. Because of her attitude and faith in me, we gained gifts from each other. She was so sure that my psychic abilities would help her that I soon lost my fear of relaying the information I picked up about her life, and as I worked with her, I gained confidence. What I had been afraid of up until that point now became a blessing.

We all like to think that we are in charge of our lives, and sure, we all make certain decisions and feel like we are managing our pathways, but sometimes I wonder. Is life a series of unplanned coincidences leading us to the lifetime that we signed up for before we arrived? How does life unfold sometimes with so many unexpected synchronicities, and are we all steps in someone else's great plan? There are no answers, of course, but my mind is forever curious. What happened next was one of those events that really made me stop and consider. Did I make the choices? Really? Was it just a case of dominoes all falling into place so that someone else got the help they needed? Was there a bigger plan? Like I said, there are no answers. None, but I had a heck of a lot of questions.

Chapter 13

The Little Girl and the 'Miracle of Trust'

In desperation a friend of my client asked to bring her stepdaughter to see me, a little girl about three years of age who was suffering serious trauma. This little one had stopped speaking after her birth mother, along with her boyfriend, had abused her. She screamed uncontrollably at night, wet the bed, and would become hysterical if her father and stepmother cuddled or kissed in front of her. Their very touching would send her into hysterics.

Prior to the abuse she had been well adjusted, happy, and dry at night. At this stage she had done the rounds of police, counsellors and social workers. She was still in therapy. It didn't seem to be working. Her beloved father and stepmum had followed all legal channels and therapist suggestions, but they were getting nowhere. The child remained severely distressed, and her emotional health appeared to be deteriorating as now she would allow no-one but her father, and her stepmother to actually touch her. I couldn't imagine what was happening in the little darling's mind. The story of her abuse shook me to my core and made me physically sick.

I asked why on earth they would want to bring her to me. Once more I emphasised that I had no qualifications, and even less experience, as I didn't even have a child of my own. This was their child's mind they were risking in their quest for help. Were they certain they wanted to do this? Trust that an unqualified stranger might help her where so many had already failed?

Desperation is a horrendous state to live in. I was to experience it myself for different reasons later in my life, but at this point I was searching for reasons that made sense within my own experience. They rang back several times. Each time I gave them the same spiel. I just wasn't qualified.

Finally, after a very tearful phone call from the stepmother I gave in, but to say that I was nervous was an understatement. I was terrified. Such a personal appeal had touched my heart, and I have always loved children. To me they were and still are such precious bundles that we are meant to protect and nurture. Nothing bad should ever be allowed to touch them. As I dwelt on her story my horror and disgust were to help me overcome my fear of my own perceived inadequacies. I became riled up, angry. I wanted justice. I wanted fairness and retribution. By this stage I wanted to help even though I had zero idea of how I could. Could anyone take away her pain? Even some of it? I was sure that I couldn't, but I had seen some very strange things happen in the past few years. I was trying to conceive myself, and I found myself thinking, 'What if this was my child? What would I do?'

Her stepmother had told me that the child psychologist desperately needed her to express either through pictures or speech what was going on in her head as at that time this was necessary in South Australia to convict the adults involved. I forget the details of how that worked but it was vital to the little girl's case as well as to her healing. My heart physically hurt for her, a girl that I had not yet met, and so, after making an appointment time for her to come and see me, I went to bed that night and turned to the unknown and asked for help. I believed I couldn't help, but I wanted to. If something was to help though, it would have to come from somewhere bigger than myself.

I awoke the next morning with only an 'nth' of my normal pain. My mind was fresh, totally clear headed and quite business like. I was surprised. This was not my normal state at all. I know now that I was geared up to meet the challenge ahead and that adrenalin was pumping through my system, but I didn't have such knowledge back then. I felt like I was on a high and that anything was now possible. Within minutes I was in awe of this woman who had jumped out of bed. Who was she, and why couldn't I feel like this every day?

I phoned the stepmother with a plan that I had no knowledge of making. It come to me while I was asleep. I told her to arrive around 10 am for morning tea and to be prepared to stay a long time. It would take as long as it took. 'Treat me more as a friend than a stranger. Nothing can or will happen until everyone is very relaxed and comfortable so we will spend quite a while just chatting. Please find things to talk about; make a list if you need to. We can't have any awkward moments. You can also bring your friend, my client, if you think that will make it easier for you. I will pay very little attention to your daughter, but you are to be perfectly normal with her. I don't want you to try to get her to talk to me or interact with me in any way that you haven't always done when she meets a stranger. When and if the time is right, I will attempt to earn her trust. This will take time. If I succeed and feel that I can do something more, then I will take her to the nursery room and show her the animals on the walls.'

The stepmother immediately interjected, 'She won't go with you. She'll scream. She won't leave me.'

'Relax,' I heard myself say, 'If she comes with me then we will go alone. If she doesn't want to come with me, then we won't go at all. The important thing is that she feels safe and that she wants to trust. It's not about what we want to happen. However, if she does come with me, I want you nearby. If she panics, you need to be right there, so, I will need you to go as quietly as possible out of my back door and around to the nursery window. I will make sure before you arrive that the blinds are tilted so that you will be able to see in, but she won't be able to see out. I will also make sure that the window is wide open so that you can hear every word spoken, it is essential that you are present, and that you can see that she is safe with me too.

'Now, I know you don't know the layout of my home, but the nursery, which was beautifully decorated by the original owner, has wonderful decals of animals all over it so is the perfect magical place for a little child. It is off to the right of the lounge room, but I will remind you of everything a bit at a time while we are chatting over tea and cake.

'Remember nothing at all might happen, and you might have to bring her back here several times before she trusts me or anything positive eventuates, if in fact it is going to.'

We talked about the stepmother's fears for a little while, reconfirmed the appointment day and time, and ended the call.

I was going to rely entirely on my intuition to guide us through the day, step by step, minute by minute. My initial adrenalin rush wore off as the day progressed, and my nervousness returned. I am a worrier by nature, but this was such an important thing for the little girl that I was deeply concerned, and so, while somewhere in my head I had this deep sense of calmness, the rest of me went on worrying.

For the next three days before our meeting took place, I worried myself sick during the daytime and received messages in my dreams at night. The night before her visit I saw her standing on my doorstep holding a doll, and I woke up soaked in tears. Once they abated, I found myself still nervous but at the centre of my being was a sense of profound calm. I felt that I was to do my bit, and all would be okay. Did I know what that meant? No. What I did know was that it wasn't up to me; I just had to trust.

They arrived. I opened the door and there was the little girl, clutching her doll, just as I had seen her. She clung to her stepmother's skirt and tried to hide behind her the moment she set eyes on me. We adults greeted each other as if we had known each other for years. I said 'Hello' to the little one and then proceeded to ignore her. I found that enormously difficult. I love children!

I did what I was guided to do. That was my job. I could feel the tension from the other two ladies, so I made tea and small talk then more tea and more talk and gradually everyone but the little girl relaxed. Seriously I have never worked so hard at getting visitors to relax in my own home. Social niceties are not my forte, but I pulled out all stops for this one. I knew it was desperately important that the child felt friendliness between us. I also knew that the words weren't really the important thing here. She would have been making decisions about me from the moment she set eyes on me so my whole body had to tell her subtly that I cared, that with me she was safe. I couldn't rely on my natural affinity with children. I was the one the adults were asking for help, but to the little girl I was the one under scrutiny, and if I didn't measure up to her needed standards then this whole experiment would fail. I had one chance. Just one.

The little girl eventually emerged from behind the folds of skirt that she had continued to bury herself in even after her stepmother sat down and made herself comfortable. She came out hesitantly, slowly, carefully, and to my surprise she looked straight at me. This was the child from my night's dreams. Having looked once, she clutched at her doll and hid her face again. She resisted all attempts by her stepmother to get her to eat or drink, and just as I'd planned, we carried on around her mostly behaving as if she wasn't there at all.

It took over an hour of small talk before the adults lost their tension and the energy and vibration in the room lifted noticeably. As it did so, I felt a gentle electric current flowing softly through my body. Even more subtly I began to feel like an observer to a strange piece of theatre, involved on some level but not on others. I felt everything, every nuance of emotion, with an enormous and increasing intensity, and yet, at the same time, I felt as if I had moved away from them all. The nearest sensation I have ever had to this was while I was being put to sleep with anaesthetic, only I didn't drop off to sleep, and the intensity of awareness, if it was possible, kept increasing.

Feeling I was losing control over my body and slightly afraid I would run out of energy and exhaust myself before I was able to see any results, I silently asked for all the help that the universe could give me, and I switched my attention indirectly to the little girl while still continuing to converse only with the other adults.

I began a one-sided conversation about dolls and how I liked them in pink dresses, and I talked about how many dolls I had as a child. I talked about what my dolls had worn, what they looked like and what I had called them. I covered their personalities in great but simple detail. It took some minutes before the other adults even realised that I'd switched tack and that although the conversation didn't seem so, things had become serious. I saw them glance at each other as realisation hit them almost simultaneously, and a silent acknowledgement passed between them as I slowly drifted into stories about an imaginary little girl, describing the little girl's fears, how big the world seemed to her, and a million other things that were pertinent only to a small child.

I talked for at least twenty minutes, and as I did so, very slowly, perhaps only a centimetre at a time, the little girl crept closer. Sometimes she moved back to her stepmother, touching base for reassurance, but always she returned, closer and closer. Eventually she arrived at my feet, very carefully not touching me. Her brilliant round eyes never left my face. Not once had I acknowledged her, nor had I spoken to her directly.

'I like dolls,' she whispered, 'I like animals too.' She softly touched my knee. I acted surprised and delighted at this information, pretending it was the first time I'd heard it. She was talking to me. This little darling who had, until now, been refusing to talk to others, was giving me her trust. I felt my heart burst open with a deep warmth, and I choked back a few tears threatening to spill. Was there anything more beautiful?

I questioned her gently for the next few minutes. What was her doll's name? What sort of animals did she like? Did Mummy (she called her stepmother Mummy) like them too? What about Daddy? Did she like the sun? What about flowers? Did she like them? She replied to all my questions, softly, timidly, occasionally looking back at her stepmother for reassurance that everything was right in the world, and, receiving her smile and a nod or two, she continued.

I had earlier established that she liked butterflies, so it was easy enough now to guide our conversation in the direction I needed it to go. 'I have a beautiful room here that has butterflies on the wall. Really pretty ones. Would you like to see them?' I asked. I fully expected her to retreat to her stepmother and she did, straight back to hang on to her knee. It was what was to happen next that mattered.

'Mmm, I would like to,' she answered hesitantly.

'Well, my room has white clouds in a blue sky, and giraffes up the walls and it's even got bumble bees playing in flowers,' I told her, and I gave a deliberate little giggle. 'Only the bumble bees aren't real, they're only pictures and they are really pretty,' I assured her. 'The butterflies are my favourites though. They are this big!' I held up my hands to show her the size.

She returned to my knee. 'Not that big!' she exclaimed, 'not big!'

'Yes they are!' I smiled down at her.

She put her hands on my knees and leant forward. 'Not that big,' she repeated. I began to describe the butterflies floating across the blue wall and the lovely white clouds above them.

Suddenly the electric current flowing through me stepped up its charge. I heard my voice deepen, and I looked straight into her eyes. I heard all that followed as if it had nothing to do with me. I put out my hand, not touching her, waiting. 'Would you like to come and see my butterflies?' I waited. The other adults in the room held their breath. She hesitated. She looked over at her stepmother who, bless her heart, summoned up a very reassuring and loving look that said both, 'It's okay' and 'How exciting!'

Ever so slowly the little one placed her hand into mine. Tentative trust, but trust nonetheless. I stood up and she almost changed her mind when she registered that we had to leave the room. I heard my voice coaxing her, entrancing her, mesmerising her, reassuring her all at the same time. 'Mummy can come and see the butterflies too,' I said. Her eyes clouded over. 'Please help me,' I begged silently. Another rush of electricity swept through me and around me. I felt floaty as if I wasn't fully present at all. Her eyes looked up into mine and suddenly lit up. She smiled, and hand in hand we walked through the door.

I have no real memory of the short walk up the corridor only that I started telling her again about the beautiful animals and butterflies and how much she was going to love it, trying to give her no time to think about what she was doing or where she was going outside of the pictures that were likely passing through her mind. I had a vague awareness, checked that box, of the two adults moving to the outside of the house, keeping their word to keep her in their sights as much as possible. Then I opened the door on what was a magical world for a child her age, and I immediately distracted her by pointing out one of the taller animals.

Low down at her height was a giraffe, flowers and some bumble bees. There was a tiny butterfly. 'Butterfly,' she exclaimed delightedly.

'Isn't it pretty?' I asked her, 'I think it's beautiful.'

As she gazed around, I could feel the tension beginning to rise in her body. She touched the butterfly and then quickly put her hand back in mine. With only a slight hesitation, I suddenly knew what I had to do next. I told her that the best and biggest butterflies were up high. Without giving her time to protest at my touch, I picked her up and swung her, not so easily, onto the top bunk bed from where she could both see and touch two giant butterfly pictures.

In a flash I saw momentary fear crash across her face at my touch and then her whole body tensed rigidly, and she trembled. I had let her go in the instant that she reached the bed but did not stop talking. 'See there they are. Aren't they the most beautiful butterflies in the whole world?' Again, momentarily, she forgot her fears. Her eyes widened and for a minute she caressed the picture.

Then the atmosphere changed. I felt a cold iciness descending on the room. She sat back on the bed, very still, her eyes focussed on the butterflies. I didn't speak. I let her process whatever was going on in her mind. Silence. Slowly she turned her head as if in a daze and looking me straight in the eye she said, clearly and loudly, 'He stuck his...in me. He hurt me.'

Her little eyes looked like those of a wizened old woman, they were so pained, so disbelieving. She promptly burst into tears and threw herself forward. I caught her gently but firmly and swooped her down off the bunk speaking soothingly to her the whole time. She was by now hysterical, her body fully rigid as, in floods of tears, her stepmother reached her side and taking her from me, wrapped her in her arms and rushed her from the room.

I stood alone in the nursery. Stunned. Unsure of why or how it had happened. Deeply saddened, tears flowing down my face. The electricity that had carried me through this event had gone. Did it go suddenly, or had it slowly seeped away? I couldn't tell you. All I knew was that I wanted to curl up there on the floor, turn foetal, and cry my heart out. Even though I had already been told in less direct terms what had happened to the little one, the words when she spoke had both shocked and filled me with instant revulsion. Reliving the scene now, I desperately fought waves of nausea and faintness. My knees gave way. It was only the shock of hitting the floor that snapped me out of my own emotions and back into cold reality. I hadn't finished my job. They may have had the breakthrough they wanted, but my part wasn't yet over. Instinctively I knew that. I didn't know what came next, but shakily I went to join the others.

The stepmother was crying both with relief and amazement. Six months of therapy had been unable to produce this result. Nobody had been able to get the child to talk about the incident, and yet she had just stated clearly what medically had been known for months. The little one was still sobbing in her arms and we were all in various states of shock.

I motioned them back into the garden, and we all sat on chairs I had placed out there on the off chance they might be needed. Hundreds of white butterflies seemed to have descended on our garden! I often wonder about this. How much was coincidence? Synchronicity? Some kind of magic? I had used the butterflies to capture her imagination, and now she was outside surrounded by literally hundreds of them.

I silently questioned, 'Were there always this many?' No and certainly not at this late time of day. Much as I love butterflies, I couldn't say that I'd ever seen so many.

Quietly I pointed them out, talking gently, ever so calmly. Slowly the sobbing ceased. A little wet face emerged from the safety of her stepmother's chest, now soaked in tears, and she hesitantly looked around seeking the magical butterflies. I remember one of us made tea and got the little one a drink which she sipped between small gulps of air. She looked at me warily from her safe place, and I went back to my storytelling.

This time I talked about a little girl who had been badly hurt by grown-ups and how frightened it had made her. How she was very afraid of being hurt again. How, because of these 'naughty' grown-ups, she thought that perhaps all big people would hurt her. I told her how this beautiful little girl, who also loved butterflies just like her, had a lovely kind daddy and mummy who were very angry with the people who hurt her. How they would never have let her be with the bad people if they had known how awful they were going to be to her as this mummy and daddy really, really, loved her, and they were going to help her to get rid of the hurt and make her feel all better.

The story took the best part of twenty minutes to tell but her eyes left my face only once, to seek confirmation that my words were true from her stepmother. Then I told her that I really loved her dolly and that she was very beautiful. By the time I had finished she was completely calm and exhausted, the sun was sinking, and the day was coming to an end. They took her home.

I was shattered, emotionally drained and utterly exhausted. I cried and then I cried some more. The world seemed such a horrible and awful place to me that day. So much injustice, so much pain. Such a tiny and innocent little girl.

I felt humbled and incredibly inadequate after this event. This was all so much bigger than me. Did I feel that the day had been successful? Yes, I did. These people had got what they needed. 'The experts' had said that the little one needed to express what had happened to her for healing to start. They had also said they needed her to express herself more clearly, in a way they could document, to strengthen the impending court case against her offenders. There was no doubt that offences had been committed, but to create a water-tight case, the little one needed to speak. Both these things had been achieved and hopefully she would continue now to speak out or perhaps express through art therapy what she had experienced and how she felt inside.

I was so deeply affected by the experience that I cried off and on throughout the next couple of weeks as I worried about how she would deal with this opening up, and I wondered what the aftereffects of the experience would be on her. On and on my mind went, and I lost a lot of sleep. Life was to teach me that adults cope far worse than most children. Children are so resilient and accepting, especially if surrounded by love the way this little one was. I didn't know that then, and so I continued to worry.

Two weeks later I met her father. He'd asked to meet this strange lady who had got through to his daughter where others had failed. He was a very pleasant and caring man, but I had no answers to the questions he threw my way. I didn't and still don't understand what happened that day but still believe that I was the tool of a larger energy source.

Three months later, just before I left town on yet another work posting for my husband, I received feedback from the stepmother. The little girl had attended her therapy session the following week and the story had spilled from her in words as well as artwork. Her therapist had been delighted at this breakthrough; the child could now begin to heal, and the legal case was watertight. The little one had now stopped wetting the bed and she was chatting normally again. Her mummy and daddy were allowed to kiss and cuddle without any hysteria on her part, and consensus was that given more time she would eventually be alright. Hearing this, I stopped worrying and finally took some pleasure in what I had been a part of. To this day, I occasionally wonder what happened to her and if she is now living a good life and has a family of her own. I certainly hope so.

Chapter 14

Losing and Winning

I had learned through this experience that on their own my abilities were useless, but, combined with someone's desire to be changed or need to be healed, they became powerful. Because of this realisation, I was feeling more secure with them and a little more confident in myself. I think sometimes learning about your 'self' is one of the hardest things that you do in life. I still thought that I was unusual, and I still wondered how it felt to live a life without strange visitations and premonitions. I imagined that it would be far more relaxing than how I lived my life as I had also started to realise that I lived with an above average stress level as I struggled to cope with living in what I felt were two completely different and yet related worlds.

I had good days and bad days with the whole concept of this unusual mind experience, and on the bad days I continued to think that maybe I was a little loopy. The good days were very different for although I still questioned the arrival of premonitions and other unexpected insights that were proved to be truths, and while I still tried desperately to analyse the why of them and to discover their source, I had discovered that forewarnings and sudden personality insights were often very useful. I came closer to accepting them more positively.

My previous experiences, particularly the one involving the little girl, made me more aware than ever of the responsibility involved with helping others with their lives. To me, the depth of their problems was far too complex for my learned abilities. I'd been raised to both act and think from an academic point of view and despite my apparent successes, it was from this point of view that I saw myself as untrained and therefore inadequately prepared to help others. The more I thought about the responsibility involved, the more frightened I became.

Our time in Adelaide was an enormous period of spiritual growth for me. It was in the early-to-mid eighties, and with no internet, no New Age Movement and only magazines to glean information from, I had not heard of such things as spirit guides and crystal healing and all the other adjunct paraphernalia that was soon to flood through Australia and open up the whole concept of psychic awareness, mind-body healing, and many other alternative practices.

Qi Gong became public knowledge here for the first time because it was tried by our then Prime Minister Bob Hawke's daughter when she travelled overseas seeking healing for an unidentifiable illness from which she was suffering. We were relatively ignorant, and almost everything except modern medicine was considered 'weird and alternative' and spoken of in scathing terms, if at all. Times were different then, and I didn't know we were on the brink of change. All I knew was that weird stuff happened to me, and it went against logic and everything that I had learned growing up.

It was with some trepidation then, that shortly after my session with the little girl and her family, I acknowledged the presence of an American Indian male standing in our bedroom doorway at night. The first time I saw him, I was scared witless. He was as clear as day. This was a different experience entirely to those of my childhood, but perhaps it was my childhood experiences that stopped me from screaming out, or perhaps I was just too scared to make a sound? By now I was well and truly an adult, and my logical mind largely ruled my world and my reactions to it. My perception of 'visitors' had completely altered. As an adult I was fully aware that these people weren't 'real'. They weren't solid. I was confused by this. Why did my brain keep telling me they were there if they really weren't? I was uncomfortable with this situation, but now it seemed different to what I experienced in childhood.

The first night I saw the American Indian in my doorway, looking for all the world as if he was casually waiting for a bus, I nearly died of fright. He was not the chief of my childhood encounters. I had been asleep and, sensing a presence, had slowly forced my eyes open to encounter this stranger in strange-to-me dress. On reflection, what was interesting was that it wasn't as if I hadn't already known he was around as he had appeared on occasion when I was doing polarity healing or massage on someone. The problem was that during a healing session, he was always just a dim impression, someone who was 'just in my head' and therefore easy to ignore. I had accepted him then because when I did healing, I moved into a semi-meditational state in which his presence was vague but also perfectly acceptable, normal even.

Now though my mind thought that this was not at all acceptable, not in the middle of the night with the bedside clock giving out it's dim light and obviously keeping perfect time. Nor was it acceptable that he should be perfectly clear against the dim light that was always left on in the hallway when I went to bed. In the beginning, he bothered me so much that I woke my husband, but I soon realised that I couldn't keep doing this as he worked long hours and was often exhausted. Instead, I made a pact with myself that if he moved out of the doorway towards me, I would scream; until then my husband could sleep. In retrospect this amuses me. Did I seriously think my husband could do anything to protect me from something he neither saw nor heard?

Every single time he appeared I got a fright. This didn't seem to bother him in the least, and he began to appear more and more often. Sometimes he would smile at me. More often, he was completely serious. Now this was a good ten years or so before it become trendy to relate to Native American Indian tribes, and their culture was popularised by the growth of New Age groups. I knew very little about them. I had read one book in my last year of high school that spoke of the horrendous massacres of their people and had been utterly horrified, wondering how on earth white men could be so brutal, and how that brutality was also exhibited by some tribes. I had questioned what on earth was wrong with us as people that we could behave that way, but I certainly didn't identify with the race.

Then, unexpectedly, one early morning while thinking about his previous night's visit, it dawned on me that I did indeed know this man and that I had seen him once before during my childhood. Interestingly I hadn't questioned why he was there then either. I simply wanted him to go away.

My fear grew greater with each sighting or visit until one night, startled from my sleep, I saw him standing silently and formidably in the doorway of my room. I instantly sat up and screamed at him. 'What are you trying to tell me?'

Why did I think he was trying to tell me anything? The screaming woke my husband. Poor man. Half of him believed my story and half of him obviously thought I'd gone bonkers. This was such a difficult time for him as he still struggled to believe what I was telling him about the strange events in my life, none of which sat well with his own Catholic belief system. This night, though, having first helped me to calm down, he offhandedly and not without some humour, suggested that I ask to be given messages they wanted delivered in a more amenable way. At first, I thought he was just being a smartass, but after thinking about it I took his advice and mentally asked to be given the message in a different way, preferably one that didn't involve 'visitors' and also didn't scare me.

My request partially worked as the Indian stopped appearing, but he was replaced immediately by nightmares about a baby with a grotesquely formed head. The child was male and always fair-haired. Instead of waking in fear, I woke up sobbing that something was wrong with my baby. This was a different type of fear entirely. Once again, I tried to logic my way through it. We had been trying to fall pregnant for eleven months at this point. We had been told that we needed to fall pregnant within twelve due to my medical condition, and so I told myself that the dreams were merely representing my fear of being unable to conceive. I couldn't convince myself of this, and my gut churned every time I thought about it.

About three weeks later I bounced out of bed and over to the dressing table mirror to pick up a hairbrush. I stopped still in utter shock. I was pregnant. I don't know how I knew, but I knew beyond all doubt. There, on my neck, where my head should have been, was the face of a fair-haired baby boy. I blinked. The vision didn't disappear. I blinked again. Now it was my face, but it was different to yesterday, rounder somehow. In an instant I felt like I had been kicked in the stomach. I was sure I was pregnant, I should have been ecstatic, but I was also just as sure that something was dreadfully wrong. I took a very long shower, and I cried. I wanted a baby with all my heart, but I knew that this one was only going to bring pain. I wanted to be excited. I wanted to be thrilled. I wanted to look forward to pregnancy tests and the thrill of telling my husband. I couldn't. I simply knew something that I should never have known.

The psychic life is interesting in some ways; it tends to attract others with more psychic awareness than most. Sure enough, a couple of hours later I opened the door to a lady who had come for a massage. Her first words were, 'Hello. Oh, you're pregnant, aren't you. Congratulations! How long have you known?'

Now I'd met this woman only once before, and I knew she was psychic, but her words still gave me a shock. Quietly I explained that I didn't know and yet I knew, but that it was too early to have the pregnancy confirmed by a doctor. I did not tell her of my misgivings nor my early morning experience with the mirror. 'You are pregnant and it's a boy,' she exclaimed cheerfully. My face fell, and I turned to ice. Surely this wasn't happening?

When the pregnancy was confirmed, I struggled to find enthusiasm. What should have been a cause for celebration was met with fear. I plucked up my courage and told my husband, who was overjoyed, and then I burst his bubble by sharing my mirror experience. It was too much for him to grasp. He assured me that it was just all part of my nightmares and fears and the baby would be fine. Of course, I didn't really want to convince him otherwise. I too wanted a perfectly healthy baby and from that point on, I lived silently with my thoughts, and we got on with life as any two parents-to-be would.

This was one of those times when being psychic, having clairvoyant ability, was definitely not such a good thing. Knowing that I was going to lose our baby, or that it would live and be severely deformed, did not help me deal with the normal human emotions of love and caring that flourish while growing a much-wanted child inside me. Knowing too that there was not a single soul that I could talk to who would understand, nobody who would not dismiss my fears as normal for a pregnant woman, was an awful burden to carry. It was so isolating. How could I show all the normal joy and anticipation of motherhood when I felt it would be ripped from me? In the end, I put on an act because, despite all the knowing, I wanted to be wrong. I wanted everyone else to be right. I so desperately wanted to be wrong! Every day I got out of bed, looked at my stomach and said, 'Well little one, that's one more day that you've survived,' and I hoped. Oh, how I hoped.

A second early scan due to my medical history showed no heartbeat, and two days later, on my twenty-eighth birthday, I miscarried. I was not meant to have this baby. The medical world had called it a baby, but in one sweep it become a 'blighted ovum', a thing, a nothing. Despite my psychic warnings, I was devastated. No matter how hard you might want to, no matter how psychic you are, you just can't stop being human.

The miscarriage was, itself, a spiritual experience. After being checked out at the hospital I was sent home to 'lose' my baby. I was in a great deal of pain due apparently to inflamed endometrial tissue, and I was already grieving. I crawled into bed, and my husband came and sat by my side. Suddenly through the pain and grief I stilled. Calm settled over me and the room filled with visitors as it had when I was a child. A woman stepped forward out of the mist that seemed to be everywhere and held out a shawl which she then draped across my stomach. She lifted it up and as she did, I saw that she was cradling a small baby. Smiling, she stepped backwards. She spoke and yet didn't speak words, 'We will take care of him now. He will return to you.' The visitors gathered closer around the bed. A feeling of great peace came over me, and then, suddenly, they were gone. I turned to my husband. I felt healed, as if some of my overwhelming pain had been taken from me. 'Did you see them? Could you see them too?' I asked him.

'Yes,' he replied with a puzzled look on his face. 'Well, not really, I more, well, felt them. I knew they were there,' he floundered.

I told him what I had experienced and to my amazement he shook his head and in a bemused voice replied, 'I kind of knew that, but I felt more than actually saw them.' He was perplexed by his senses and his feelings, but he had felt the love and the peace that filled the room. That was enough for me. Just as well because in those days the emotional and psychological effects of a miscarriage were only just starting to be recognised, let alone researched. To the medical world when you miscarried an early term baby, it wasn't really a baby and didn't count for anything. Because of this, you were just dismissed and expected to get on with life as if nothing had happened. These days we know better. Every parent who wants a child bonds with that foetus from the moment they know they are pregnant. To them it is a baby. When that baby dies, they grieve the child they will never hold in their arms. The emotional reality is that they have lost a child. The grief is real. Together we grieved.

We were lucky. Two months later I was pregnant again. I suffered Hyperemesis Gravidarum (constant vomiting) and had one heck of a tough pregnancy, eventually being hospitalised. Type 1 Diabetics do not do well when they are vomiting multiple times a day for months on end. It's more than a tad difficult to balance blood sugars. The hyperemesis is enough to put most women in hospital and with my husband again working long hours, and no family or friends to support me, coping with the medical aspects alone was incredibly exhausting. This was a price I was willing to pay, even when it involved vomiting and crawling around while blind, on my hands and knees trying to find the jellybeans I'd dropped on the floor during a bout of low sugar. I was determined to carry this baby to term, and soon, mission accomplished, our first daughter was born. We were over the moon.

Late in my pregnancy, I had had another spiritual visitor of a different nature. I had experienced a few bad days with several bouts of low sugar, and my husband was going to be absent for another twenty-four hours. Dealing with hypos can be draining at the best of times, and I was exhausted. It was about 7pm, and I had been lying on my bed for about an hour when I felt the now familiar electric sensation pass through my body.

This time, I buried my head into my pillow and started to cry. I wasn't up to this, couldn't take any more, emotionally or physically. Surely they weren't dumping more bad news on me? Regardless of my trying to hide, the current increased until I felt a strong and inexplicable urge to turn and look at the bedroom doorway. I would not do it, I decided. This time I was going to be the one in control. 'Go away,' I said silently but firmly. 'I don't want to know. Can't you see I'm ill?'

I began to feel scared. There was someone there. I was being watched. I tried to resist the urge to look, but fear overtook my willpower. What was worse, I started to tremble. I have always found it easier to look what I am afraid of in the face and deal with it, and so, with a great sigh, I gave in.

Tentatively, with some difficulty due to my size, I rolled sideways and looked towards the door. There, as clear as day, stood my husband's grandfather. My two dogs moved slowly from the bedside towards the door. They stopped, tails wagging, about a metre away from him, then slowly moved back to the bed and paid no more attention. Startled by what I saw I remember thinking, Pop? But you're real! You're still alive. It can't be you. I never see real people.

142

The figure smiled calmly and lifted one arm towards me just as Pop always did when he wanted to draw you to his chair at home. I pulled myself up to a sitting position and shook my head violently from side to side to clear the image. It couldn't be Pop. Pop was alive! I was going nuts, completely losing my mind.

'No!' I screamed at the figure and snatching a mug from the bedside table, I hurled it at the image in the doorway. 'No, you can't do this to me, I can't take it,' I screamed loudly. The figure vanished momentarily and then reappeared as the mug bounced off the wall next to the door and rattled, without breaking, across the floor. 'No!' I sobbed and then a wave of calmness came over me, passed through me, and realisation dawned. Pop was dead! The figure that was Pop smiled warmly at me. I had received the message correctly. I sank back onto my pillows and curled into a foetal position, rubbing my swollen belly for comfort. I knew I would hear of his death soon. I knew that I would be the one to tell my poor husband of his loss. I cried softly, 'Why now, Pop? Why me?' I sensed the figure move across the floor. His hands reached out. One touched my head, the other my back, and then blackness. I was asleep.

I awoke the next morning after my best rest for months. I was so calm and relaxed. It felt luxurious. I felt healed. There was no other way to describe it. It felt very similar to the feeling of being reborn when I emerged from my illness at eighteen. I momentarily wondered if I had gone insane the night before. Was I crazy? Had I imagined it? There on the floor lay the mug I had thrown, unharmed. There was a slight dent in the wall where it had hit. That was real! I got up and went about my day but before my husband returned that night, I received a phone call. His grandfather had died. I would have to tell him.

Even today these messages affect me. Back then I was always horrified and scared. Now though I see that they have some value, distressing though they are, as no matter what sadness they bring, they do prepare you. When the phone call or the message of bad news arrives, you are already geared up and expecting it on some level. You have the advantage of not suffering the same level of shock, which leaves you in a better position to help others, or even yourself. They can be a great help.

Chapter 15

Babies

My dreams were vivid during my pregnancy, which is normal, but so were my premonitions. I dreamed that an uncle, who lived in Wales, would come out to visit Australia. Surprise! He came, unexpectedly to everyone else, after the baby was born.

I also dreamed that my baby had died and left an empty room with a picture of a teddy bear on the wall. I was worried, as any mother would be. Was it just fear? I had by now figured out that some of my premonitions didn't have to happen, some were warnings of things to avoid. As it turned out I started to spot three days after the baby dying dream, and, against my husband's wishes, and for the first time in my life, I took myself off to see a naturopath. Three days later I no longer required my doctor's prescription anti-nausea medications, and I had no more nausea for the rest of the pregnancy. Four days later the spotting stopped and there were no more problems until I was hospitalised near the end of my pregnancy.

Our baby though, contracted staph in the hospital after birth, and was sent home with a lump on her leg and one on her spine despite my protests that this was not normal. We undertook multiple trips back to the hospital, as she experienced an increasing number of lumps and raised temperatures. They refused to admit her, claiming despite the evidence that there was nothing wrong with her. We were turned away to manage alone. Eventually, her fevers broke, and we finally got in to see her specialist who had been on holidays during her battle. He diagnosed her with a severe staph infection, now cleared, but admitted that he didn't even know how she had survived.

We did not sleep more than two hours out of twenty-four for three weeks. We slathered her lumps in drawing ointment, manually cleared her nose and throat of mucus for hours on end and placed her in and out of regular cooling baths as she continued to scream or sleep restlessly. We took her to multiple doctors including private general practitioners, and we attended the hospital several times. It was horrendous, but the main thing is that, even without their help, she survived.

A few months later we found out that the hospital was under investigation. Several babies had died because of staph infections picked up while patients there. Their refusal to diagnose staph was because giving the diagnosis would have resulted in the hospital being closed until it was cleared of the infection. We felt so blessed to still have her, but I lost a lot of my faith in the medical system because of their lack of care. We reported several times that our daughter had turned blue and that she was running temperatures of thirty-nine and higher for more than two weeks, but every time we took her to the hospital, they would take her temperature and then turn away without showing us the result. They would claim that she was fine without disclosing her temperature.

It turned out that my dreams weren't entirely correct this time. She didn't die, but she so easily could have. According to the paediatrician, she should have.

Our country prides itself on its hospital system. How could this have been allowed to happen and continue for so long? Disillusioned, I realised that I still had a lot to learn about life.

With my second daughter, I was to have a spiritual experience that was extraordinary, even for me, and it will remain with me, a treasure in my heart forever, perhaps even more important because it was partially confirmed by medical staff who, upon her birth, couldn't believe that she had survived.

The pregnancy had proceeded as normal, and I had discovered that there could be joy in growing a baby inside you. I had even, after the first three months of nausea, developed a wonderful pregnancy bloom.

Waking one evening from a light sleep I saw my grandmother standing at the foot of the bed. She spoke my name, as if to ensure that she had my attention. It literally felt like she had dropped in for a casual chat, and yet, I hadn't spoken to her in person, nor seen her, since I left Wales twenty years before. She wrote to my father and occasionally I had written to her, but we had very little communication.

She told me that I was about to become ill and that she would do everything that she could to save my baby's life. She said that she had come to say goodbye and that once she had done what she came to do, she wouldn't be able to help me again, and I probably wouldn't see her. I remember watching and listening to her in awed fascination while feeling the same bond with her that I had experienced as a tiny baby when she held me in the hospital, and I had looked into her eyes. She gave me more reassurances about my baby, said her goodbyes in a calm but loving manner, and with no distress to either of us, she was gone.

Immediately I felt completely alert and wide awake. I looked at my husband sleeping beside me. I looked again at the space at the foot of the bed where she had just been. Feeling a sudden urge to go to the bathroom I put my feet over the edge of the bed, and as my toes hit the floor the shock hit my mind. 'What was going to happen to my baby?!' I was going to get ill. Was I going to miscarry? Would I lose my baby? Would my sugar levels get out of control? Grandma was going to try to help, but would she succeed? Would my child survive? Distressed now by what I had heard, I silently prayed and hoped that our baby would be fine. *Please let her be fine.*

The following morning, after very little sleep, I told my husband that I was certain my grandmother had passed away, and I waited for the phone call I was sure would come from my parents. It didn't come. Two weeks later they called me with the news, having only just found out themselves as they had been away on holiday. If I had any knowledge that they were going on holiday, I must have forgotten because I was more surprised by that than the news of my grandmother's death.

Of course, as always, my spiritual visitor was correct. I became ill with the winter flu. I was bedridden for several days, and my baby stopped moving. It was two days and late at night when I realised how much time bub hadn't moved for. I fought not to panic. I lay there waiting for the tiniest tremor from within. None came. I felt too terrified of what lay before us to even share my fears with my husband, and with hands still on my stomach I fell exhaustedly to sleep in the wee hours of the morning begging whatever might be 'out there' to 'please fix my baby'.

You can't begin to imagine my joy when I awoke later than normal the next morning to the sensation of a jab to my rib cage, and then my whole stomach moved titanically from side to side as the cherub within rolled completely over. From that point on I made a slow but happy recovery.

It wasn't until her birth that the miracle of her survival was fully realised. In the words of the doctors present, 'At some point during the pregnancy the tube connecting the baby to the placenta had torn completely away and somehow managed to reattach itself!' There was a mass of scar tissue to indicate what had happened, and this being a relatively rare event, my placenta was whisked away for research. Silently I thanked my gran.

I felt extremely lucky to have my new daughter, and I felt an almost abnormal need to protect her right from her birth. This feeling was much stronger, and different to, my need to take care of my first daughter whom I adored. I wondered often why I felt this way as although she was technically a miracle, she was also perfectly safe now. I found myself looking into her open eyes and promising to take care of her, no matter what. No. Matter. What. I heard myself speak it aloud and a fizzle passed down my spine. I registered it as odd, whispered that I loved her and cuddled her close. That promise would come to haunt me just a few years later.

In the meantime, I was a very busy mum. Having children brought out my creative side, and I was always happy to down tools to play with and entertain them. I thoroughly enjoyed making up magical stories for them when playing was just physically too demanding for me. Those were tough years in a physical sense, as I was, like most mums of young children, constantly on the go but also fighting the muscle pain that seemed to roll around my body in never ending random patterns. If I was constantly tired too, then I blamed the demands of motherhood and the 'absence' of a full-time dad in their lives because even when he was home, he was working. He was determined to succeed, determined to carve out a new future career path, and now juggled both a full-time job, that required him to be away from home for weeks and sometimes months at a time, and study for an entirely unrelated degree. I threw myself into motherhood and gave them my all because I figured that they were only small for such a short time and, because of my own childhood memories of a mum who seemed to be constantly doing housework, I didn't want them to remember their early years as a time when mummy just constantly cleaned and fussed. Slowly though it became my husband's job to take them to the park or on walks when he was home, as I was finding it more and more difficult to walk, and my fatigue and pain increased.

By the time my eldest was three years old, despite my lack of energy and my pain, I was mentally unfulfilled, and recognised that while my emotional cup was full, my brain was missing learning. I stressed over the fact that I was not happy with what I had and needed more. A part of me missed my adult life and the career I would have liked but couldn't physically hold down. Was this all there was? Holding myself together, playing at being happy while my husband pursued his dreams? Like most women I needed something that was for 'me', not 'the mother,' nor 'the wife', but the individual with career aspirations who had been buried under other demands. I missed thinking!

There were no intellectual challenges for me in motherhood and I discovered that I needed them. I filled this unused space in my brain by initially doing a bookkeeping course by correspondence, figuring that it would at least help me to re-enter the workforce when our youngest was a little older. I was always trying to be practical and approach life with logic. To my alarm, I found that brain fog was now a major issue and while I could learn, my memory retention was extremely low, and two weeks after completing a lesson, I sometimes couldn't recall ever doing it. I found this scary.

My psychic world had gone quiet, or so I thought. My tarot cards had long been packed away. Spiritually I think I was sleeping, doing the job that was most important in the minute with no energy to expend on others. What I didn't know was that I was about to be woken up with a jolt.

As per my norm, the next psychic event happened at night. I slowly became aware that I was tossing and turning, then that I couldn't breathe. Something was over my face. My mind panicked. He was holding me down. He was suffocating me. I was losing it! I prayed for help. He backed off for a moment. I was dreaming of a strange man. He was tall and strong and had a large face. He was now standing in the corner of my room and trying to get my attention. I didn't want to talk to him. I wanted to sleep. He became impatient and took a step towards my bed. In the dream, fear prickled down my spine and drew me closer to consciousness. He spoke, I replied. He was irritated with me and took a sudden, and to me, threatening step closer. Terror instantly raced through my body. I sat bolt upright in bed and as I opened my mouth to scream, I realised that the sheet was wrapped tightly around my neck preventing me from breathing. I was choking to death and already giddy from lack of air. It was the horrific screams of my eldest daughter that brought me fully to consciousness though. Awake and choking, with some difficulty, I managed to untangle the sheet from around my neck and then raced to comfort my child.

She was hysterical and shaking violently, and as I held her close, she continued to scream at the top of her lungs. It took a good ten minutes or more before her sobs quietened, but she continued to cling to me like grim death. As I whispered words of comfort to her over and over, I realised that I too was shaking. Eventually she gasped out, 'The man! Where's the man, Mummy?'

'What man, sweetheart? There's no man.'

'The man in your room. He was by your window. He was going to hurt you, Mummy, he was! He wanted to hurt you!' She dissolved into gulping tears once again.

'Mummy's fine, sweetheart. There's no man. You had a bad nightmare. I'm here cuddling you. I couldn't do that if someone was here to hurt me, could I?'

She still clung to me as if I was about to disappear. In the end I got her out of bed, and together we inspected the whole house, including checking her little sister who had remained fast asleep throughout the incident. It was nearly an hour and a half later before her shaking stopped, and I lulled her back to sleep in my bed.

The maternal-infant bond is an amazing thing. This whole incident had me scared stiff and my daughter's words frightened me further. I had put on the good, calm, in charge mother act for my daughter, calmed and soothed her, and even patrolled the house with her. My child came first, my own personal fears overcome in the face of my child's needs, but I too was a mess. I was thoroughly shocked. She had shared my nightmare. Had she picked it up from me or vice versa? If she had picked it up from me, then how had her little mind tuned into mine while asleep? In the previous hour and a half, she had described both the man and his actions with spine-chilling accuracy, and his location was exactly as she had said, 'by the window'. I couldn't just dismiss this as a nightmare caused by almost choking on the sheet as I would have if it hadn't involved us both. What had happened? What was the human mind capable of?

I had so many unanswered questions. I still had sheet marks around my neck. I had almost choked to death. The consequences of this for my children would have been horrendous as my husband was away for another two weeks, and we had no visitors. Horrified yet again by this thought, my mind raced, and I eventually fell asleep just after dawn. I would later learn that approximately 800 people die every year after becoming tangled in their bedsheets, unable to free themselves. Who knew? How awful! The incident had such a terrifying impact on us that for the next few years we both needed a night light on to feel secure.

Years later, after I had further developed my alternate skills, I wondered if 'the man in the corner' was not actually trying to hurt me but to save me. Firstly, he had very dark hair, like my Native American Indian night visitors. Secondly, since my mind was being starved of oxygen, perhaps our 'mind to mind' talk wasn't possible, especially since I immediately started to panic. That would leave him no option but to use body language to wake me up and give me a chance to save myself. When it became obvious that this was sending me into deeper panic, how else could he wake me up than through the mind of my sleeping child? How much of a 'last resort' was this? I could have easily died but I didn't. Thinking about this from a different perspective changed my views on how we perceive spirits and think of them because that's what religion teaches us; spirits are evil. What if it is our fear that stops them from giving us the help that they are trying to give and they are not evil, not trying to harm us, at all?

At the time though, apart from scaring me, the incident reawakened my interest in psychic phenomena and the spiritual world. I sometimes think that if I had been a little smarter, I might have let it scare me off, but, as always, I wanted answers. I wanted to know the why and the how of it all. I wanted to understand, and to do that I had to delve deeper. On the practical front, logical as always, it made me extra careful with our home security. Every experience has multiple uses.

My next step was to buy a book on fortune telling using playing cards. I have wondered why I didn't just pull out my tarot cards, but I think it was to do with my thirst for new knowledge, the need to come at this from new and different angles. Books on the subject were hard to come by; it was the early nineties and they were in short supply in Brisbane, and so I jumped next into trying to learn the playing cards. Three weeks later my visiting sister-in-law became my voluntary guinea pig.

The book I had found assigned four or five meanings to each card. You had to use your intuition to choose the one you felt was correct, and then join the chosen words together to make the interpretation or story. My experience was that as I wrote the words down a television screen opened on the inside of my forehead. At least, that's the best way that I can explain it. When it appeared, I focused on the pictures instead of the words.

Now, despite being a willing volunteer, this sister-in-law is a private person, and consequently I had some trepidation about telling her what I was picking up. She was single at that time, and the pictures were about the males in her life. I carefully and tentatively told her what I was seeing and with hesitation she confirmed it was true. Encouraged, I gave her more details about a man she had not yet dated, and she self-consciously confirmed that she was interested in him. I explained that from what I was seeing he would become a constant in her life. Well, a couple of weeks later they started dating and thirty years later, they are still together. Sometimes it isn't about the words in the book but about trusting what comes into your head when you read them. Trust your intuition. Always.

My husband went to work overseas for three months leaving me with my damaged body and two babies to care for. On his return he was home for just a week and then he was sent away again for a couple more months. I thought I might physically snap in two at this time, and I hated what his work schedule did to our family life. Our eldest daughter started to complain that Daddy always left us behind. She too was hurting.

Then, fortunately, it was summer holidays, he was home, relief was at hand for me, and for the first time in four years, I got a day to myself. I went out to the January sales feeling very odd at not having my little charges hanging off me and asking a thousand questions. It was an enjoyable morning, a day I desperately needed, until, over a quiet lunch, I started to feel uncomfortable. Initially I put it down to not having my babies with me. Three years is a long time to be joined at the hip and then suddenly separated. Within half an hour I decided I had to return home because the feeling of discomfort became stronger and stronger. So much for a day off; my gut insisted that something was not right.

As I walked into our home, I was greeted by my husband's beaming smile and knew from his look that something significant had happened. You get to know 'the look' when you live with someone. That special face they reserve for when they've done something and are excited about it but somewhere in the back of their head, they subconsciously know that you may not be quite as excited about it as they are. This was one of those moments.

Within minutes I was in shock. While I was enjoying my day of freedom, he had been both offered and accepted a study post in the UK. No consultation with me. No chatting about the difficulties of moving two children and a dog. Nothing. We were going to the UK. He was ecstatic. I just wanted to cry. I couldn't find my sense of adventure. I was exhausted. I didn't feel up to moving anywhere as I'd not recovered from the months of parenting alone while battling my chronic illnesses. Carting a two-year-old and a four-year-old across the world, unsettling them yet again, and all for my husband to lose himself in yet more study, was not on my list of things that I wanted to do with my life, and now there was a massive list of things to organise for who knew what lay ahead.

To cope, I decided that I had a really bad attitude due to fatigue. It's not that I didn't want to go to the UK; it was my home country which I still loved, and I had relatives there that I would love to see again. I was just so tired. So very tired. For the first time I seriously contemplated telling him to go on his own, but I didn't see how I could make that work. If he went overseas alone for the year because it was my choice, I would have no support from my parents and no-one to turn to. I was certain that his parents would be mightily unimpressed being an ex-military couple themselves. This meant that life would become exactly like it had been the previous three months of single parenting, and I would also have to find childcare, another rental property, and a job as I doubted that we would be allowed to stay in our current military home while he was housed separately overseas. It's not that I didn't love my husband; it was just all too much. I was overwhelmed.

I had been diagnosed with fibromyalgia and chronic fatigue when we were in Adelaide and told to not mention it to anyone by the Dutch doctor that had diagnosed me after he had attended a fibromyalgia conference in Holland. At the time, health authorities in Australia considered it a psychiatric 'all in your head' type of condition. Having learned all about it in Europe, my doctor was certain it wasn't a mental illness and didn't want me categorised incorrectly. In Europe it was already acknowledged as a physical illness that required further scientific investigation to positively identify and categorise, and it was being seriously researched.

Here in Australia most doctors were in denial if a patient presented with the symptoms and gave them the brutal diagnosis that they were making it up, telling them that it was all in their heads. Regardless of the years I had already struggled with it, and the weeks I'd been bedridden I had gone on to have children and dutifully said nothing to anyone other than my husband. If I was curled up in a ball on the floor next to our girls while they played, if Mummy had a hot water bottle on her back in the middle of summer while she read stories, if Mummy couldn't walk to the park, well, that was just how Mummy was. The children knew no different.

So, despite thinking of refusing to go with him to his 'dream job', I squared my shoulders, drew on reserves I had no idea I possessed, and trying hard to muster a better attitude, I gathered up the children, packed our possessions, and followed him across the world. If I'd been up to using my skills in a serious way and seen what was ahead of us, then despite the obvious advantage of showing him my home country, this junior psychic would never have boarded the plane.

Chapter 16

The Haunted House

I f it could go wrong, it went wrong. We all got the flu and were holed up in one room of a bed and breakfast in the UK for a few weeks after having to skip my husband's planned dream holiday in Turkey. We were eventually moved to a hotel which made life more pleasant, but I although I've long forgotten the name of the bed and breakfast, the couple who owned it could not have been kinder or more helpful. They made our stay as comfortable as possible. Without them it would have been a disaster. As we had arrived too early for our posting, our designated future home for our time in England was still occupied by another Australian family who would soon be returning home.

Once we were sufficiently recovered, they invited us to dinner and filled us in on the quirks of village life. Having lived in Wales until I was almost eleven, I was quietly amused to be given lessons on the differences between us and the locals, and remembered thinking that I would probably still fit right in. They assured us that they had had a wonderful year and the practical advice they gave us on how the UK military system worked in our village was extremely helpful.

Then it was time to move in. Our fellow Aussies had packed up and cleaned the day before. All that remained was for us to meet at the house at 9 am, and with the caretaker present, sign the paperwork and receive the keys from them. When we arrived the next morning, no-one was there. Just after 9 am the caretaker turned up but eventually left to attend to a handover at another house. We waited. Time passed. The children were getting irritable and thirsty. Time ticked on. No-one turned up.

Eventually the caretaker returned with an offsider and passed on the message that the current renters had misplaced the house keys and were still searching for them in the hotel they had stayed at overnight.

He smiled as he passed on the news and glanced at his offsider. Something unfathomable passed between them. They weren't at all irritated by the delay that this was causing them. 'They'll turn up,' the offsider said with a grin, 'They always do.'

'They always do?' I repeated.

'This has happened before then?' queried my husband.

'Oh yes, countless times,' was the reply. I replayed the look that had passed between the caretaker and the offsider, trying to fathom it's meaning. Something about the situation amused them. Unlike them, however, we were getting impatient. We had no choice but to wait for as long as it took.

The family eventually turned up, a couple of hours late, apologising profusely for the delay. They professed amazement at where they eventually found the keys, which had somehow become lodged between the top and bottom mattress of a king-size bed. They had absolutely no idea how they had got there. We too wondered how a set of house keys could crawl between such heavy mattresses. Their children certainly were too young to perform such mischief—they could never have lifted the weight of the top mattress—and it wasn't something an adult could do accidentally. In our rush to get into the house that was to be our home for the year, we really didn't register just how strange the situation was. That night, I was going to wonder just what we had been given the keys to; we were in for one hell of a year.

The brick house was solid and functional and consisted of two semi-detached residences that appeared to have been joined together to make one larger home. The layout meant that some of the activities that were to occur within should have been impossible. As we stepped through the front door, we were met by a view of the stairs to the upper floor. To the left was a small area that led to the downstairs toilet. Further to the left was a bedroom or office. To the right of the doorway and stairs was a short corridor that had a door to the kitchen on the left and led straight into the dining room before continuing to the lounge or sitting room. From the kitchen there was a door to the garden.

There was a turning and a landing halfway up the stairs with two doors directly off to the right. The first became my husband's office, second was a bathroom. You then walk straight ahead up the stairs and at the top was a long corridor to the left and a toilet immediately to the right. The corridor had two doors off to the left leading to what we used as a bedroom for our youngest daughter and the second led to the master bedroom. As you continued walking past the master bedroom there was another bedroom door at the end of the corridor, directly facing the toilet. We chose this room for our eldest daughter.

With keys in hand, we entered our new-to-us home and checked it out. I can only describe my feelings as strange from the moment I set foot in it. Something was odd, and I didn't have the words to describe it. 'A cold house' was perhaps the closest or 'No heart.'

The girls, happy to explore, immediately chose their bedrooms. We then went out and picked up essential supplies for the night and returned home where we ate and unpacked our suitcases, made beds, bathed, and all settled down for the night. We were exhausted, still recuperating from our awful bout of flu. Thankfully the central heating kept us warm and toasty and within minutes of having the children settled, my husband and I drifted off to sleep ourselves.

It was the screaming that woke me. My feet didn't touch the floor as I flew into my eldest daughter's room. She was sitting bolt upright in bed, eyes glazed with terror, one arm out pointing at some invisible-to-me object ahead of her. Just as she had the night she had 'seen' the man in my room when I was choking, she screamed and screamed and continued to scream. I held her but she didn't register that I was there. I thought, 'My god, if this is night terrors, it's petrifying.'

She continued screaming. I talked, but she couldn't hear me. I put my hands in front of her face, but her stare didn't falter, and she continued to scream. I yelled for my husband. He didn't come. 'Surely, he couldn't sleep through this noise?' I thought. I screamed out his name. He still didn't come. She kept screaming.

I felt panicky by now; this was way too weird. She'd never done this before. Why wasn't he coming? Her noise alone could have woken the dead. I continued to hold her tightly, speaking firm words of reassurance, the sweat breaking out on my brow. How long could she keep this up? Her screaming continued. I lost track of time and only registered the 'never ending' feeling of this when, despite the sweat that had broken out all over my body, I realised I was shivering and the room was ice cold. Had it been that way when I first came in? I hadn't noticed. Hadn't it been warm? I put out my hand and winced as it contacted the boiling hot, central heating panel. I was now sweating and shivering at the same time. I realised that my daughter too was icy cold. 'Shock,' I thought, 'she's probably in shock.'

Then as suddenly as that thought had passed through my mind, a chill went down my spine as my daughter's screams faltered and her eyes followed something invisible towards the doorway. I glanced away from her face to see what it was that she was looking at. As I did so, I received the distinct impression of a man. I blinked. 'There's no-one there,' I told myself. I looked again. The air was clear. I shifted my position at the bedside, cuddling her and talking now to reassure us both, rather than just her. 'What is it darling?' I probed gently. Receiving no reply, I tried to lift her up. She was a dead weight and solid like a stone. Frozen. I couldn't move her.

"No,' she whispered. Thinking that she was talking to me, I stopped what I was doing. 'No. No. No,' she whispered desperately, and then burst into tears.

The tension drained from her body, and her porcelain-white face flooded with colour. At the same time the room became unbearably hot. I reached across to turn off the control on the heating only to find that the panel itself was now stone cold. Frissons of fear raced through me. My brain whorled. Nothing made sense. I just had to get out of there. Trying again to move my daughter, I now found it easy to lift her, bundled her up and ran for the safety of my own room and my husband. As I plopped her none too graciously down onto our bed, my husband rolled over sleepily and asked, 'What's up? Is she sick?'

The poor child promptly renewed her loud crying, tears pouring down her face as I replied, 'Nightmares, or rather "night terrors", I think. I don't really know!'

Between us we comforted her back to a settled state, but

she didn't want to go back into the room that she had originally chosen. As she calmed, genuine fear flickered across her face as she realised that her precious teddy was still in there. Her dad went to get it. On his return, after we got her off to sleep and still unaware of what I'd gone through, he said thoughtfully, 'You know, it's odd. The heater is burning in there, but the room is as cold as ice. When we put her to bed, it was just as comfortable as this one.'

Quietly I relayed the full story of what I had experienced. I decided that her behaviour must be night terrors. She'd never had them before but perhaps all the change in her life had been too much for her. I couldn't explain my impression of the man. Imagination maybe? We pondered the idiosyncrasies of the heating system and decided that we would get it checked out. The following day we arranged for just that, but despite her dad taking her into the room and showing her that there was nothing in there, nothing wrong with it, nothing to hurt her, our daughter refused to set foot in it.

Remembering what I had experienced, I too felt uncomfortable, but I told myself that I was being ridiculous and tried to brush my feelings aside. Our daughter decided that from now on she would share a room with her little sister who had taken the bedroom on the other side of the main bedroom, the first one near the top of the stairs. We repositioned beds in there as they both insisted that they needed to face the door. After trying out the acoustics of the house, we went out and bought a nursery monitor that day. We wanted to be sure that we could hear them from downstairs as neither my husband, nor our youngest, had heard any of the previous night's noise. Odd. If you spoke in the end bedroom you could hear some noise if not make out the words in the main bedroom. Screaming, especially over so long, should have been a bother. It was not going to be the only time when screams went unheard....

Within days of moving in, our children's behaviour had altered dramatically. They became insecure and did not want me to leave them at night. Within a week they demanded that we place both beds together and from then on, when we came upstairs to go to bed, we would either find them asleep in each other's arms or holding hands. They were close but they had never been that close. They would no longer sleep with a nursery light on either, it had to be a full room light. Gradually over the next few weeks they exhibited more and more fear of being left alone. Initially we put this down to what we thought was natural insecurity. A new home, a new country, and so on. We thought that with enough comfort and reassurance it would pass, but it didn't. This played on my mind at odd moments throughout the day.

On the periphery of my brain, I also became aware that there were other things that were odd about the house; things that I couldn't bring forth clearly and couldn't find the words to express, so I pushed the thoughts away time and time again, making excuses that I too was tired and still in recovery mode myself. Gradually the question reared its ugly head, 'Why weren't my children improving?'

We tried turning the now spare upstairs bedroom into a toy room, in an attempt, to get my daughter over her fear. It was lovely when the sun shone, a perfect playroom once the toys were all sorted and in place. It failed. We were soon to notice that the youngest would dart in, grab the toy or toys that they wanted and then dart out again to play in the corridor outside it. Within a couple of weeks, she herself refused to enter the room without an adult. They called it 'The Cold Room'.

Then one day, as my youngest played on the floor of the main bedroom while I folded laundry on the bed, she spoke to someone. Realising that she wasn't speaking to me, I continued with my chore and just listened. She was a two-year-old, so she was bound to make up little friends for her games. She spoke again and then burst into tears. I thought that she had somehow hurt herself. 'What's up? Did you hurt your finger?' I asked her.

'No Mummy, it's the little girl.'

'What little girl darling?'

'The little girl from The Cold Room. She's sad.'

I was a little perplexed by her answer, but I picked her up and gave her a cuddle. What was going on in her head I wondered? Pictures slowly slid through my own, and suddenly I knew exactly what she was talking about. But did she? Was I right?

'Describe her to me. Tell me what she looks like,' I said gently. She proceeded to describe exactly the image that had come into my mind, an image that I had seen several times over the previous weeks and been trying to ignore.

Both girls had, at separate times, talked about this young girl. The eldest had mentioned her weeks before, but I hadn't been ready to acknowledge the images. Now I heard myself saying, 'I think the little girl would be happy if you said that she could play with your toys. I think that she's sad because she hasn't got any, and she really likes yours.'

I didn't feel this little vision that I had seen in my head was a threat, and if my daughter could see her, then right now she needed reassurance. I would pretend that this was perfectly normal. My daughter beamed, climbed off my lap, and set out her miniature bears as if there were two children playing. I sat and puzzled over the incident for some time while she and her invisible friend happily played by my feet.

I had seen the little girl several times, but I had told nobody. I think part of me didn't really believe it, or maybe I just didn't want to acknowledge it. It takes quite a mental jump to accept that things happen on a different level to what we call normal, and my trained to be logical mind wasn't going to jump easily, even now.

The first time the girl appeared, I had been tidying away toys, putting them away in the bedroom that our girls had nick-named The Cold Room. They were having their afternoon sleep in their own room when we reached for the same toy at the same time. I had been thinking of other things and with my mind far away while I worked the little being caught me unawares, so much so that I said, 'Oh sorry sweetheart, did you want that one?' before I'd realised that she wasn't one of mine.

On numerous occasions I had been putting things away or generally cleaning up, when a hand had gently touched my leg or bottom and I had turned to smile at my youngest, only to see this spirit child instead. Slowly I started to absorb the fact that something odd was happening but, initially I put it down to being overtired and run-down from the move. 'Just seeing things,' was an easy way to explain it away. Now, however, I became quite nervous and uncertain.

I had not consciously decided that there were spirits, or that I even, in spite of my previous experiences, believed in the spirit world. In my own spiritual growth, I was a fence sitter. I experienced things, both good and bad, but I had not yet taken a stand one way or another. Starting with my acceptance of this little girl, the events that were to follow during this coming year were to change that; they were to change me.

To my knowledge the little girl never came past our bedroom doorway. If she was at my heels as I made my bed, she would stay in the doorway as I made theirs. If I turned right towards the stairs as I left their room, she would simply disinte-grate. She never came when invited, she only appeared when it suited her. She didn't frighten me, nor did she appear to frighten the children, and I never questioned them when they mentioned her. In time I became very comfortable with the idea that there was no harm to this little thing and decided that the best way to handle this was with gentle acceptance and absolutely no fuss.

Life couldn't be that simple though. Not for me, not for us. There was more going on in that house than just a little girl who wanted to play. Sitting in the lounge room at night we would both hear heavy footsteps walk down the corridor towards the toilet. One of us would dash up the stairs to make sure that a sleepy little girl didn't make a wrong turn and fall down the stairs. Most often it was me, as my husband would be ensconced in his study. When I reached our girls, they would either be fast asleep or adamant that they'd never gotten out of bed.

Since it was too easy to tell when they were fibbing, we were left with no choice but to believe them. Besides, the footsteps were too heavy to belong to a child. My husband brushed it off as something to do with the acoustics of the house, but I gradually became more nervous. This was more than just acoustics, and I wasn't going to buy into his belief.

This became more of an issue when we also began to hear the upstairs toilet flushing. To reinforce that I wasn't imagining it, I would make my husband check. Not only was no-one there, but the toilet was completely quiet. We became more and more puzzled. Then, one night, as my husband and I sat silently reading side by side in the lounge room, the footsteps sounded loudly upstairs. My husband sat up and listened intently. I glanced at the nursery monitor and then at him. We had forgotten to turn the machine on! We had checked the girl's monitor but not the downstairs receiver. In a flash, almost knocking each other over, we rushed upstairs.

The little one was in her sister's arms in bed. Their eyes were wide, and their faces were pale. 'Who got out of bed?' I asked.

'I didn't!' They both spoke at once.

We could easily see that they weren't lying. They were scared out of their wits. I sat down on the bed to talk to them. My husband, sure that we had heard adult footsteps, searched the whole of the top floor including the wardrobes. There was no-one there, but the children were visibly upset about something. Careful not to suggest anything or to lead the conversation, all we learned was that the eldest was 'a bit scared', but that was all, no other information.

We sat with them and read stories for an hour and watched as the girls stared at the door and had to be continuously coaxed back to looking at the pictures in their books. This was very unusual. Eventually two exhausted little girls drifted off to sleep, both with their faces to the door, and we crept downstairs.

My husband's reaction was to remain as cool as ever. Convinced he was hearing the footsteps but then finding no-one there, he again brushed the event aside with the statement, 'Old houses do funny things.'

I was not at all reassured by his words, but logically he made sense. After all, there was no-one there, right?

The old house kept on doing 'funny things'. The upstairs toilet would flush at random times. I would pop upstairs to see if it was our eldest and check to see if she was okay only to find that the toilet was not flushing, and not refilling, and that all was quiet. Soon the sounds of the toilet flushing happened randomly, both day and night, and we heard heavy footsteps walking along the upstairs corridor increasingly often.

Despite gentle, random questioning, the girls were obviously keeping secrets and were scared by something upstairs, but they wouldn't talk about it. They wouldn't go up there without one of us. It began to get to me, making me nervous of what wasn't at all logical, but my husband continued to brush these abnormalities aside and wouldn't discuss them. He was simply going to pretend that the 'funny things' weren't happening for as long as he could. Maybe they would all stop?

Then I became afraid to step out of our bedroom door at night. On reflection it was a very gradual thing. I had been hesitating for weeks before I registered my fear. Almost every night, around 2 am, I would get up to go to the toilet, an annoying habit that was proving difficult to break. I would be at the bedroom door before I was fully awake. One night I became aware that I looked left and then right before scuttling like a nervous rabbit to the toilet at the end of the corridor. I would remain nervous until I was back in the bedroom where I would let out a sigh of relief. I finally registered that I was behaving like a frightened child. The corridor was kept lit to allay the children's new night fears, so it wasn't as if I couldn't see clearly the whole way. Deciding I was being silly, I made up my mind to put this childlike fear aside and act like a grown up from now on. There was no reason for it, and it had to go.

Less than a week later and still half asleep, having spent the past few nights only looking in the direction I needed to go when exiting the bedroom and deliberately making myself deal with any sense of vulnerability by leaving the toilet door open while in there, I turned around from flushing the toilet to clearly see a man standing at the other end of the corridor. He was in his late thirties or early forties, tallish with a slim build. He wore out-of-date clothes and sported a haircut to match. His collared shirt was white, his trousers dark. I froze with shock. Before I could scream, he disappeared. I took an instant to dislike him. His figure emanated danger. I also felt that he wanted something from me. He certainly didn't create a pleasant atmosphere like the little girl. I moved back to our room in a kind of trance registering only that the corridor was now chilled. I touched the heating panels as I went by, and they were like ice. I darted the last few feet like a hunted rabbit, and then sat shaking on the side of the bed. My husband slept peacefully on.

On some level, I knew the man wasn't real. Regardless, I was still a mother, first and foremost, so, scared as I was, I couldn't go back to bed before checking on the children. After some minutes I forced myself back into the corridor and into their room to find them sleeping peacefully and their room warm. I went back to my own bed and huddled under the covers and thought about what I had seen. What was going on here? Was I mad? Was I so tired that my brain had somehow created a solid picture of my fear, or had I been seeing on a different level? I was still thinking when the alarm went off and we started another day.

That night was a turning point in my spiritual development. I really wanted to get to the truth of this and finally had to acknowledge to myself that I was having some kind of mediumistic experiences. Feeling a bit silly, but still too scared to keep it to myself, I told my husband what had occurred. To my surprise, the man who had brushed everything off up until this point was open to believing me rather than dismissing the whole event. We discussed the odd events, and my husband shared that although he never actually saw anything, he had become aware of odd feelings in parts of the house not always associated with the unusual noises. Neither of us had any logical explanations, but he no longer brushed my fears aside. This was a lifesaver for me, and I sometimes wonder even now If I would have coped at all with what was to come if he hadn't been there to provide the support that I needed.

Having acknowledged that I must be 'a bit of a medium', I recognised that since I felt so much fear, I would need to do something about it, something to protect myself. I knew very little about psychic protection, but I had read about 'white lighting' in my earlier years when I had taught myself to read tarot. So that is what I proceeded to do, or at least tried to do because no matter what I did, I could only white light half of our house at a time. Not once did I succeed in mentally shrouding the whole house in white mist or white light. Always, I would get halfway around the house, and then I would meet an impenetrable blockage.

I puzzled over this as, using my logical side, I felt that white lighting was merely a creative use of the imagination. You imagine that the objects that you wish to protect are completely surrounded by a protective white light, or a white cloud if that is easier. At any one time though I could only cover half of the house. Since it was up to me to create the picture of light surrounding the house, I couldn't understand why half the house remained uncovered with the white cloud disintegrating in my imagination as fast as I placed it on the other half. I had no problems white lighting either my family members or the car. I couldn't grasp why the house itself was an issue. There were no answers, no-one to ask, and so I just kept trying, and we got on with life there as best we could.

I began to sense or to see the male figure more often. Mostly he partially appeared when my husband was at work and realising this fact, I first analysed myself. Was I afraid of him and therefore conjuring up an imaginary figure out of fear? I concluded that this was not the case. Yes, he could frighten me when he appeared unexpectedly, but I wasn't untowardly frightened of him per se. He couldn't be real. He wasn't real. I couldn't touch him. I was never thinking of him when he appeared, so I wasn't obsessing over an unrecognised fear, and I wasn't conjuring him up. I eventually decided that if I was to stay sane then I would do my best to simply ignore his appearances. Admittedly, given a choice, I'd have moved out because the children were affected, and the atmosphere of the place was

unsettled rather than homely, but we weren't in a financial position to move out. Whatever was going on here, I would just grit
my teeth and either face or ignore it as I saw fit.

In retrospect, I wondered if the experiences were more
unsettling because they were random rather than every day.
Sometimes a whole week would pass before he appeared and
ruined the normal atmosphere. I'd be lulled back into a sense of
security and be happy and relaxed. The house itself would
settle and become calm, reflecting the mood of the family once
again. All would be as if nothing had ever been wrong, and life
would cheerfully muddle along. Such was my state of mind
when the following event came out of the blue.

Chapter 17

The Man

I t was a beautiful day. My husband was hard at work in
the upstairs study, and the sun was shining through every
window. Our eldest was at school and the little one was
watching a video of *Playschool* in the lounge room. I folded the
washing and then trooped upstairs to put it away, humming
quietly to myself. I ducked my head into the study. 'Still alive?'
I questioned and grinned at my husband's cheeky response.

I started singing a current pop tune and continued onwards
towards the bedrooms. As I entered the main bedroom, I
screamed loudly and threw the basket of washing into the air. It
scattered all over the room. From the doorway I saw, clearly,
vividly, in full colour, The Man! He was lying stretched out on
my side of the bed, legs crossed and arms folded behind his
head. He grinned at me, and trust me, it was not a pleasant grin.

It took only seconds for my husband to reach my side. I was
shaking and crying. My legs had given way, and I was sitting on
the floor surrounded by clean underwear and shirts. His eyes
darted around the room as he helped me up asking what had
happened.

He believed every word I told him. I don't think I would have coped at all well if he hadn't. He was very comforting, confounded but comforting, and slowly I regained my composure. He got off the bed where we both sat, and mumbling something about it being cold, he moved to close the window. Our eyes met and understanding dawned on us. Every time The Man showed up, it became ice cold in that area. Within ten minutes it would be warm again. My husband slowly stuck his arm out of the window only to find, as he'd expected, that the temperature was a great deal warmer outside. He returned to the bedside and hand in hand we waited. Sure enough, every so gradually, the warmth trickled in. 'I think I'm going nuts,' I whispered.

'No, you're not. You're just sensitive. I wouldn't be you for quids though!' he smiled gently down at me.

From then on, I was nervous to walk into and out of the upstairs rooms. I felt stretched and tense, always on edge. My personality was affected, and I withdrew quite a lot from outsiders, more for fear I'd mention something about our strange experiences and look stupid than any other reason. I felt like I shouldn't be there. We shouldn't be living in the house. It was as if we were doing something wrong. I found it difficult to be a happy mother and wife. I was constantly aware of the atmosphere upstairs. Downstairs was fine, but I became gradually more and more aware of the heaviness that was upstairs.

Because I was always completely myself away from the house, I found reasons to go out and stay out. I probably saw far more of the local villages than I ever would have if I'd not been completely spooked. It's ironic really that something so wonderful could come from something that was so frightening, but I am, in retrospect, very glad that I got to do all the sight-seeing that I did. My life became a routine of dropping our eldest at school, and then armed with a box of munchies and drinks to keep the youngest happy, I would drive as many miles as my fatigue levels on the day would permit. Together we would pop into the most gorgeous villages along whichever route I'd impulsively taken, and we would visit all the craft shops and bookshops they contained. I may not have had any money to spend when I got there but my love of craft gave me a purpose for being there and that was all the excuse I needed. I got myself mildly lost a few times, and mildly panicked about being back in time for school pick up, but after safely finding my way about three times my confidence grew, and I realised that since I always had a map, a wrong turn just meant a different turn or two up ahead.

Then things started to go missing. That's not strictly accurate. I should say that our things, grown up things, started to go missing. The children's toys had been disappearing constantly since about two weeks after we moved in, but of course, because they were little, we assumed that they were forgetful. We had suffered increasing bouts of impatience with them as it happened far more than was normal, but soon even we came to know that if we had seen a doll or a book in a certain place just five minutes before then it wouldn't be there when we went to get it for the child.

The missing toys often turned up somewhere obvious, and always somewhere that we had already checked. They were always upstairs too and could be found sitting in the middle of a smooth, well-made bed, or on the wide windowsill in the hallway. Very occasionally they were on the floor on my husband's side of the bed as if one of the girls had been sitting there playing. It wasn't until our keys and our mail started to also disappear and then reappear upstairs that the toy activities were really questioned.

Our mail was delivered at lunch time. My husband also

came home around this time, so he would pick the letters up off the mat inside the door as he entered. We would check through the items and then leave the bills on the kitchen table and move through to the dining room for lunch, taking with us any letters from friends and family back home.

We had finished lunch one day when my husband said, 'I'll pay that bill on the way back over to college,' and went to get it. He couldn't find it. I looked but to no avail. It had simply disappeared. He was cranky, and I was puzzled. I searched high and low. No sign of it. He went back to college without it. When he came home that evening he emptied his briefcase, just in case, but no, he hadn't absentmindedly dropped it in there when he came home for lunch. We pulled out the refrigerator to check in case it had been knocked off the table and fallen behind or underneath it but no, no luck. That night as I cleaned my teeth at the basin in our room I was still worrying about where it could have gone. 'You'd better arrange for a copy to be sent to us or see if we can pay without one,' I told him.

'Yeah, I'll do that tomorrow,' he grunted, unimpressed about the inconvenience.

He didn't have to. The next morning as he adjusted his tie in front of the basin mirror, he said, 'Oh good, you found it. Where was it?'

'What?' I mumbled, trying hard to ignore his voice and stay asleep.

'The bill!'

I opened my eyes to see him waving the bill before my face. I was instantly wide awake. 'That's not funny. I'm glad you found it, but you didn't have to wake me up to tell me. It's not that important.'

'I just saw it on the hand basin and wondered where and when you found it, that's all,' he replied.

Suddenly I was fully awake, aware that the bill had just

176

reappeared overnight in a spot that we both definitely knew it wasn't in when we retired to bed. We added it to a list of strange events in the house and said a laughing 'Thanks' to who knows what for returning it. Once again, we got on with our lives.

A once off is kind of funny, amusing even, but it began to happen with greater and greater frequency. It became so frequent in fact that we started to deliberately leave mail on the kitchen table to test our ghost. It became a joke, a party trick if you like. This wasn't frightening or threatening; it was just curious and bizarre. If anything went missing, we checked the bedroom first. It started with letters and moved on to keys and jewellery.

One earring from a pair went missing from the table. Thinking that it had been knocked off we searched the floor, then the fridge, and under the dishwasher. No earring. We checked upstairs. Not a sign of it. It turned up long after I'd forgotten about it, right under the sink in the bedroom. There it was, sitting on the freshly vacuumed carpet as if it had just been dropped. No footprints on the freshly vacuumed carpet. No explanation.

Toy movements became more frequent and obvious, and it didn't take us long to figure out that children who had been out of the house all day couldn't possibly have moved toys from one room to another, or that teddies neatly stacked on beds don't walk on their own to sit in hallways and doorways elsewhere. The incidents became annoying and frustrating, but they weren't scary, so we said nothing to the children, although we did occasionally hear them making up explanations for their toys' behaviour. Things that went missing always turned up and the incidents didn't seem to be connected to The Man. I contemplated the possibility of multiple ghosts haunting the house, but I still didn't really believe in such things. I was just constantly performing random mind searches for logical explanations that weren't forthcoming.

By the beginning of August sightings of The Man were becoming more frequent, and I had come to dislike the house immensely. Fortunately, it was August holidays, and having saved hard all year, we took the girls Eurocamping in France and to EuroDisney, which had just opened. As we left for our trip, I remember thinking that all the stresses and strains, all the loneliness, all the late nights and long weekends of study that my husband was putting in while I crawled slowly up the wall, all the lack of support, was completely worth it just for this opportunity alone. As young parents, we could never have afforded to take our children to Disneyland if we had remained in Australia, and now we were off on the adventure of a lifetime. We were ourselves again, stress free, with nothing more difficult to worry about than how to order a croissant from a French patisserie. Bliss!

France was wonderful, and I loved it almost as much as I loved the UK. It had this amazing atmosphere, in the countryside especially, that I found almost impossible to define. Away from the house I was relaxed and happy, but I found that the psychic in me didn't switch off. At Disneyland in particular, I was intrigued to find that incidences I had previously dreamt of occurred, and I discussed them with my husband. They weren't big and important except perhaps for the moment that I realised that someone had taken my daughter's hat off her head while she was in the stroller at my feet. She was asleep at the time, her hat firmly positioned, the band under her chin. I glanced at her, looked quickly at people walking to the right side of her, turned back and glanced again, but the hat was gone. It was not even visible on the head of anyone in the light crowd. It made me very security conscious for the rest of our visit which may have been the whole purpose of it happening.

Hats, fortunately, are easily replaced. The fact that this occurred in an identical manner to my dream a couple of weeks prior was the big stand out for me and added to my belief that I was waking up psychically to a skill that could be useful.

After a fabulous holiday we returned to the UK feeling relaxed. We continued our break with a short holiday in defence accommodation in Scotland, a place where none of us had been before. I fell in love! Scotland is amazingly beautiful with outstanding scenery and very friendly people. My psychic mind, now relaxed and open, produced *deja vue* after *deja vue*.

So clear were my premonitions and dream memories that at one café I was able to tell my husband not to have his first choice of meal, a type of pie that he really wanted. 'Remember my dream?!'; I hissed at him across the table when he initially wouldn't take my advice to make a different choice. Shortly after this he was highly amused when he overheard the couple at the next table grumbling about their not so good meal. They had eaten what had been his first choice! He thoroughly enjoyed his eventual choice, but I'm not certain if it was tastier because of the inside knowledge that had saved him from making a mistake. Such a silly thing to have dreamed about, but it made life a lot pleasanter. This short trip was over way too soon, but it did make us determined to revisit Scotland before we returned to Australia.

We were home again and back into our routine when my sister-in-law arrived for a holiday with wonderful news. She was engaged to be married. Her husband to be looked exactly as I had predicted a few years before when reading her cards for her. He was indeed the vision I'd seen in my lounge room. I was quietly thrilled about this as it gave me a little confidence that these things in my head weren't contrived nonsense from my imagination. My sister-in-law's visit proved to be the most pleasant time we were to spend in the house as while she was there, The Man was quiet. Occasional footsteps were heard but sightings were rare indeed. I was out and about even more with my visitor, so he could only bother me at night anyway, and I continued to be more relaxed than I was before our trip to Disneyland.

Despite my introversion, I managed to make a few acquaintances. I am naturally a loner but when you live in an army village you are forced to socialize even when you prefer to be left alone. The nature of my husband's job meant there were social occasions to attend. I didn't generally enjoy them. I am not good at making friends in casual situations. I give out little of my real self, which leads people to believe that I am a very different person to who I am. Over the years I have been classified as either a snob or boring. I know because people say too much, especially when they've had a few drinks. Their attitudes occasionally bothered me, but not sufficiently that I ever tried to fit in. I've always been a 'like me or not, it's your choice' type of woman.

One of these acquaintances seemed to more adopt me than make friends with me, and slowly a friendship formed. When her grandmother died, my friend, who was Australian and like me doing the 'accompanying the husband on yet another posting' thing, was understandably very distressed. Her distress touched me. We weren't really friends at this point, more acquaintances, but I felt for her, and I wanted to help if I could. A couple of weeks later when she had expressed her sadness once again, I volunteered to do a reading for her. This was most unlike me as I'd not done readings for years, and I never mentioned my clairvoyant or psychic abilities to anyone, but there it was, out of my mouth, unplanned, an offer to read. She was immediately interested so I warned her about my seeming mediumistic abilities and how I had no control over them. She was fine with this, so we arranged for her to visit one evening when the children were asleep.

It was an interesting evening; the first time I'd seriously put my untrained, and mostly undiscovered abilities, to any form of test. Feeling a little nervous I tried to concentrate. I think from memory that I was holding a piece of her jewellery at the time as a point of focus, a ring, but I cannot recall exactly. Firstly, I received a lot of general information about her grandmother's life. Then came more specific information about her possessions, information about a ring, information about other relatives, all of which she could relate to and place in her current life. I was gaining confidence with each recognised description I received, and she was getting more and more excited as the information came through.

Suddenly the atmosphere changed, and a young man appeared next to her. I recall taking a big deep breath and shaking a little as I slowly described him. He was dressed as a fighter pilot. She identified him as a close relative of her grandmother's. He proceeded to pass on information about her relatives including their names. Since he was from a generation with whom she'd not really mixed, there was some information that she couldn't confirm, and he mentioned events from before her time, but he assured me that there were people in her family that could confirm the information. I passed this on. Eventually I had to stop as I was too tired to continue. I thanked the man and he faded slowly away until nothing was visible inside or outside my head. It had been a very satisfactory evening, and she left feeling much more at peace with the loss of her gran.

She spoke with her mum back in Australia a couple of days later, told her what had eventuated and passed on the information that she didn't have the answers to. To our delight, her mum was able to verify almost all of it. I think, from memory, that there was one small piece of information that she said she had no memory of as she too had been young when it was claimed to have occurred. I was excited by this experience, and I gained an acceptance of my abilities I'd not had before. After all, now I had a really good use for them.

The evening was interesting from another perspective also. Although I was so nervous of the vision of The Man upstairs, I became aware that to 'read' downstairs in the dining room was no problem at all. I didn't know why, but for some reason the downstairs area seemed safe.

It was also interesting to logically work through the emotions I'd experienced and the physical changes that went through my body during the reading. I have mentioned before that I analyse everything, and this was no exception. I was aware that I'd had been very nervous before my first ever deliberate sitting as a medium. The nervousness had, however, been accompanied by anticipation and excitement. The energy that flowed through me had been both exhilarating and exhausting, but overall, it had given me a feeling of being alive like nothing else really did. When it reached what appeared to be a natural conclusion, my body was exhausted, but my mind remained buzzing for several hours.

Later I would learn that this was, for me at least, a normal state during readings, but back then it contained the wonderful thrill of all new and exciting experiences. To be honest, I have never really lost that thrill. When I occasionally do a reading for someone now, I am usually left with a feeling of completeness tinged with that original thrill of excitement, coupled with a deep sense of satisfaction. I am left feeling like I have done what I was born to do.

More visitors arrived about a month later for a brief stay. Before they arrived, I found myself in a quandary. Should I put the two sisters in the room upstairs where the children refused to play? It was the only empty room by this time as we'd given in and moved the girls' toys to the downstairs study and converted it into a convenient playroom. I admit that I felt guilty about putting our visitors in a room that had given us so much trouble, but in the end, knowing that my friend was very religious and didn't believe in any spirt other than the Holy Spirit, that's the room we allocated the pair. I personally thought that with her religious beliefs either nothing would happen to her, or she simply wouldn't be aware of anything unusual, and I was willing to take the chance as it assuaged any guilt I felt.

Besides, I was now almost certain that The Man only had business with me. I had figured that out because he kept appearing in front of me or staring at me down the corridor. He must want something from me, in particular. I had also realised that he had me so scared by this time that I couldn't address whatever it was he wanted. I simply couldn't go there in my mind. I had contemplated trying to talk to him to figure out what was wrong with him, as to me something obviously was, but I'd decided I had too little knowledge in the psychic field to take what could be a huge risk. I wouldn't dabble. All would be okay if I left him alone. Our visitors would be all right!

Their first night in the room I plied them with extra blankets, assuring them that the room could be very cold. Was it? No, of course not. True to course it remained the hottest room in the house the whole time they were there. One night they even had to open the window to cool off even though it was bitter outside and the temperature in the rest of the house was set at 17C, comfortable for us Aussies. This was how we rolled!

The second night of their visit I felt a little edgy and kept getting the impression that I was being watched. I commented to my husband later that I had felt like a naughty little girl, as if someone was angry with me, although nothing had gone wrong, and we were enjoying the company of our visitors. The only change was that the week before I had taken to wearing a gold cross that had been given to me by my uncle when I was a young child. I felt the need for protection and had emotionally automatically fallen on my own religion-based childhood choices.

During the evening there had been lots of intelligent discussions and chatter, and the sharing of different childhood memories between friends. It was as perfect as time with friends can be, relaxed and filled with laughter until reluctantly we all retired happy to our beds.

I had hidden my growing nervousness and insecurity, consciously pushing it to the back of my mind, trying to ignore it. The company had made it much easier. Now, alone with my husband, I couldn't explain the feelings of vulnerability that gradually crept up on me, and so I silently white lighted myself and, although not overtly religious, I prayed. 'I don't know what I'm praying for God, but if you're really out there I need help that's bigger than just me.' I felt foolish. I found myself playing with my cross as I got into my nightdress and then went to check on the children.

Three times I got out of bed over the next hour and the third time, glancing at my visitors' bedroom door, I registered somewhere in my mind that they were completely safe in the odd room. No nightmares for them. It was as if I suddenly knew something that I hadn't known before, and it came from deep inside me. Finally, I tried to sleep, to relax deeply, but something was still bothering me, and I couldn't put my finger on it.

I must have dozed off eventually because I awoke at 2 am with a raging thirst. We didn't drink tap water unfiltered as the taps to the building were too old and the water tasted awful. If I wanted a drink, I would have to go downstairs to the kitchen and get it. Slowly I shrugged into my dressing gown and slippers and glanced at my sleeping husband with envy. I knew that if I woke him, he would go and get it for me. Bless him, he knew how scared I was of having another confrontation with The Man. I didn't feel the need to wake him though; it would be mean to rouse him from his much-needed sleep. I stepped outside into the corridor and listened for a moment to the breathing of the house. It was warm and cosy, everyone seemed to be happily asleep. There was nothing to be concerned about, so off I trotted. Automatically I checked on our girls as I passed. They were more than okay and looked as cherubic as only sleeping children can. It was with thoughts of them glowing in my head that I started to descend the stairs.

I had rounded the landing by the bathroom and study and was at the top step of the main flight down, with my foot extending downwards to the next step when it happened.

In a split second I saw him slightly behind and to the side of me. His face was manic, his eyes glassy and distorted. A lock of hair flopped down his forehead. As this vision registered in my mind, my back buckled as if someone had pushed hard into the small of it. At the same time, my right foot, which had almost reached the next step, took on a life of its own. Toe still pointing it went up in front of me, right up, higher than my head. I looked on in shocked amazement. It all happened in slow motion, which was amazing, but I also seemed to be outside of myself and found myself thinking, 'How the heck did I get my foot that high?'

I have had extremely stiff joints and muscles since my near-death experience at eighteen. My movements were tight and restricted, something that I worked hard on hiding when in public, but even before my illness I had never been able to get my leg up there! Then, just as slowly as it went up, it came down from its skyward ascent and went backwards behind me.

My nose pointed for seconds towards the floor at the base of the stairs. Fleetingly I thought, 'Please God, help me. I'm going to die if I fall like this.' Bizarrely I felt no pain at all at this point. I knew that this was my body, but I can't say that I really related to it. I didn't live a life without being in pain. What I did know was that if there was a good way to fall down a steep flight of stairs, then this was certainly not it.

Then the slow-motion feeling stopped, and everything went into high gear. My backward flung right leg now snapped in towards my body, the ankle and shin twisted violently sideways and at the same time my left leg, which had remained frozen in the normal position of anyone who is about to descend a staircase, suddenly gave way at the knee. Instead of hurling me face forward down the stairs, it too took on a life of its own and I watched as the foot shot out in front of me, throwing the weight of my body backwards. I heard myself scream in fear as I slithered to the bottom of the stairs with my left leg extended to the front and my right shin twisted somewhere behind my bottom. I distinctly recall thinking on the way down that the bumpy staircase should be a lot more painful as I was acutely aware of the bumping sensation but felt absolutely no pain. Fleetingly too, I remember the sudden knowing that the pain would arrive when I stopped at the end of the downward flight.

The pain didn't come immediately. I landed with a soft thud and registered surprise. The next thing I became fully aware of was the icy coldness, a bitter, biting coldness. Then I felt myself become whole again, as if I had stood apart from myself while all this happened. As I blended back into myself, the pain hit me. I was badly shaken, and for several minutes I simply couldn't move. It wasn't an option. Where was my husband? Why hadn't my screaming woken him? It seemed that I hadn't even disturbed my children or my visitors. Shock set in then, and I shook violently, but I couldn't move. I knew that if I moved now, I would vomit everywhere, so, I just sat, freezing, shaking, crying with pain and waiting for the nausea to pass.

As the initial shock receded, the pain increased exponentially. I called out to my husband, now in too much pain to care who I woke up as long as I got help. I think though that I could have called for the rest of the night as it seemed that nobody could hear me. After some time, and now sobbing from pain I figured out that help wasn't coming. I also slowly registered that I was still thirsty, and that not just my ankle but the front of my head hurt badly as well. I still couldn't move and so I remained still and relived the accident over and over in my mind trying to figure out why and how it had all happened and the sheer eeriness of watching my foot extend fully upwards in front of me to maximum stretch.

Then anger bubbled up from deep inside me, out of nowhere, as unexpected as the accident itself. 'You rotten bugger! You're not going to break me!' I exclaimed, The Man's face clear in my head. The yelling finally brought back my sense of reality. I couldn't sit here in this state and freeze all night and obviously help wasn't coming. I should also be checking my sugar level after such a shock. So, slowly and very painfully, crying quietly, I turned and crawled on my hands and knees up the stairs. Ever so gingerly, one slow and painful movement at a time, I edged my way along the landing and corridor to our bedside. Every couple of feet, in increasing pain, I called out to my husband as loudly as I could muster, too distressed to care if I woke anyone or everyone, but the household slept on.

Even in the state I was in a part of my brain found this unbelievable. How could nobody be disturbed by my noise? By the time I made it to the side of the bed my foot and ankle were three times their normal size. My husband still slept soundly. I couldn't get myself up off the floor so I pulled as hard as I could at the bedclothes trying to get leverage. 'For God's sake,' I spluttered between tears, 'will you please just wake up and help!' Someone must have pressed his buttons because in an instant he was wide awake. He reacted as if someone had slapped him, leaping out of bed, fully conscious and asking what had happened to me. My hero wakes up groggy from every sleep and stumbles for a half hour afterwards, but this time, there he was, ready at last for action.

Fixed up at last and story told to my husband, I finally fell into a deep sleep. I spent the next day in bed with my ankle firmly strapped and iced. We explained to the visitors and children alike that I had fallen down the stairs. Exclaiming over the bruised lump on my forehead and bruises on my cheeks, my friend asked if I had fallen face first. That was one thing I was clear about. I hadn't. We couldn't explain those injuries nor the ones that appeared on my upper arms.

Later, when I had healed and our visitors had left to continue their holiday elsewhere, my husband and I once again checked out the acoustics of the house. Just as when our children had cried when we first moved in, it didn't seem to make sense that nobody could have heard my scream nor cries that night, and yet our attempt to find a logical explanation for at least one part of this event failed. Just as we had already known, there was absolutely no reason why I shouldn't have woken the whole house.

Because of this incident, I was now seriously scared. Where I had been nervous, worried, and uncomfortable before, I was now a hundred times worse. My logical self was taking a back step. In the daytime, I relived and replayed what had happened, or had appeared to happen, pretty much on repeat, as I went through my days. I was both scared and incredulous. Why? What for? What if anything did The Man want?

This last question became louder as the more I thought about it, the more I came to believe that he wanted something. The idea had slowly grown. It had grown so slowly I'd been almost unaware of it until one day it became a certainty. He wanted something. The trouble was that the more scared I became, the less likely he was to get his message across.

I alternated between feeling like a person who was extremely scared and a person who felt perfectly normal in every way but for that one glitch in my mind. Since the glitch appeared to be 'all in my mind', I feared that I was literally losing my marbles. I seriously considered going to the local doctor and telling him what was going on. I pictured myself fronting up at his office and telling him the story, and I realised that getting help was not an option as he was bound to think that I had a mental health condition, and I'd be off to see a psychiatrist before I could blink. I knew inside me that this wasn't madness. I didn't want pills nor counselling. I just wanted to feel safe in my own home, and I wanted all this nonsense to stop. In even more distressed moments, I demanded that my husband get us all away from the place. 'Take us away from here,' I would angrily demand, 'this is a crazy house, and it's driving me crazy with it. Take us all away from it right now!'

We couldn't go. We couldn't afford to move out. Besides, my husband still had a couple of months to work in his current posting. I could just see him fronting up to his superior and saying, 'Sorry Sir, permission to go back to Australia early. Wife got pushed down the stairs by a ghost! She's not happy, Sir!'

It sounded ridiculous, even to me, and it would make him the laughingstock of his regiment. However, imagining him doing just that made me laugh, and with the laughter always came the re-establishment of common sense. I would then tell myself that I could do this; the end was in sight. I would give myself a stern talking to and once again go back to stoically counting down the days until we handed back the keys.

Our visitors were in Germany when they phoned to say they had left an expensive cardigan behind them and wanted us to post it on. They were 100 percent certain it had been left in the house, specifically in the bedroom. We hunted high and low but to no avail. That cardigan was never seen again. We wondered if this was a mistake on their part or yet another case of things that disappeared in this crazy house.

Chapter 18

The Babysitter and the Children are Scared

Shortly after this my new friend came to babysit for us while we attended a compulsory work function and although I didn't usually enjoy functions, I was desperate for some down time with my husband. I was looking forward to the evening away from the house and the general drudgery that was motherhood. We had a lovely night, but unfortunately my friend, at home with the sleeping children, did not.

An hour or so after we departed for the evening the phone rang. There was no-one on the other end of the line. This happens, so my friend thought nothing of it. Then the footsteps started. Upstairs she went thinking that the girls were awake and playing up. The nursery monitor was on and there were no voices to be heard, so she assumed they were just sneaking around. When she got to their room, however, the children were fast asleep. Back downstairs she went, puzzled.

Half an hour later the footsteps came again. This time she stood by the monitor and listened. She realised that the sound was coming through the ceiling rather than the monitor, so she went back up again. The children were still asleep. She went back downstairs.

The next minute, a child burst into hysterical sobbing, and she rushed back upstairs calling out that it was okay she was coming. Again, when she arrived, the children were fast asleep.

We had never mentioned the goings on in our house to her. She hadn't been forewarned so couldn't have been nervous and therefore created these events in a tense mind. We arrived home to find her a little spooked. She told us, 'Your house is very strange. I might not rush to babysit for you again! It's a bit scary here.'

We were concerned by what had happened but as she and the children were okay, we took it in our stride. The place was weird, and the fact that she had experienced some of its weirdness somehow made me feel a little better. It wasn't just us that weird stuff happened to. It had happened to someone outside of the family. I felt a little relieved, but from this night on things took a turn for the worse.

The upstairs toilet started to flush itself. When we went to check, the water would be running or the tank refilling. The telephone rang frequently with no-one on the other end, not even a hanger on who didn't speak. We never heard the sound of breathing. Just nothing.

When our eldest wouldn't go to bed one night, we asked her why, and she burst into tears. Then came her confession; she didn't like the man in the corridor. A chill ran down both our spines as we heard her words. Taking a big breath, I asked her what she meant. Both girls proceeded to describe the exact man that I had been seeing, and they told us that he often walked up and down the corridor at night but that lately he had started stopping and standing in their doorway. 'That's why we always sleep together,' they told us. 'We are safe when we are together, and, Mummy,' said my now almost three-year-old, 'he doesn't like the little girl.'

The horror I felt was enormous. I could cope while I felt that this thing was all to do with me, but to know that all along my children had encountered and instinctively feared The Man was too chilling to contemplate. The fact that they saw him as a danger and that he was getting closer to them by standing in the doorway induced primeval feelings of protectiveness in me.

We dealt with this as logically as we could and kept things calm. Our first job was to make our children feel safe again. We did not refute what they had told us. Rather we told them that The Man couldn't hurt them because he wasn't alive, that he was lost and that he did like the little girl, but he just couldn't find her.

'He's her daddy then! He's not angry. He's upset because he can't see her when he looks for her!' our littlest exclaimed cheerfully. To them, daddies were warm and loving and so they accepted this idea, but they still didn't like the thought of any man standing in their doorway. I told them that they could tell him to go away and that he would go, that I would also give him a good talking too myself and make sure he left them alone. Their trust in Mum to keep them safe was so beautiful, so innocent, and within minutes we had them settled down for the night. We sat with them until we were certain they were fast asleep.

From then on, with only two weeks left in the house, we sat with them every night until they slept. Almost every light in the house was left on. This strategy worked as they did not talk about The Man again until they were back in Australia. I avoided going upstairs in the daytime as much as I could and waited for my husband to come home from work before taking up even the washing. A crazy way to live. I still felt safe enough downstairs at this point, but upstairs was mentally out of bounds even during the day. Did I think I might be neurotic? I sure did! I would tell myself that if I didn't snap out of this mindset, I'd find myself locked up and in a straitjacket in the very near future.

I had to admit though that the children's ability to see The Man had both frightened me and somehow reassured me of my own sanity. After all, I wasn't really imagining this if more than one of us was seeing the same thing. Remembering when I'd almost been choked by my sheets and our eldest had screamed about the man in my bedroom, I had to wonder: could they be seeing The Man because of me? I eventually decided that I wasn't the cause, only because if I'd thought for a minute this man was standing in their doorway even for one night, I'd have been in the room with them. The thought of him watching them hadn't entered my head.

The toilet continued to flush and my husband, who had fixed several toilet malfunctions in the past, gave up trying to fix it himself. The caretaker organised for a plumber to come and sort it out. He put a new seal on it just in case and commented on the way out the door that it was strange because the previous occupants had the same problem and because it was impossible to fix they had put in a new toilet for them. My husband and I just looked at each other, both thinking, 'This is not just happening to us then!' New toilets don't flush themselves. The house was weird!

The odd phone calls continued and logically I assumed that they were just from a prankster. It was unnerving and unsettling, but at least that I could logically explain. Toys and letters, especially bills, kept going missing, and then turning up again in odd places, no longer just on the bedroom sink. We were feeling the pressure of all these odd activities.

Then the smell of fire started. When the fire smells started the footsteps promptly stopped. The fire smell was very distinct and occurred randomly. One day it would come from the bedroom; the next it would be downstairs in the kitchen. It was so distinct that even my husband, who suffered from chronic hay fever and blocked sinuses, would suddenly launch himself out of his chair to check the kitchen or check upstairs. Twice we woke simultaneously in the middle of the night believing that the house was on fire because the smell was so strong.

Before my marriage I'd lived through one house fire, caused by a faulty electrical board. While there hadn't been much damage at all, the experience meant a house filled with the smell of smoke triggered a very real fear in me. Now though, there was no fire.

On one occasion as we sat together watching TV, I smelt a light smoky smell and at almost the identical moment my husband looked up and exclaimed, 'Is that smoke?'

I glanced up to see that the lounge-room appeared to have light swirls of smoke close to the ceiling. He didn't wait for my answer but bolted through to check the kitchen which held almost all our major electrical appliances. Seeing that all was fine there, he went straight upstairs to check the top floor. He came down looking nonplussed and we stood there staring at the ceiling yet again. We went outside in the freezing night, checking for smoke in the air. There was no smoke smell out there; it was still and fresh. We came back inside and stared up at the ceiling, and as we stood staring in stunned silence, we watched the swirls of what appeared to be smoke move around the ceiling and then slowly vanish. When we looked away, our eyes met in shock. 'What the hell is going on?' my husband spluttered. We had no answers.

I can't honestly say that I was coping any more. Surviving

each day was a more honest description. I was severely stressed and questioned my own sanity several times a day. All that kept me together was the fact that my husband was living through the same experiences and openly acknowledging them. We only had two more weeks in the house, and they couldn't pass fast enough.

About ten days before leaving my husband had to attend a function without me. It was short, just an hour long. Hating to leave me and the children alone in the house at this stage, he promised that he would be back as soon as he could. I braced myself and like all animals sensing danger, my main instincts focused on keeping our children safe. Fearing that if a man could appear in their doorway, he could probably disturb them in even worse ways, I didn't like to leave them alone upstairs at all. So, before my husband left the house, I set up the ironing board and a radio in our bedroom and prepared to make myself useful while he was away. I would be right next door if the children needed me.

I had been ironing for about twenty minutes when the phone rang. I hesitated, thought about not bothering to answer it, and then went downstairs to do just that. What if it was my husband? It stopped before I could pick it up. Back upstairs I went. It rang again. Downstairs I went, but when I picked it up there was no-one there. Back upstairs, I ironed one item before the phone rang again. Back downstairs? Not likely I thought. I let it ring. It rang out. That wasn't very clever, I thought. If someone is casing the house then they'll think that no-one is home. I checked that the curtains were closed. If someone was watching the house, they couldn't tell where I was inside it.

Several minutes later the phone rang again. I went downstairs. Dial tone. I took the phone off the hook. Back upstairs. More ironing. I forced my mind to think of other things, nice things like the trip home to Australia. Singapore stopover. Hotels. I managed to lose myself a bit in this daydream, looking forward to a couple of days in a nice hotel with no washing and no cooking to do. It would be bliss.

Then I smelt fire. Sniff, sniff. I snapped out of my daydream. The corridor air looked hazy, smoky. I checked the upstairs rooms. No fire. *Relax.* I still smell fire. I turn off the iron thinking that maybe it was the cause of the smell. I checked it thoroughly but there was no sign of any fault or damage; it just smells like a hot iron. I thought I'd better check downstairs even while my mind told me that this fire was not real, was in fact as unreal as all the others we had smelt previously. I headed downstairs, cautious as always since my accident. There was no smell of smoke downstairs. Back upstairs I went.

The phone rang loudly, and I jumped. My heart missed a beat. I remembered the phone was off the hook. It couldn't ring! I came to a dead halt. I froze in place. I could still hear the sound of the phone ringing. Loudly. The front door, at the foot of the stairs, opened, and my heart jumped into my mouth. My husband called out, 'It's me, love. I'm home,' as he walked inside. Briefly he looked up the stairs, saw me, and then glanced sideways towards the telephone. 'Funny, I thought the phone was ringing,' he commented as he walked over and placed it back on its cradle.

I stayed frozen on the stairs. The next minute he was holding me close. I was shaking from head to toe. 'It's okay,' he said, instinctively understanding what was wrong with me. 'I heard it too!' Some of the tension ebbed out of my body. It was okay. I was no longer doing this alone. I was still sane, still myself. I was wrecked, but he was home. I was safe.

One week to go, and we were still there. We were nearly

out of there. Out of this madhouse. My husband wasn't sure about us staying as he really wanted us out of that crazy space, whereas I was counting down the final days and certain that we could make it, as long as I avoided stairs in the middle of the night. I had my logical and organisational mother and partner hat on; to me this was now just another 'preparation to move to another posting' week. Logically I thought that since we were going to leave in a few days The Man would leave us alone. He'd be glad to see the back of us, surely?

My husband had one last function to attend before we escaped. By coincidence this was also our last evening in the house. He would be absent for about three hours. We were almost completely packed, with only a few remaining overnight essentials to throw in a box the following morning when the removalists arrived. I was excited about escaping and looking forward to being in a motel by the following evening. My focus was on our future, but my husband was seriously concerned with the present. He was openly anxious about leaving his family alone in the house for as long as he was away. Only a year ago he'd have scoffed at anything to do with ghosts or spirits; to him, back then, the paranormal simply didn't exist. He'd experienced so much during the year that his thinking had expanded, and he admitted that while he may not be able to 'see' like the girls and me, he was very unhappy about what he could 'feel'. He had no choice but to attend the function, however, and he walked out the door promising to be home as soon as he could get away. We hoped that if The Man had an issue with someone in his space, he would leave us alone on our last night since we were obviously leaving soon.

I focused on this belief as I locked the door behind my husband, half laughing as I did so at the fact that I was probably in more danger from inside the house than I was from anything outside. I glanced warily at the phone and wondered if I should just take it off the hook, mentally double checked my thinking and chose to be brave and leave it on for that just-in-case phone call my husband might need to make. I went upstairs, checked in on our sleeping girls and then went back to ironing our clothes for the next day in our bedroom next door. I ironed as quickly as I could. The bedroom got warmer, so I took off my cardigan and assumed it was because of my activity. The temperature however continued to rise, and very slowly I realised that it was making me quite drowsy.

I was halfway through a pair of trousers, struggling with my heavy eyes, when the phone rang. I jumped. I had been miles away, contemplating our journey home. Although I hesitated for a second, I went cautiously down the stairs to answer it. As I crossed the hallway to the phone my mind registered that I'd not turned off the iron. No doubt though, there would be no-one on the other end, and I could go straight back up there. Sure enough, only the dial tone greeted me. I felt no surprise, no fear. The heat upstairs had half drugged me. Rather than being upset my quirky humour got the better of me. 'Who are you going to pester tomorrow night?' I questioned aloud with a bit of a chuckle in my voice. Freedom was so close!

I was just two steps up the staircase when I smelt the sickening smell of acrid smoke. I looked upwards, about to bolt towards the iron. On the landing stood The Man leering down at me. Instead of bolting I froze and instantly wanted to vomit. The smoke was visible. It swirled around him, thick, yellow, and grey. I took a backward step without thinking and almost lost my balance. I looked up again, expecting for some reason that he would have just disappeared. This couldn't be real. It couldn't be happening. It made no sense.

I started talking to myself. 'You're not real. The fire is not real. You can't hurt me. You can't touch me. The fire isn't real. Get out of my way!' The figure, still visible, raised one arm as if to hit or threaten me. His hand almost disappeared into the smoky cloud above his head. His face was dark with blood curdling anger. Once again, I froze to the spot and an enormous chill crept down the stairs towards me. My racing mind suddenly recalled reading that people who were confronted by unreal or frightening images should always pray, and simultaneously I realised that this thing was between me and my children. I needed to get past him. My children were up there. I had left the iron on. Could he really start a fire? No way could I risk that possibility.

So many thoughts, so fast, and then a recollection of my God figure that I'd seen in my near-death experience. Without hesitation, I walked up the stairs reciting 'The Lord's Prayer' very loudly. Did I think the volume would make a difference, or was it just a form of bravado?

About two steps from The Man, my voice faltered and broke. The smoke quickened and swirled. Suddenly, from the very pit of my being lurched a deep and ferocious anger. My core released my strong fighting spirit and an equally strong determination not to be beaten. I'd had all I was going to take of living in fear. It rose with the force and velocity of an erupting volcano. My kids were up there, and I had had enough!

Looking The Man straight in the eyes, I yelled furiously. 'If this is about purity of spirit, then you can't touch me, so go to hell!' I was bloodcurdlingly angry, and nothing was going to stop me.

His arm descended from nowhere. It held what looked like a smooth block of wood. I switched quickly back to the last line of 'The Lord's Prayer' and threw myself forward up the last two stairs. I stopped abruptly. There was nothing. No smoke, no Man, nothing. I felt no pain. He hadn't hit me. He was simply gone. I was stunned. Shocked. Numb. This was madness.

The place was like ice. I was badly shaken. I checked the

bathroom to my right. No Man. I checked the Study. No Man. Tentatively I went on to check the toilet. Nothing. 'I'm acting like children do after a nightmare,' I thought to myself. 'Well, if it's a nightmare, it only happens when I'm awake.' I checked my girls. Holding hands and fast asleep. Even acoustically this house was abnormal. How could so much screaming and yelling never disturb them? My world didn't make any sense.

I went into our bedroom and switched the iron off. I noticed that, strangely, the dial was turned right down low. I must have done it automatically because I had no recollection of doing so. I touched the soleplate hesitantly, and it was cold. The temperature in the room itself was comfortable, but I certainly wasn't. I returned and checked the girls again, checked that the monitor was on, and when I exited their room, I closed the door. I knew I would be in trouble if they woke up, but somehow it made me feel they were safer. As was our norm, the hallway lights were ablaze.

Nervously I went back downstairs. Intuitively I felt that the children were completely safe. It's an odd feeling to get in the middle of mental confusion and distress, and I was aware of that at the time, but the feeling arrived out of nowhere, and I was as certain of it as I was of my own feet walking down the stairs. Realising that I was still shaking, I made myself a cup of tea. I felt weak, and I needed to sit down. Cup in hand, I settled onto the couch in the living room. I was utterly exhausted. I sipped my tea and checked my watch. Hopefully my husband would return within the hour. By the time I drank my tea, I was struggling to stay awake, so I gave in to my fatigue and lay on the couch. I glanced at the ceiling. No more footsteps. I listened to the sounds of the children breathing through the monitor and then, from sheer exhaustion, I dozed off.

I was dreaming. I had slept late. I had to get up to go to her funeral. I didn't want to face it, but he was there. He wore a dark suit, and I heard him calling me gently as he stood back and knotted his tie. His voice became impatient.

'I'll make you some tea,' he said gruffly, 'perhaps that will help you wake up.' He called me by name. That wasn't my name? I'm Lynne. Didn't he know that I was Lynne? My mind moved forward, still dreaming, to the funeral, and a wall of grief rose to meet me. This was painful heart-splitting grief the likes of which I'd never known. I pulled the blanket higher and turned my face into the pillow. She was dead. My little golden-haired darling was dead. Sobs wracked my body. I couldn't go. I couldn't see that little coffin, that awful box. They would lower her into that cold hole. Her and her teddy. I had cried when I had given them that. I hadn't wanted them to take it away. He had stared at me. That cold stare that he used only with me. He hadn't understood that it was part of her and that I wanted, needed, to keep it with me. It was all that I had.

He was back now, shaking me none too gently with one hand and holding a cup of tea in the other. 'You'll be late,' he said roughly. 'Pull yourself together. Sit up and drink the tea.' I pulled the blanket away and realised that he was now holding the cup of tea right in front of my face. I saw his knees. The dark trousers. My tearful gaze travelled slowly up his body. He seemed so tall from here. Wiry, I thought detachedly. My eyes continued to follow him upwards. His Adams apple moved in his throat as he spoke. I didn't hear what he said. My gaze travelled over his face. It was hard and set. He was angry. Why was he angry with me? My tear-filled eyes met his. Shock coursed through me.

Instantly I was wide awake and screaming hysterically. It was him. The Man! I launched myself upright, swinging my feet over the edge of the couch. I had to get away from him. He was dangerous. He'd killed her! I knew beyond all doubt that he'd killed her. Not the woman whose body I'd just been in, but their child, the little girl.

I had reached the lounge room doorway before I stopped, and now completely awake, I looked back at where I'd been lying and realised that it had all been a dream. It wasn't real. There was no-one there. It was a nightmare. Awful as it had seemed, it really had been just a nightmare.

Nervously I began to talk to myself. 'I'm not going nuts. I don't know why this is happening, maybe just stress, but it will all end when we leave here. You are a strong and smart lady. It's not your fault that you're mediumistic, but you are going to live through this. We are all going to be okay.' It flashed through my mind that if he could come downstairs, The Man could go anywhere. No, I had just been dreaming. He hadn't really been in the lounge room. I quickly brushed the thought aside. No! He belonged here. This was where he would stay.

I went to the kitchen and glanced at the clock. My husband was later than we had both expected. He should have returned by now. I needed him. I made myself some coffee, determined to stay awake. I couldn't bring myself to go back into the room to get the nursery monitor, and I chastised myself for being so childish. I went and sat at the foot of the stairs right in front of the front door.

Sipping my coffee, I tried to push the dream out of my thoughts, but it kept returning. 'Deal with it!' I thought to myself. Look at it. Let it go. So, I stopped pushing it away, and, leaning my head against the stair post, I relived it and analysed it as best I could. I decided that he must have killed the little girl. He had pushed her out of the window in that room? Had it been an accident? Was it done in temper?

The teddy. The teddy in the coffin. That really hit home. The bear belonged to my baby, my real-life child asleep and probably hugging it right now upstairs in her room! As I pondered this, I acknowledged that it was a dream and therefore some images would be from real life and some from fiction. The teddy in the coffin with a golden-haired child who looked similar to my daughter was just an image. It wasn't her in the coffin, just her bear. Slowly, like a small drip of water that eases its way through the tiniest gap, something shifted in my chest.

Very slowly, a softly creeping, ugly dawning thought connected in my brain. My child was going to die. If I wasn't careful, I would be too late. This was a message. A strong message. Maybe I didn't have it right? Maybe my interpretation of my dream was wrong? I tried to stand back emotionally and analyse what had just happened and what my brain was processing. It wasn't easy. I didn't want my child to die. This couldn't be true. Surely not? I didn't want it to be true. It was just a dream. Just a nightmare. It wasn't a message.

Denial is great. You can hide behind it all you want, but eventually you have to face the truth. My truth was in the knowing. I knew that my child was in danger. That this was some kind of message. This was what The Man wanted me to know. I had no idea what the danger was or when it would appear. I had to be 'awake' though. I must not miss it.

I pondered the fact that one day my littlest had stood on a box at a closed window upstairs, and her elder sister had shouted at her hysterically that she would die if she did that. It had taken an abnormal amount of reassurance to calm her down, but then, her reaction was abnormal.

We had given them rules about the windows as they were dangerous. They opened outwards and had no childproof locks, but nothing we had said to them should have untowardly scared them, and besides, the window had been shut. Their father had told them they might break a leg or an arm if they fell through, but our eldest was correct; they might easily be killed if they fell to the pathway below. Did she also know that her sister might not live? That her hold on life might be more tenuous than most? After all, she had tuned into me previously; anything was possible. I felt sick at the thought that something could be wrong with our baby. That we could lose her. I so hoped that what felt like a certainty was not, and that the stress we had been living with had just produced a dream about what is naturally a mother's worst fear. I could hope.

Is that what happened to The Man? I wondered to myself. Had he done something silly? Lost his temper perhaps and pushed the girl too hard? Had she been sitting on the wide windowsill? Or had he done it on purpose?

A hand touched my shoulder. My head shot sideways to check my shoulder. As clear as day and as cold as ice, I saw a man's hand. His touch was soft and gentle. His voice spoke from behind me, ever so quietly, 'Please.' He said no more. I didn't give him the time!

Jumping up I let out another bloodcurdling scream, spun around and flattened myself against the front door. I was now facing directly up the stairs. I looked up at him, tears streaming down my face and shaking from head to toe. He stood on the fourth step and seemed way too tall up there. He was no longer angry and wild. His eyes were instead soft and sad and very tired.

'I can't help you,' I said, 'I'm not ready for this. I can't cope. Leave me alone.' I was almost pleading. He put his right hand out towards me and slowly turned the palm upwards. I continued speaking through my tears. 'I can't. I can't deal with this. Please,' I begged him, 'leave me alone!'

I began to pray. He dropped his head and moved slowly backwards up the stairs. As he did so, I felt a deep and dreadful sadness fill my body. 'I'm sorry,' I heard myself whisper, 'but you frighten me. I'm just not ready.' Slowly, very slowly, he disappeared. My knees finally gave way, and I sank to the floor. The house was still now, the only sound my quiet crying.

Ten minutes later my husband put his key in the lock. 'Who's that?' I asked shakily.

'Only me, love,' he sang out. I unchained the door and stood aside to let him enter. 'Good grief!' he exclaimed, 'What happened to you? You look like....' He never finished his sentence. I collapsed into his arms.

While this experience was by far my most upsetting in the house, it opened so many doorways in my mind and left me with far more unanswered than answered questions. My idea that The Man wanted something seemed to have been correct. Why had he become gentle? What was he wanting from me and why did I suddenly feel deep compassion for him after the nightmare? Where did my words to him come from because I certainly had never thought like that previously?

Why did he show me my daughter's teddy in the coffin? Nothing else in the dream was real, so why the bear? His daughter had died, that much seemed certain. She was the little girl we saw upstairs, but they seemed to wander the same house without ever meeting. Had she fallen out of the window during play? There were no answers, but the sight of my daughter's white teddy bear in the coffin would continue to haunt me for the next few years. Was it really a warning? Was my knowing correct yet again? Only time would tell.

Even after this nightmare the house wasn't completely done with us. The next day the removalists came and emptied our weird home. We had arranged for a carpet cleaner to come through the following day. It was a long job, and as we had done all that we could do at that point, the cleaner, who was a regular and known to be trustworthy to Service Personnel, offered to return the house key to the caretaker's office when his job was complete so that we could just leave. We were delighted to not have to hang around a moment longer, and so, after checking with the caretaker that this was fine, we went off with a huge sigh of relief to spend the night in a motel.

We returned the next morning for what is called handover to the new family whom we had previously met and dined with. They were a lovely, and I dreaded the thought that they too might have to live through events like ours. I wanted to warn them, and I had been pushed far enough to not care if I looked and sounded like an idiot in their eyes. After all, I wouldn't have to see them again. My husband and I argued about this for some time. He insisted that we say nothing to them as they might not be 'like me'. They might not have any trouble. They might neither sense nor feel anything. More importantly, he didn't want to be thought crazy. He had a point, but I wasn't for it. The wife was from Papua New Guinea, and if anyone was in touch with the spirit world, I thought surely she would be, as spirits are a large part of their culture. I continued to argue my point, but eventually I gave in, not wanting to be responsible for placing him in an embarrassing position. We kept quiet.

Despite this, I found the morning somewhat uncomfortable. We were doing a regular handover. What I hoped would be a quick ten-minute job took considerably longer.

As it turned out, the key had not been delivered to the caretaker's office, and, as happened when we moved in, there was a long wait to retrieve the key. Several times during the wait I almost spoke up about our ghosts. I found myself squirming as I felt so guilty keeping quiet about the house and its crazy happenings. I reminded myself over and over that I would embarrass my husband if I spoke, but still, I felt it was the right thing to do.

Despite the caretaker's assurances that this mistake with the key had never been made before, it took a bit over an hour to retrieve it from the carpet cleaner. In the meantime, the care-taker went back to his office to sort out other house handovers, so when it finally arrived my husband went over to the office to inform him that the key was there and that we could complete the house exchange. 'So sorry to hold you up. This key is a damned nuisance,' my husband said, thinking back to our own arrival.

The two caretakers looked at each other and grinned. 'Not at all unusual for that house,' one said, and both chuckled. 'Didn't have anyone in it for a year once. Nobody would stay there.'

'Always terrible trouble with the toilet upstairs too. I'm surprised that you've not had to call us out more often to fix it,' said the other. 'The last lady who lived there was always calling us out.'

If I'd heard any of this conversation at the time, I'd have blurted out everything that had happened, warning the soon to be occupants of the house's oddness, but, as only he could, my husband didn't speak a word about it until we were safely on our way back to Australia. Men! It was then too that he confessed to other strange happenings. 'There was often someone standing behind me when I shaved at the basin in our room. I never really saw him, but I was always aware that it was a man.'

His clothes had been rearranged in his wardrobe too. He had always been meticulous about the order of his clothes, and I recalled him arguing with me early in our stay over the way I'd put his shirts away 'out of order.' I had lost my cool and from then on, he had put away his own clothes. I would simply hang them on the wardrobe door after ironing. The problem kept happening, but wisely, he had decided not to spook me further and kept that information to himself. Often someone stood outside his study door too. He said that he frequently found himself telling me to 'come in', only to find out that I wasn't there when he checked.

We were glad to have moved out and to get on with our lives, but a few years later, I was to really regret not informing the new family about our ghost, as we now referred to him. During an accidental meeting at work, our husbands literally bumped into each other. The gentleman who had moved into the home after us questioned my husband as to whether he had known there was anything unusual about the house. When my husband replied that the house was weird and seemed to be haunted, the gentleman became instantly angry. 'You should have told us. We would never have moved in there, especially with my wife's background and culture.' He did not explain further but stormed off down a corridor.

I felt terrible when I heard this and guilty about not speaking up. Intuition. Instinct. Call it what you like, but it is always right. These days embarrassing my husband would not be an issue. I've had more life experience and have more confidence. I would broach the subject and risk ridicule rather than stay quiet.

House issues aside, we loved our year in the UK and relished every opportunity to explore. We visited many of the delightful towns and villages around us, and my husband, never having been there before, was overawed by the many castles and old towns we set foot in. While we were delighted to leave the actual house behind, it was with deep regret that we left behind the thatched cottages and some of the most beautiful scenery we had ever viewed. Whereas previously I had been the only one in love with the UK, now it was a family love affair. I had been extremely happy to return to my homeland and for my family to meet my old friends and relatives. In some ways, I felt whole in the UK, but Australia was my little family's home, and I was glad to return.

On our return our relatives were inundated with tales of our haunted house, and shocked that instead of talking about our many travel trips, we wanted to talk about our ghost and our weird house. While some were intrigued, you could see from most of their faces that this wasn't what they expected, nor were they comfortable with it, so we decided that 'you really had to be there' and dropped the subject.

Chapter 19

Psychic Awareness and Growth Continues

I was back in Australia. I had returned to my homeland, reconnected with its beauty, marvelled at the ties that my birth country still held for me. Relived the memories of my first ten years of life, and then, firmly closing the door behind me, found myself once again on Australian soil.

Did the experiences in the UK change me? I had lived in a haunted house, travelled and seen my home country through my husband's eyes and watched him grow as a result. Of course they had. This time though, it was 100 percent my choice to be in Australia. Much as I loved the wonders that the UK held, and as strongly as I felt the ties to my native land, I realised that the lifestyle in Australia suited me far better. Economically life for my family was easier in Australia, and I couldn't even imagine how we would cope in the UK full time.

Also, after the year that I had endured, I no longer felt young. It was a more mature woman who had taken the plane trip home. Despite the magic of the country itself, our home life had worn me down. I felt so strained that I no longer enjoyed playing with my children as I once had; a lot of the light-hearted joy had been knocked out of me. I rarely made-up stories for them now. It was easier to read straight from a book. One night, when my eldest asked me to tell her one of my 'special stories', I found that nothing came to mind. I was empty. I tried starting with the traditional 'Once Upon a Time', but the next few words didn't flow the way they always had. I felt that I had no interest in make believe any more. Claiming fatigue, I got her to fetch her favourite book and together we read from that. This situation left me feeling sad and empty. Where had my creativity gone? When it failed to appear in the next few months, I wondered, 'Was this what happens when you finally grow up?' I wasn't too impressed if it was. I missed my creative side.

We were to have three homes in the next two years, moves were made due to landlords wanting their houses back to live in themselves or, in one case, we had to move out due to health issues. Our stress levels remained elevated because of this. During the first year I made new enquiries about studying naturopathy, but once again I was disappointed although this time I did have the complete support of my husband. Naturopathy was rapidly gaining in interest and popularity, and the fees had increased dramatically; we just couldn't stretch to them. I wondered how many people's dreams died due to a lack of finances. I still do sometimes.

Life is all about choices. Being with my children and supporting my husband through his studies prevented me from working and saving the finances I needed to pursue my own career. Living with chronic illness meant there were simply no spoons left at the end of my day now anyway, and so I faced reality and put my dream aside. I got on with the life I had. I believed that if it was meant to be, the opportunity would come; if not, something else would appear.

The psychic experiences didn't stop happening once we

were back in Australia. I'd been warned about having to move from the houses and landlords changing their minds. The problem was we had a dog. It's hard to find rental properties with a pet, so we had to take the homes, especially when some closures on the lease gave us short notice.

I experienced many *deja vue* events over the next couple of years. They were all relatively common place to me after our English house and the interactions with The Man, but I did spend many hours when occupied with mundane chores thinking about how these things worked. How did predictions appear as information and then come true? How did spirits appear, be there and yet not there? Why could some people see them, and some people sense them while others did not have a clue but would comment on rooms getting chilly or odd smells around the place?

I analysed anything that defied logic, but as always I found no answers and had to be content in finding some level of acceptance and a little more understanding that these events happened, and how we reacted to them varied. I realised that I had learned more than I had realised during our English adventure. It had changed me. I no longer hesitated to admit to myself that I was psychic, clairvoyant or mediumistic. I talked more freely about all sorts of unusual experiences and found it almost amusing if people frowned. I think that it was around this time I started to enjoy being 'odd'.

During one of my ironing sessions when my mind had wandered once again down these pathways, I reached the conclusion that I wouldn't have encountered these experiences if I didn't have the capacity or the knowhow to deal with them. I made up my mind that should anything like the ghost encounter happen to me again, heaven forbid, I would deal with it appropriately, seeking help if I had to, but otherwise sorting it out for myself.

I told my husband. He laughed. 'That's not going to happen here,' he said. 'Our houses are too young for spirits!' I wasn't so sure of that myself. I didn't know if age had anything to do with hauntings, but I was determined not to live through such a nightmare again.

It was our second year back, and we had just completed our second house move. The children had survived yet another school change, and I must have had enough down time as strange things began to happen yet again. It was obviously time for me to do more growing.

It started with the sense of a man standing behind me. He was not a threatening presence as we'd had in the UK, so I didn't pay much attention at first. Then the person started to come and sit opposite me when I settled down to read at night. The energy felt like that of my grandfather, not the same, definitely not him, but kindly. I felt nothing to be afraid of.

I was not comfortable though when I started seeing a hanging man whenever I opened the door of my walk-in robe. After a few of these visions I started to let the fear get to me and began to dislike the whole bedroom. Then, one day, after slamming the door on my apparition I decided that it was time to confront the issue and deal with it. I understood that what I was seeing was not real. I sat down on the edge of the bed and stared hard at the wardrobe door and deliberately brought back the image I had encountered minutes before. I burst out laughing.

This was not a hanging man but The Hanged Man. He was hanging by his foot not his neck! Nothing funny about a man hanging in your cupboard, but The Hanged Man has a completely different meaning. It is a picture from the tarot and is merely a symbol. Throughout history it has been allocated many meanings but the most common is that your life is currently at a standstill and that you are in limbo. On a different level it means that there are changes taking place within you that cannot be seen yet. This was exactly how I viewed my current circumstances and perfectly apt. I took the vision as a signal to pay attention to myself, and not just give endlessly to my family. It was time to grow. I acknowledged that I'd become very discontented with the mundaneness of my life and that negative energy was building up inside me. What to do? What interested me? What could I afford to learn next?

I went through the newspaper seeking courses that might interest me, and out jumped an advertisement to learn tarot. I had only ever used the mythic tarot properly and that had been a good ten years back. Could I handle tarot again? I had had two very scary experiences doing readings for friends during those ten years, and they had frightened us out of our wits. Did I want to walk that pathway again? I could afford this course, and I would surely learn something new. It would get me out of the house and alleviate my boredom. My mind went back over some of my past experiences.

In 1987, the year our first daughter was born, I was reading for a dear friend when a pair of alabaster white hands appeared between us. Both of us waited for the other to acknowledge that they were there. Both of us wondered if we were the only one seeing this apparition. Neither of us had had an experience like this before. Neither of us knew what to do. Should we speak up? Say nothing? My girlfriend was the first to give in to her fear, and she remained frightened even after I told her that I could see them too. Relieved but nervous, we both watched for a couple of minutes until the hands slowly dissolved. We had no idea how or why this happened. We had no idea what, if anything, it meant. Consequently, when the hands disappeared the reading came to an abrupt halt. We were more than a little spooked. We marvelled at what we'd seen, but my friend was scared. I never read for her again, so I'm unsure whether this was the product of our combined energy or simply a one-off experience.

The second incident had been terrifying, frightening me enough to make me put my cards away for a very long time. It occurred in Brisbane about four years after the incident with the lady's hands. A man appeared behind the friend I was reading for. I started to describe him to her, believing that he was only visible to me, when, unexpectedly, his hands shot out, grabbed her neck and began to choke her. I watched stunned and frozen to the spot as her face changed colour and her eyes bulged. Then, as her head twisted towards one shoulder, I raised my eyes in shocked horror and saw the man's insane face. I realised in that moment that real or not I had started it and therefore I was the one responsible for stopping it. I had to take control. It was up to me! My first reaction was to yell 'NO!' as loudly as possible. This proved useless of course. My second reaction was once again to pray. I recited the Lord's Prayer. Not necessarily accurately I might add as it was a long time since I'd stepped inside a church. The figure slowly disintegrated as, still praying, I made it around the table to my friend in time to catch her as she fell from her chair.

We were both in shock, although she was in a far worse state than me. She had experienced the whole event as if it was real; there were even marks on her neck where his fingers had been. It took about fifteen minutes for the finger marks to fade but a lot longer for us to recover. Our friendship was more than a little strained after that. I learned that using the psychic gifts that I'd been born with came with a large amount of responsibility, and I wasn't sure I wanted to take that on. I had literally been shaken to my core.

Despite this, tarot still held a great deal of fascination for me. I loved its symbolism and the psychological aspects of it all. I read the advertisement for lessons at least a dozen times and rehashed both good and bad previous experiences. I thought about how I dreamed about books and films before they were even released. I thought about how my husband, once one of the great disbelievers, now totally accepted that If I told him I'd dreamt an amazing, interesting, or amusing plot, then he could expect to see the movie released within two years, or the book in the bookshop with the new release cover exactly as I had described sometime in the months ahead.

I knew these experiences were driving me crazy in an entirely different way to what had happened in England. I had always escaped into books, but now I could no longer do that as books become something I read through quickly just to see if the story was exactly as I had dreamt it. I kept buying them, but by about the third chapter the visions from my dreams would come flooding back, and I would know the rest of the plot no matter how convoluted or unexpected the author had made it. I had reached the stage where I was now buying books that I wouldn't normally read in the vain hope that I would find one that I didn't have this annoying insight into.

A few times my dreams had even given the book two different endings, and while only one could show up in the book I would always come across interviews after the book was released in which the author talked about their planned original ending and how they had changed it to the published version. It seemed to me that while there was no point in knowing the end of a book in advance, it was one way for something greater than me to pay attention to my mind. Perhaps it was something I was just going to have to live with, perhaps it had a yet undiscovered purpose. It was very irritating, especially as no matter how much of the story I knew, I still had to read through it all to find out if it was indeed a copy of what I'd dreamt.

Logical as always, I reminded myself that I had used my strange abilities to help people even if it wasn't often. Perhaps, I contemplated, there was a bigger purpose, an actual use for this. Did I only dream of trivial things because I wasn't using my energy constructively? What if it could be channelled into something useful? I felt a growing drive to use these abilities, and I was ready to admit that I was definitely attracted to this other world where there were lots of questions and very few answers. I think I liked the fact that this was a puzzle that needed solving. I am intrigued by mystery in general, and I love to learn; in addition, I knew so little about this area. Fascination carried me forward, and I signed up for the classes.

The tarot class was fun. There were one or two naturally developing clairvoyants amongst us, but on the whole it was a group of young women searching for something more, seeking to grow and to learn to sort out their worldly problems from the inside. I have always loved to observe human behaviour, and I thoroughly enjoyed observing the sharing and individual development during the course, almost as much as I enjoyed the course itself.

The teacher was a pleasant, mature lady, and as I'd discovered in many earlier interactions in my life, she quickly saw me as some kind of challenge or threat. Kind and gentle with the others whenever it was my turn, I would be ordered to speak, commanded to explain. If not for my well ingrained upbringing, we could easily have butted heads on many occasions. It startled many members of the class, and by the end of the course, a couple of people had asked why the teacher didn't like me. I laughed it off and explained that I was used to people reacting to me in this manner, but I couldn't explain it. The tension between us was palpable at times, and during our last class became quite alarming.

During this last get together, the teacher laid out her own cards and asked me to read them. I felt like a deer in the headlights of an oncoming vehicle. Not one to back down to a challenge, and feeling that it would be rude to refuse, I carefully did just that. I felt so ill. The minute she'd thrown down the cards I'd seen that she was going to die. Not only was she going to die, but she was going to die suddenly and quite soon. Now, to be clear, the cards have a thousand interpretations, and it was not the cards themselves that let me see this awful future. I also had no experience of seeing death in the cards and no reason to think that she would die as she was in her early fifties by my estimate. There is also an unspoken rule that if you do pick up a death, you keep it to yourself as naturally you could be misinterpreting the cards.

I gave her the reading, working around what I saw as her obvious imminent demise. I was shocked and sickened by what I felt and saw, but I desperately tried to keep my cool throughout. To complete the reading, I warned her that she needed to get a health check in the immediate future. She dismissed my words with, 'Oh yes, you're right, I have an appointment next week with my GP.'

She spoke about her general feelings and then stopped, and, staring directly at me, she told the class how she'd had nightmares while away the previous week. Every night for three nights she'd dreamt of her deceased parents knocking on the windows of her hotel room and being unable to get up to let them in. Being an intuitive herself, she had wondered if she was going to die. The class was aghast, and this started a lot of chatting and reassuring. A few people gave other interpretations of the symbolism in the dreams, and slowly we moved on to other topics. Meanwhile I'd retreated inside myself, hiding from my own shock of seeing death and not knowing how to process it. I was scared I would be right. The knowing I'd had previously in other circumstances came from deep inside of me, not from a reading, so I didn't know what to do or how to manage this situation. I soothed myself with the fact that she was seeing her doctor in a few days, but when the time came to write down my interest for a more advanced course, I didn't sign up. I couldn't. In my mind, it wasn't going to happen.

With the course completed, I was once again left to read only for myself, or my little family, and it was with a sickening feeling in my stomach that I casually tossed the cards out on a table one day to find them telling me that once again I was to move house before the end of the year. We had moved from England to Canberra, and again moved within Canberra in the space of only fourteen months. The thought of another move was depressing and overwhelming. I told my husband what I saw, and he shook his head. He certainly wasn't willing to believe this one. Politely he reassured me as best he could, and I put the cards away. They stayed away. It's fascinating how the mind tries to run from situations it simply cannot face. Maybe I thought that if I couldn't see them then the move wouldn't happen? Anyway, they became back of the drawer items for some months to come. I was literally not dealing!

If I'm not learning or working with my mind, I get antsy. It's not that I get bored so much as I have this energy that drives me, even when I'm unwell, to seek out information, something new, something useful. The creative in me was crying out, and so I signed up for a cake decorating course at the local college. Eventually I graduated and successfully made an intricately decorated wedding cake, but this didn't fulfil me in the least. It was another notch in my creative belt but not something I would choose for a hobby let alone a career. It helped to fill a void, soothed my needs for a short time, and no doubt would come in useful at some point, but it was time to move on.

My inner drive was becoming stronger, getting harder to live with. I was getting harder and harder to live with. Fortunately, my husband was too busy with work and study to notice, and if I'm perfectly honest, once my time at college was complete, I channelled most of my pent-up energy into keeping him on track. You see, after all these years, he had almost completed the university course he'd started before being posted to study something entirely different at university in the UK. The incredibly long hours he'd put in there, learning subjects he had no previous education in, had paid off, and he'd received an award never before gained by an Australian serviceman: he became a fellow of the London City and Guild. He returned home needing a break, wasn't able to take one and was now burnt out. He looked and acted like he might break. I was doing whatever I could to support him through his last couple of subjects.

I often thought of my original fears about my husband studying and the negative effects this was known to have on any marriage, exacerbated if the family also had young children. I don't think that we even really knew each other that well any more, as we had both changed a lot over the past six years, and we had spent very little quality time together. Fortunately, through the magic of chemistry, we were still 'in love', and I marvelled over this fact. I was determined that we would make it to the other end together; we were after all a team. Jokingly I told him that I would carry him to his last exam in a wheel-barrow if that's what was required to get him there and that the children would stand on the sidelines waving flags and cheering him on. He knew I was just crazy enough to follow through on my threat, and with the girls thinking it hilarious and prepared to join in, he laughed out some of his tension.

In this last semester of his degree, I signed up to study jour-nalism through a college in Sydney. It was something I both wanted to do and something that I hoped would fill my silent evenings once the girls were in bed. Whatever I did had to be by correspondence due to my husband still being absent for a couple of weeks at a time on frequent trips interstate. He was simply not available to help with childcare between work and his studying. I already held a Bachelor of Arts, and I enjoyed writing stories for the children on occasion. The next step seemed obvious. I would study freelance journalism.

My husband quipped about decorating the walls with my diploma collection. He pointed out that I appeared to be making a hobby out of studying. 'Since we've been married, you have attained a secretarial diploma, a massage diploma, a book-keeping diploma, a certificate in polarity therapy, a diploma in tarot and a cake decorating certificate. Why did you get a degree in the first place if you're not going to use it by getting a job?'

I froze, and then erupted. 'I've got to do something with my mind while I wait for you to be done following your studies and career path!' I sniped. I was not a happy camper.

There are moments in your life when things change on a pin. Someone does or says something and sends your mind down a pathway, seemingly accidentally, that leads you into territory that you might otherwise not go to. When my husband questioned my need to study, my near-death experience once again raised its head. I started to worry. Was I doing what I had promised to do, or was I still to find it in the future? What if I helped my whole family succeed but failed to succeed myself? This was not a prospect I liked at all. What if I didn't fulfil this promise that I couldn't recall? I felt a sense of responsibility to complete this one thing even if I didn't know what it was. How was this even possible? My mind continued spiralling into question land, self-analysing, disassembling, and I realised that the me who wasn't a mother, or a wife, was lost.

I had drowned somewhere in the morass of daily life, and nobody had noticed, not even me. I realised, too, that my interests were very different to my family's, both close and extended, and they had no idea that this other me existed. Although I joked to myself in this lightbulb moment that it wasn't like me to do anything quietly, not even drowning, I realised the seriousness of my situation. It had happened so easily, so silently, and it was the greatest source of my personal dissatisfaction. This was an awakening moment in my life. I was not happy to find myself in this position, and the little Welsh girl still living deep inside of me was not happy to realise it either. This was not how I was meant to be.

When the *Sydney Morning Herald* published my first article in their *Good Weekend Magazine* in December 1994, I was jubilant. I came alive again. I had needed to prove that the real me, the individual who had given up so much, was still there, and that she still had potential. When my tutor phoned from Sydney to ask how I had pulled off such a coup, I knew that I was well and truly alive and kicking. Confidence I hadn't known I'd lost returned. With it came the acknowledgement that my husband liked the me that he had helped mould during our marriage, but I truly didn't. Of necessity there was a gradual shift in our relationship as I emerged from what was a self-made chrysalis.

By the time this article was printed, however, we had moved house yet again. Just as the cards had predicted several months before, our landlord decided that he wanted to live in the house himself, and so we had to go. Luck was on our side this time.

The owners of our new rental were the parents of one of our daughter's classmates. They were about to be posted overseas and needed someone to rent their property. I had found out from my daughter that they were moving overseas and immediately felt compelled to ask them if they were going to rent their house out. I felt this needed to be done urgently. I followed through with it the next morning when I saw the lady at school drop off. We had barely said more than good morning to each other before this. As it turned out, the couple were happy to have tenants they knew, and we were happy to have a lovely home, conveniently located nearby. Once again though, we were to learn about something odd. The lady of the house was herself stunned at how events turned out.

Earlier that year, before her husband was told he was being posted overseas, my husband had delivered our daughter to their home to attend their son's birthday party. When my husband drove off, she had turned to her own husband and said, 'I know this sounds silly, but that man is going to live in our house.' They both clearly recalled the incident and told us when we signed the rental paperwork.

I was changing more than just homes. The strange events that had already happened to us, coupled with my own accurate predictions, were making me more and more convinced that none of us are in control of our own destiny as I had been brought up to believe. Our lives were looking more like they followed some pre-ordered plan. This lady's accurate premonition added to my belief.

Chapter 20

Becoming the Teacher

The owners went overseas, and we were handed the keys to their home immediately which meant that we could start moving in before the exit date at our current property. I started a routine where I would pack a few boxes during the day and my husband would transport them at night after work. I noticed from his second trip onwards he always took our family dog. Thinking that the dog would be more of a hindrance than a help, I queried the sense of this. He looked a little sheepish, but he merely replied that he liked her company. I thought this odd because the little minx would always run away if not kept on a tight leash and no amount of training had convinced her to behave differently. Surely this would make moving boxes into the house from the car diffi-cult?? Wouldn't she just be in the way? I didn't voice this thought, though, as the house was set well back from the street. Apart from a small circle of light on the porch it was very dark at night. You would never have got me up there alone at night before the house was occupied.

I never felt any discomfort about this house move. I can

count on one hand the number of times that moving house has excited me, and I have had nineteen house moves in my lifetime, most of them since my marriage. I really liked this house in a way that I only ever liked one before it; the one that we had lived in down in Adelaide, in our pre-children days.

We were all excited when moving day came and the children went off to school from one house and went home to another with big smiles on their young faces. They were delighted to live in the home of their friend.

The first night in the house we settled the children, and my husband settled in for some study time. I opened a box or two and then, exhausted, started reading a book. As was my norm, I was certain that I knew the ending of the story, and probably a fair bit of the plot, but I was determined to read the book from cover to cover. It was a new release, only in bookshops for four days before I bought it. I think, looking back now, I might still have been in denial that the human mind could have the abilities that it did, and so, in my own small way, I was trying to remain as normal as possible and hoping to be proven wrong.

I had been reading for about ten minutes although I wasn't fully aware of the words as I was so tired, when a slight, cooling breeze, wafted through the room. It had been very hot all day and the breeze was appreciated. 'Must be a storm brewing,' I absentmindedly thought as I glanced outside. However, the air was still and hot and such was my fatigue that I didn't register the importance of the sensation of the cooling breeze. The leaves on the trees and bushes weren't even moving. There was no sign of a storm. Unperturbed, I went back to my book.

A man, dressed like a wealthy country landowner in a Tweed jacket and moleskins with polished boots, appeared at the top of the few stairs leading to the open dining room, divided from the lounge by a waist height wall. 'Hello,' he said pleasantly as he walked towards me, 'welcome to my home.' He was very polite and quietly spoken yet distinct.

'Hello,' I responded automatically and continued reading.

'Who are you talking to?' My husband's voice came from the kitchen through the doorway. I looked up at the figure and gave a little yelp of fright. He smiled slowly, turned, and walked back up the stairs. As he reached the dining room, he smiled down at me again and then simply disappeared.

'Oh my God!' I exclaimed loudly.

My husband rushed in. 'What's up?'

I explained.

'Sounds like we might have another ghost,' said my master of understatement. we weren't impressed by this thought at all. I kept repeating to myself throughout the rest of the evening that at least this one wasn't unfriendly. After all, he had welcomed us to his home, so surely things would be fine.

Over the next few days we were too busy to give but a passing thought to our unexpected housemate, and so, when our wedding anniversary rolled around and our daughter's godmother volunteered to babysit, we happily accepted her offer and looked forward to spending some quality time together for once. It didn't enter my head to tell her about the man I had encountered on our first night. As I was the only one who had seen him, there was still the possibility that he was the result of my overtired imagination.

We had a really, lovely evening in an excellent Italian restaurant and returned home relaxed and happy. Before we could even get the key in the front door lock, the door opened. There stood our dear friend, obviously nervous and shaken and with her bag at her feet to hasten her departure. 'Lucky you're home now as I was about to put the girls in my car and take them to my place. I was going to leave you a note on the table. This place is strange. Weird. I won't be babysitting here again!'

I was instantly worried and intrigued. Relaxing a little now that we were home, she followed us up the long hallway to the kitchen at the back of the house assuring us that the girls were fine, but that she herself had been completely spooked by something. She couldn't stand with her back to the dining/lounge area as she felt that someone was there watching her. Right now, though, she said, she just wanted to get out of the house and didn't want to say more. Worried, we thanked her profusely and walked her out to her car, agreeing to talk the following day.

Her behaviour rattled us completely as she was the last person that we would have expected to behave this way. She was one of the most grounded people we knew, extremely down to earth, so whatever had happened must have been serious for her to behave like this. She was obviously very scared.

The following day she returned to explain. Everything had been fine until she'd put the girls to bed. After that she kept hearing noises, as if one of them was getting up to go to the bathroom. She would get up to see if they were alright only to find them fast asleep. On returning to the lounge room at one point, a cool breeze had passed through the room, and she had distinctly felt a man's presence. She had retreated to the kitchen thinking that she was being a bit silly, but the feeling of being observed increased.

Increasingly nervous, she had packed her bag and prepared to wake the children and make her escape. 'If they had been awake already, we wouldn't have been here,' she insisted, 'it was just too spooky!' She was so scared by this event that she couldn't sit with her back to the dining/lounge doorway even in broad daylight. 'I just need to see what's coming,' she said with a nervous laugh.

She was so open and honest with us that I thought I should

share my own experience. I recited the story of the man welcoming us to the house, and how I didn't think that he was at all harmful. 'I don't care. I'm not babysitting until you get rid of him. How can you bear to share a house with something so spooky?' After the house in England, it still surprises me that I wasn't scared myself, although I admit, her fear certainly made me nervous.

The man wasn't harmful, but he did become bothersome. He also began to come closer and closer to me. I would turn around to see him standing in the middle of the room, in a doorway, and eventually just a couple of feet behind me. It was when I began to smell cigarette smoke in the dining room that my memories of our ghostly visitor in England played on my mind. It was time for this gentleman to go. I had made myself a promise back then, and it was time to keep it. I was especially concerned that at some point the children would sense his presence. They were happy here. They felt safe, and I didn't want anything to change that.

Of course, I had no idea where to turn to deal with ghosts or spirits. I knew no more than I had experienced so far in my life, and I didn't know where to start to get rid of this Gentleman. So, I started by asking him to leave whenever he made himself visible. Then I asked him to leave whenever I felt his presence regardless of if he was visible to me or not. I soon learned there is nothing like talking to an empty space to make you feel like a complete fool. I meditated. I prayed. I lit candles. Instead of doing what I wanted, the opposite happened, and he appeared more and more frequently.

He caused me to have accidents, dropping glasses and crockery with gay abandon when startled by him in the kitchen. It was when I went outside to clean the floor to ceiling windows, my mind focused on a list of chores I needed to complete that day, that I really decided it was time to get serious. There was I, cloths and a bottle of window cleaner in hand, a shopping list forming in my head, and there, clear as day, looking back at me from inside the house, was the Gentleman. I was done! This was no longer his house even if it had been once. It was time to evict him!

So, still using what I knew, I meditated every evening for a week with a candle burning on the table in front of me. I asked during meditation that his spirit be removed from the house. He didn't appear for a couple of days after that, and I naively thought we might be safe; that it had worked. About three days later I went to the dining room to close the curtains and saw him on the other side of the glass, looking back at me from the darkness outside. The sight of him was so unexpected that I screeched loudly and jumped back from the window without thinking. He seemed completely real, solid as any other man or woman. I was now shaking just as I had in England, and this triggered my anger. I was not going to go through that situation or anything like it again. No more sitting on the fence unable to decide if these things really happened or not. Nothing was going to spoil this home for us. Time for forceful ghost busting. I was not going to let a thing use fear to control me again.

The next day I went to see a leader of the local spiritual church. I needed help and this seemed the most likely place in my universe to get it. I was a bit uncomfortable at the thought of discussing this topic with a stranger, and even climbing the stairs to their office, I was still asking myself if I was even vaguely sane.

'Light candles every night and pray. Ask him to show his face. If he appears, ask if he comes from the Light of Christ. Unless he answers with a definite yes and looks you directly in the eye then he is lying. If he avoids your eyes, or avoids answering, then you will need to pray for his soul to be delivered to the light. He will then disappear. You will need to do this at 4 am.'

Four am! Light of Christ! Ask him! Conjure up his face! Was she some kind of nut case? What was I thinking going to this woman for advice! What she had told me served only to justify my earlier thoughts. 'I am quite mad!' I exclaimed to myself. 'This is the true meaning of insanity.'

I felt completely overwhelmed by the kookiness of the situation, and it was doing my rational head in. I had finally plucked up the courage to step out of my comfort zone and ask someone to help me get rid of a ghost, and this was the advice I was expected to follow? Seriously?

All the way home I berated myself. 'You went to talk about a ghost. Call that sensible? Why would you get sensible advice about something that doesn't make sense in the first place? What had I expected her to tell me to do? Spray him with pesticide and watch him lie on his back and kick his legs until he died like a cockroach?' That last thought amused me and chuckling lightly, I calmed down.

Thinking about it more deeply, I realised that I could either take her advice or ignore it. What did I have to lose if I took it? Nothing that I had done had stopped the thing from appearing, so was there a chance that this apparent idiocy would? I figured that no one but my husband need ever know. Hey, even he didn't need to know! After all, what were the chances of him being awake at four in the morning?

Eventually I decided I was a tired mum still getting up at night for our youngest and nothing was going to entice me to get out of bed to play games at four in the morning unless I absolutely had to. I decided that I'd skip the 4 am routine for as long as I could and try to achieve the same thing of an evening instead. No 4 am starts for me, thanks.

Famous last words.

I took the lady's advice. I was neither brave nor confident; that's almost impossible when you feel like a complete idiot and are very nervous, but two weeks later, after evenings of candles and meditations had failed to bring about a safe confrontation and with the unexpected encounters increasing, I folded. I had been feeling increasingly pressured, but my sense of humour held up until one afternoon I lifted a tray of small cakes out of the oven, turned to place the hot tray on the kitchen bench, and came face to face with my gentleman farmer. I don't know how loud I yelled, but I do know how far the cakes flew, and the majority were scattered across the floor to the other side of the room. I was shocked and angry. I had reached my limit. Enough was enough. Four am suddenly didn't look so bad.

That night I put it in the hands of the gods. Before I went to bed, I spoke aloud to no-one in particular, 'If you want me to get rid of him, then you'll wake me at 4 am. I am not disturbing my husband's sleep with the sound of an alarm.'

I have always believed that you can program your mind to wake yourself at set times, an easy use of self-hypnosis, so when I awoke suddenly at 3.50 am, I was mildly amused. I turned over to go back to sleep.

I quickly found that I couldn't as I was as wide awake as if it was mid-day. Groaning softly, I reluctantly got out of bed. I had said I would do this thing if I woke up, so I'd better get on with it.

I picked up an aromatherapy candle from the dressing table and moved quietly to the door. 'Maybe insanity runs in the family, and they've just never wanted to tell me,' I thought humorously. Always able to stand apart from myself and see the ludicrousness of any situation, I had momentary movie-like pictures of what I'd look like to an observer pass through my mind, and I got the giggles. Oh well, insane or not, I was going to give it a try. You never know, it might surprise me. I might learn something, or not. I expected not.

The house slept. I turned on the lounge room light and sat

on the floor by the fireplace. I lit the candle, prayed, and asked the Gentleman to show himself. Nothing happened. I repeated my request. Still nothing. A startled bird chirped loudly, probably scared by the neighbour's prowling cat, and I jumped nervously. Still nothing. Feeling very foolish, I went back to bed and slept.

The following evening when I lay down in bed, I went straight to sleep. I was too tired to contemplate ghosts or 4 am starts. I had had a rough day with a sick child and a broken car; exhaustion overtook me. At 3.55 am. my eyes opened. Someone had touched my arm. I looked groggily for one of my daughters. No one was there.

'Get up!'

I felt rather than heard the command. I crawled out of bed like a zombie, picked up the matches and candle from where I'd deposited them the morning before, and slowly went to sit by the hearth. 'Well, I definitely didn't plan this,' I thought, 'I'd much rather be in bed. What am I doing here?'

The air seemed cold. I wrapped my dressing gown tighter around me and went through the motions of the morning before. Nothing. I repeated my request for him to show himself. I felt my legs turn to lead. I needed to move them. I couldn't. I tried to flex. Nothing!

A chilly breeze wafted around me and suddenly the Gentleman was there in front of me. Well, technically just a part of him. His head. No body. He was about forty something, quite handsome and rugged with thick hair and smiling eyes. He seemed pleasant. Then I remembered what I was supposed to ask.

'Do you come from the Light of Christ?' I questioned aloud.

His face turned, and I saw it in profile. Then it turned back to face me again. The eyes were closed. 'Do you come from the

Light of Christ?' I repeated, wondering if he had even heard me the first time.

I registered that I'd begun to shake with nerves just as the face doubled in size, and within seconds, it transformed a dozen or so times into different people from different ages. Fear rose in my gullet as part of my mind, ever fighting for a logical explanation, realised that I couldn't possibly have made that up in such a short time. I'd have had to plan for these changes, surely? Fear freezes me, and it took me a moment or two for my mind to refocus on what was happening.

When I did, I realised that his face had metamorphosised. He now had dark hair, swarthier skin and his eyes were bulging. He looked furiously angry. With a shock I remembered that I was supposed to pray. 'Please deliver this spirit to the Light of Christ. Please show him the way for he is lost.' Again, more desperately, 'PLEASE show him the way to the light!' In fear, I squeaked out the words.

The face grew grotesquely dark and frightening and where the eyes had been oddly blue before they now flashed a fiery red and black. Where they had been kind, they now looked like pure evil. The face moved closer and closer to me, constantly transforming from one ugly, angry state to another.

I was praying fervently. I no longer felt like a fool. I felt like my life depended on the words that I could get out of my mouth and that I couldn't get them out fast enough to protect myself. In fear I shut my eyes and mouth tight and like a child I prayed silently and fervently. 'Please God, take this lost spirit to the light. Oh God, please!'

I was completely wracked by fear but suddenly I just had to open my eyes. I had to see exactly what was happening. Opening them I was confronted by my own version of pure evil. Just as I had when scared in the English home, I fell back into my childhood experiences and 'The Lord's Prayer'. 'Our Father,' I started.

The face transformed like putty. For a second the eyes seethed with anger and then just as suddenly peace descended on the face and the eyes closed lightly down. A look of pure serenity washed over it, and, slowly but surely, the face disintegrated.

I finished the prayer. The room was now still, quiet, and completely calm.

I felt an enormous sadness wash over me. Why? I didn't have an answer even as the tears rolled down my cheeks. I realised that my body was cold and shaking. I looked at my watch. It was 4.45 am. Where had the time gone? I felt like I had only been sitting there for about ten or maybe fifteen minutes. Wanting to be warm I blew out the candle and stumbled back to bed. I felt numb both inside and out. What had I just experienced? What was it? What did it mean? Was it real? Climbing gently into bed, taking care not to disturb my husband, I fell instantly into a deep sleep. When I awoke later that morning, I felt like I'd been on a long holiday. I went out to the lounge room. The burnt candle was still there. It had really happened. The atmosphere in the room had a particularly crisp and clean feel to it that stood out. There was no longer anything there. He had gone to wherever he needed to go.

For the next few days, I thought about very little but the experience I had just lived through. I went over and over what had happened, examining and re-examining both the event and my reactions to it. As a young child I had attended Sunday School intermittently and only for a short period of my life. The last thing I would have described myself as was a religious believer. I had reached a belief that there some sort of heaven after my near-death experience, but the conclusions I had reached back then hadn't extended to the biblical concept of hell.

Yet, during this event, I had seen evil anger in the ghost's eyes and had responded with deeply felt and trusted Christian prayers, relying on them to keep me safe. Okay so I had stumbled my way through 'The Lord's Prayer', but it seemed to me that this ritual I had performed was really about intent. I intended to remove him from the house, and he intended to remain. Was it a case of good versus evil? I still didn't think that the man himself was evil.

'Perhaps,' I thought, cautiously feeling my way through the pieces of information and jumble of ideas, 'this was just how we defined things which our minds were deeply uncomfortable about accepting?' Perhaps that's what I had, in my fear, done to The Man in the house in England? Perhaps he too needed to be released from that home? What if that was what he had really wanted from me all along? I would never find out, but it was an interesting thought. It would certainly explain why he had haunted me. It would also explain the change once I had acknowledged that he wanted something. I felt sad at this thought, sad for what might have been if I'd been more awake and open to so-called spiritual events. I wished that I'd had the understanding and acceptance that I had now. Perhaps now I would be able to help him. How different our lives might have been if I had.

The confrontation with this Gentleman was also a confrontation with my own fear. I had successfully faced what I was most afraid of in an ethereal sense. It was a victory that left me both overawed and with a thirst for greater knowledge and understanding. Was this what I had promised to do? Was I perhaps on track after all? If it was then, surely this was really a build-up, perhaps even a form of initiation for something else. I wondered what learning lay ahead. I felt strongly that there was something bigger, or tougher perhaps, ahead of me.

I swore to myself that one day I would put all these events down on paper: my whole near-death experience, the spooks, the *deja vue* events, everything. There must be other people like me out there in the world, who felt like I did, like they were going crazy half the time, experiencing events that they just didn't understand. Maybe if I shared my story, it would help them to know that they were not alone in possessing these strange senses and abilities. Maybe they would see that they were all part of the human experience which our modern age mostly ignores and denies? 'One day,' I told myself, 'one day.' Not just yet though. I intuitively felt that there was more to come, more to learn, and therefore more to share, and of course, there was.

I began to attract friends who, although not involved in psychic areas themselves, were open-minded and interested in them. They were people who were able to recount at least one of their own amazing tales. Between us we discussed the unanswerable question as to whether these events were unusual, paranormal, or merely coincidental. I questioned how much imagination impacted on them. I had known since childhood that I had a creative and imaginative mind, but discussions with others reassured me that much of what had happened to me was definitely not all in my head or coming from a place inside of which I was unaware. I often wondered at my dogged determination to analyse everything that happened until I found at least a tentative logical explanation for it. My mind was split in two over these matters, and I continued to constantly struggle internally to not accept the life that I seemed to have to lead, regardless of how I felt about it. On the one hand I wanted logic to win out and explain all, but, on the other hand I was excited by the possibilities of the human mind opening to that which couldn't be explained logically at all. I was fascinated by the unexplainable.

Logical or not, it was certainly not my imagination when the smoke appeared. A local Avon Representative had dropped in early one evening with a delivery, and she sat chatting on a couch while I sat on a chair opposite her. There was a space of about two metres between us, broken only by a rectangular coffee table. I had met this lady previously on three or four occasions, and we had hit it off so the atmosphere between us was relaxed and friendly. Our talk was trivial but animated when I became aware of what looked like a whisp of thick smoke hovering in the air between us. It changed shape constantly but was never more than about thirty centimetres in length. Slowly it furled and unfurled but it didn't rise as smoke should, and it didn't disintegrate. I glanced at the hearth, half expecting to see a fire even though I knew it was summer. The fireplace was filled with a dried flower arrangement; no fire burning there.

My new friend kept talking. The whisp kept hovering between us. It was now getting in the way of my view of her face, and I found it more and more distracting. I moved my position and kept chatting. Eventually, when we had both moved several times, and I was feeling dreadfully uncomfortable, I gave in and swotted at it with my hand.

'Oh, thank goodness!' exclaimed my friend. 'You can see it too. I've been trying not to say anything. I thought it was just me. What on earth is it?'

We made eye contact, and then burst out laughing at our own absurdity. I stood up and waved my arms to disperse it. My arm went right through it but didn't alter its shape. My friend joined me and did the same thing. There was no change. 'Smoke?'

'Smoke would change shape, wouldn't it? It would move, surely?'

'Should do, but it isn't,' I replied thoroughly puzzled.

We swiped at it. We passed our hands through it. Nothing. It merely continued swirling and unfurling, remaining in the same space as if nothing had happened. Then as we both stared at it, as if someone had pressed a button and released it, the smoke unfurled, furled again and rose about fifteen centimetres higher. We watched to see what it would do. 'Have you seen it before?' she asked as we stared.

I had. A few days after our arrival, we were unpacking boxes in the lounge room when it just appeared in front of me and my husband. We both thought it was smoke and tried to wave it away. It followed a similar pattern to this only it was on the other side of the room. We were really puzzled by it but when it eventually twisted up towards the ceiling and hung there, we ignored it and got on with our chore. At the time we dismissed it as a quirk of the light, perhaps smoke wafting inside from a barbecue we could smell cooking somewhere nearby. We were puzzled for a few minutes by the smoke's odd behaviour and its lack of response to our arm movements, but it seemed like no big deal, and we were busy people.

This time was different though. This time it had my full attention. It wasn't behaving like smoke. It retained a consistent shape and swirling pattern and didn't disperse when we used physical objects to create a breeze or interrupt it's flow.

'Oooh,' said my friend with a big grin, 'perhaps it's a ghost! Aren't they supposed to do things like that?'

I laughed, more at her excited reaction than anything else. We watched as ever so slowly, it moved in a large circle between us and then rose to just above head height.

'Well, whatever it is, it's got our attention,' I said, adding impishly, 'so you can leave now, whatever you are.'

To our amusement it twirled slowly staying in place as if it was making up its mind. Then, almost unbelievably, it twisted slightly and glided past me towards the window only to stop still once again. Of course we followed it. It was too fascinating not to. We tried again, with no luck, to disperse it. Not only didn't it disperse but it still did not react to our hand movements at all. It completely maintained its shape.

We stopped joking. We were both becoming uncomfortable. As I've mentioned previously. the mind just doesn't do well with what it can't explain, and we were experiencing the inexplicable. There was no breeze. Both us and the room remained completely still. For some minutes this strange thing stayed still like a suspended umbilical cord, slightly furled, and then, with a sudden but gentle twist, it went up towards the ceiling and vanished.

My friend and I stared at each other. My friend looked back to where it had been. 'If I hadn't seen that with my own eyes, I would never have believed it was possible. What was it?'

I had no answers. Logic of course tried to prevail once again, and again failed. There was no fire, no humidity, no fog, and this time, no neighbourly barbecue. There was nothing logical to explain the apparition. Why hadn't it changed when we touched it? We remained puzzled and intrigued. We never got any answers, but it did remind me very much of the hand that appeared between me and my friend some years before. They were the same colour and had the same smooth appearance.

After visiting the lady from the spiritual church, I had taken to visit clairvoyants and psychics, wanting to learn how they worked and where their information came from. Some were so factually accurate about knowledge they simply couldn't have obtained from anyone but me, I soon figured out that there really was something to this. The human brain had an ability, generally unaccepted, that mattered and could be useful. I was no longer able to deny and ignore my own experiences using logic as a shield. I needed to understand my ability.

Interestingly, in addition to sharing facts about my life, the psychic readers also informed me that everything I would need to become the psychic that I was meant to be would be presented to me by life. Books would come into my life, people would arrive on my doorstep, situations would just seem to happen without my actively seeking them. They were general in their information, but I soon realised that they were correct. A huge number of coincidences began to fall into my life around this time. If I had a problem, spiritual or otherwise, books would leap out of me in shops. The advertisement I needed to see would glare at me from a newspaper left randomly folded on a seat in a café. I would hear two people talking about just the information I needed to hear at the time. Whenever I recognised that I'd reached my limitations and felt tested or pushed, the answers to my problems would appear.

When I thought I'd found the answers to my problems by myself though, things would go wrong. Our girls were both at school now and financially we were struggling on one wage. We managed but there was very little for treats of any type. Twice I attempted to re-enter the workforce only to be sabotaged. I was well qualified despite being at home for years, and both attempts at finding work landed me good positions, neither of which I got to fill. I tore a gut muscle while opening the garage door just a week before starting the first. A specialist warned me that the pain would likely last several months due to its position, and for at least the first month I would be walking bent over. I resigned from that position before I started.

Several months later, adequately recovered, I accepted another position. On day one, I woke up feeling extremely ill. I dragged myself through the first day and then went to the doctor where I was given a high dose of antibiotics and ordered to spend the week in bed. My employer was wonderful about it, saying these things happen. At the end of the week, I was about fifty percent recovered. However, the effect on my youngest daughter was devastating. She had been cared for after school by a close friend, the same one who still refused to babysit at our place. During that time, she regressed to the speech and behaviour of a two-year-old and was waking in tears several times a night.

My husband and I argued over what to do. Naturally he wanted our financial strain lifted. 'She will adjust!' he said.

I knew that in time she would, but my heart told me that she shouldn't have to. All my instincts were to protect her and for some reason these instincts were screaming instead of talking. I had learned to listen to my intuition, and it was shouting loudly. Five-year old's don't just suddenly go backwards because of a couple of hours childminding with someone they love. Something else was wrong with her, but what? I didn't know; couldn't come up with anything. Unwilling not to follow my gut despite a cross husband, I resigned the following Monday.

A phone call from my employer a few days later let me know that my replacement was a single mum of two children who was absolutely delighted to take up my vacated position. I felt relieved out of all proportion. It was the right thing to do, but I didn't know why. I returned to being a mum with this strange sense of calm. I felt very sure that I'd made the right choice and that everything would be fine financially.

Two weeks later, I was offered a job. Not a regular nine to five affair but a position reading tarot cards at parties. It was evening and weekend work, all at times when my husband would be at home, and if he was away, then I simply didn't have to work. Perfect. Problem solved.

The opportunity presented almost accidentally. Through a mutual acquaintance I was invited to a crystal party at the house of the Avon Lady. It was a very interesting evening. I had no experience of crystal healing and was intrigued by the information offered. The crystals themselves were beautiful and the colours appealed to me. While I couldn't see myself using them for healing, I could appreciate the idea behind it. When our host announced that tarot card readings were also on offer, I placed my name on the list of those who wanted to participate and sat back to enjoy the rest of the evening.

Several events that evening were *deja vue* experiences for me. All of them were minor, so when I entered the kitchen and sat down for my tarot reading, I did not find it unusual that I knew what the tarot reader was about to say. Sure enough, she mentioned that she had been a friend of my previous tarot teacher. She also mentioned that our mutual teacher had passed away. She never completed teaching the advanced course she had asked me to join. I felt queasy at the news. Not surprised, just ill. In the years to come, I learnt that knowing something in advance doesn't ever prepare you for the facts when they happen to include a death. Instead of her just reading my cards, the two of us ended up reading for each other. I paid her, and then she offered me a job. Would I like to share her job as she was now very busy? Would I ever? It was the answer to my prayers.

I had some serious concerns about this position. I would be going into the homes of strangers at night. It would be a challenge meeting strangers. Secondly, the continuous battle with my physical energy might not hold up to reading for a dozen people in one sitting. Would I even cope after a day of housework and childminding? I was more than willing to give it a try as it would ease our financial stress. Here too was an outlet for my psychic energy. I also knew I shouldn't knock this back as I'd dreamt this entire night two years before.

I know this is hard to imagine, but the way my dreams work is that I dream my life, seemingly randomly, way before the events occur. Some of my dreams have taken over ten years to come to fruition, but when they have, they unwind as if I'm slightly ahead of the movie and know every move in advance. This evening proved to be one of those nights. 'Living the dream' could be taken two ways that evening. I felt a thrill of excitement that I'd not felt for a very long time.

This then was how I found myself reading for dozens of people and how life went from quiet to busy in the flip of a coin. I had found myself touching on counselling issues with random students while at university, but I now discovered a depth of talent that I hadn't known I possessed. It was certainly not something that I had thought about in relation to tarot readings. To my concern, I soon realised that the majority of people who wanted readings at parties were those with serious problems and issues. There were always a few who did it for fun and took the information lightly, but the majority implicitly believed what I told them and wanted real help and guidance with their lives.

I discovered that this 'occupation', which our society tends to trivialise, and which most people don't even like to talk about, can hold people's lives in the palm of a hand. I constantly reassured people that anything I saw would remain private. I always felt the need to reassure and to help people deal with what was around them. I quickly learnt when to keep my mouth firmly closed and intuitively gauge how much bad news a person really needed to hear. I always searched for the positive, believing that no matter how bad the situation was, there was usually something that they could do to ease the strain caused. I still implicitly believe that this applies to most life situations.

The night of the party I also signed up for a crystal healing course. I didn't believe that stones of any type could heal but, as always, I wanted to investigate for myself and find out if there was something real behind this other than the power of the human mind to heal itself. Was I intending to use this in my future? No. What it did was introduce me to some terrific people who were all interested in the psychic and alternative world. I underwent an intense and swift period of personal growth and expansion. I sometimes wondered why I'd jumped into the course but, it was from this group that the first requests came for me to teach tarot classes. Was this another of life's little coincidences? I didn't think so. By now I had realised that very little in my life was really a coincidence.

I was busy fulfilling party commitments and so I didn't even consider the thought of teaching. For many months I enjoyed doing the readings but, as I'd anticipated, I found it difficult to recover from the late nights. My energy levels were in a constant battle with my commitments. Children, chronic fatigue, and the emotionally demanding party readings were not a good mix. The energy that I gave out began to take a toll physically. My mental and physical sides became way out of balance, and I suffered frequent colds and other minor infections. My mind thrived on the work, loved it, needed it, but my body was struggling to keep up. Some nights I would have to remind myself that I was lucky to be here still and to be able to do this job, as I swallowed a couple of painkillers, put on a smile and marched through my initial pain. What I had discovered was that if I could start reading despite the pain, I would soon reach a state that pushed the pain to a distance until I ceased working, at which point it would then come crashing back down onto me.

Then, one night when I arrived already tired and in more pain than usual, a stranger looked me dead in the eye and said, 'You should teach this to others. You'd be good at it, and you wouldn't have to drag yourself out in the cold.' Only then did I think seriously about running classes.

That same night I managed to get completely and utterly lost on the way home! Those were the days before we all had apps on our phones, so I pulled up under a streetlight to read my paper map. As I did so, a police car came screaming around the corner. It pulled up in front of me and two policemen rushed up to the house and started bashing the door and shouting. As another police siren sounded some distance away, I quickly pulled out and moved several streets from the trouble. By the time I eventually made my way home, I had decided I would get my health back and write my own tarot course. If teaching was what I was meant to do, then the students would appear.

I wrote the course during the Christmas holiday break when the children were home for six weeks straight. It was a time-consuming job, but I thoroughly enjoyed it. By the time school went back in 1996, I was ready to start teaching. I didn't give up the parties entirely, but I did a lot fewer of them. As if the universe knew I was home, the number of daytime reading requests increased dramatically. Now, had I wanted to, I could have filled almost every waking hour. However, my family and my body were my greatest priorities, and so I spaced the readings out and paced myself appropriately.

I found that I really enjoyed helping people in my own space and time, and I found great delight in discovering new aspects of my psychic ability. Before a client arrived for a reading, I would take their name and their age and write down all that I could intuit about them. I soon found that this covered much of their lives including everything from remembered early childhood experiences right up until the present day. It became quite normal for them to turn up intending to ask certain questions only for me to present them with the answers before they had a chance to. I found it great fun to challenge myself to do more and go deeper.

Occasionally someone would visit who was basically a user, an energy taker; a person who really didn't want to help themselves, but who wanted life handed to them on a platter. These were the ones who tested my patience. As someone who always tried to pull myself out of whatever mire life threw at me, I struggled to deal with those who only wanted to play victim and have someone else do their life work for them. They suffered stress, and they caused me to get stressed dealing with them. My husband was constantly stressed and dealing with his was enough!

I felt inadequate to deal with these types, so I added to my workload by signing on for yet another course of study. This time I would become a counsellor, and my focus would be on stress management. If I was going to deal with people with problems, then I'd make sure I was suitably qualified to do the job.

Looking back now, I'm not sure if it was the perfectionist in me, or merely an awesome sense of responsibility, but I felt I had no right to deal out the information that would, or could, affect people's lives unless I could speak from a qualified position. By now I had visited some wonderful clairvoyants, psychics and card readers, but I had also encountered an incredible number that I deemed crackpots. The latter were the ones who had something to say about everything. They put their personal opinions into the readings and gave what was often dreadful and sometimes shocking advice. If it had been up to one psychic (who was twice divorced), I would have left my husband because of his workaholic tendencies. Apparently because I was getting little attention, our marriage was doomed. She was correct about the attention due to the circumstances at the time, but that didn't necessarily dictate the outcome and never took account of the agreement that we had in place between us which was one of support. That was over twenty years ago now, we are still married, and I couldn't imagine a life without him. Imagine if I'd taken her advice!

I did not want to be another crackpot tarot reader. I wanted to help, and I wanted the security of knowing that I could do it from a professional point of view. My own internal battles between the presentation of psychic information and logical explanation were ongoing, and if I couldn't be content internally, I could at least be qualified.

People came out of the woodwork. Friends from the crystal healing course signed up for my course and then friends of friends and so forth. Word was out. So began one of the most enjoyable periods of my development. I soon discovered that I loved to teach and guide, and I was thrilled with each class member's achievements, whatever they were. Within eight weeks, attending one night a week, students who had claimed that although they were interested in learning the tarot they would never be able to do 'the psychic thing', found themselves using the psychic thing regularly. Just as often, they wouldn't realise that they had used their innate ability until it was pointed out to them. Interestingly though, they were always quick to recognise the same skill in others!

As my students gained confidence so did I. They became so accurate I frequently found myself having my personal secrets revealed by one or other of them. I never denied these secrets. I believed that they should be encouraged and to deny anything accurate that they saw in the cards would have hampered their growth. Consequently, we moved quite quickly from teacher-student relationship to friendship, and such was the depth of sharing that when the course finished, the group continued to meet and gained both knowledge and friendship from each other.

What I also learned while running this course was that I couldn't work with a group of people who were all developing their psychic awareness without experiencing a few unusual occurrences. One of these was the sighting of a spirit child. For several months my children had talked about the little boy who lived in the house and who played with their toys. My youngest called him her 'angel friend'. Occasionally, while working in my study, I would sense a child in the doorway and look up expecting to see my youngest peering around the wall at me. She was never there, but the atmosphere was like hers, so I was not perturbed. By now I didn't fear visitors unless the atmosphere felt cold or heavy, so I'd just return to my work.

Over a matter of weeks this little one gained in confidence. One evening after class, I walked out of the bathroom and almost stumbled over him. I lost my footing and bumped hard into the opposite wall. My husband, doing his usual paperwork at the kitchen table, asked if I had tripped. Laughingly I told him that I'd nearly fallen over a child in the hallway, one that wasn't there. I was stunned as I was sure that I'd seen a real child initially. My husband grinned from ear to ear and promptly and accurately described the chid that I had just seen. This little one often appeared in the doorway leading from the hallway to the kitchen when my husband worked late at night and the rest of the family was asleep. 'I always think it's one of ours and I look up to speak. Then I realise that it's not, and it disappears,' he said. As he spoke it slowly dawned on him that now he too was seeing. I smiled warmly. The disbeliever that I had married had certainly grown.

The following week one member of the group needed to take a bathroom break during class, and we all sat chatting until she returned. She was gone an abnormally long time, and just as I was getting concerned, she returned sporting a huge grin and delightedly informed us that she had just seen a child in the hallway. 'At least, I think I did. I thought it was one of yours, and I said "Hello." Then I realised it wasn't one of your girls and, umm, it wasn't really there either. It was kind of weird!' Her grin said it all. She had just had an exciting experience. Over the coming weeks the child was seen by several others, all of whom initially thought it was my youngest daughter, only to realise, as the image disintegrated before their eyes, that of course it wasn't.

One evening, after completing a group meditation, the smoke appeared again. I saw it almost immediately. It followed a similar pathway, only this time it hovered a little higher and remained for some time high over one girl's head. I tried not to look at it and continued with the class. Then one or two class members noticed it, and it became increasingly hard to stay focussed on what I was teaching. Eventually one of the girls who had her back to the area where the smoke was, twisted in her chair trying to follow the direction of our eyes. She saw nothing and asked frustratedly, 'What are you lot looking at?'

'That!' said another student, pointing to the smoke. It promptly drifted towards the high ceiling, stopped several centimetres from it and slowly disappeared. They had a lot of questions, but again, I had no answers.

A few weeks after this the Avon Lady returned and after making coffee we sat down to chat, inadvertently sitting in almost the same places as we had on her previous visit. Within minutes the smoke appeared. This time there was no need to pretend that we couldn't see it. We both took turns moving towards it and then through it. It seemed to have a life of its own. The breeze caused by our movements did not alter either its shape or its course. Once again it moved to the same area on the other side of the room and, after a few minutes, it disappeared as it had before. We were fascinated. Over the next few months, it appeared several more times to me and my husband. Its course varied only slightly and the time of day, the weather, the light, and the heating conditions all varied. The whole time we lived in the house we found neither a logical nor satisfactory explanation for its presence.

Amid this psychic world in which I now spent a large amount of time, the other me continued to be a mother and a wife. I could step out of doing a long reading and jump straight into chores. I also began to use my writing skills to help both of my children who had developed, as children do, different issues and challenges in dealing with life.

My eldest went through a stage where she was in trouble a lot at home. When I couldn't convince her that this phase would pass, and she continued to be upset, I wrote a story about a naughty fairy that was always in trouble until one night she saved a family from a house fire and became the most applauded fairy in the kingdom. It was a great hit, totally relatable, and solved her problem. Healing comes in a multitude of forms.

Of course, sisterly competition came into play, and the youngest wanted her very own story too. Since she had trouble going to sleep at night, the topic presented itself. I wrote her a story about a little girl whose parents let her stay up all night without their supervision and the antics that the child got up to in the dead of night, accompanied by her pet dog. I shared this story with friends' children as well, and they were delighted. I decided to try to get it published and sent it off to a publisher. These days, I would just self-publish on Amazon, but back then this wasn't an option.

The book was eventually rejected, not for the content but because it was considered too high a risk to invest in a new author as the work needed expensive illustrations. Although two out of the three people who assessed it, wanted to publish it, it was rejected by the accountant. It must have been decent enough as I received a personal phone call from a very disappointed publishing manager rather than just the usual rejection letter that was sent out when a manuscript was returned.

I was disappointed, but at the same time I was completely delighted to know that I could write to a suitable publishing standard. The editors weren't the ones who knocked it back. This boosted my confidence, but life was to get in the way, as it often does, and I did not pursue my writer's dream. Years later, I am still in trouble from one of my children for not having published her book! I must admit though that the spiritual world was really holding most of my attention at that time.

Chapter 21

Horrific Premonitions

Nineteen ninety-six saw a huge leap forward in my psychic development and growth. One of the talents I discovered was that I had the ability to write down a name and age and focusing on just that, pen in hand, receive information regarding the client. This came about after a pre-reading meditation one day when I randomly felt the need to pick up a pen and write. I put the client's name and age at the top of the paper and found myself writing quickly, all of it information about someone I'd not yet met including specific ages and events that had occurred to them: happy times, heartbreak, loss. It all seemed quite random, but I tried hard to trust that the information was correct. When the doorbell rang and interrupted the flow, I left it on the desk. The only way to find out if it was correct was to talk about it with the client.

I waited until the unsuspecting person was seated and then hesitantly explained what had happened. I asked if she would mind verifying the information. Startlingly, the information proved to be correct. Yes, her father had left her when she was six years of age. Yes, she had not seen him again until she was nineteen. Yes, money did play a very important role in her work. She was an accountant! The list went on. I was as surprised as she was. This was a useful tool. It became a way for me to determine if someone was going to turn up for a reading. If I wrote down their name and no information came to me, then they weren't going to attend. I would calmly go off and do something else with my time. This tool seemed to work like a spiritual privacy act. I never received information about people I wouldn't meet. My theory was that I could only gain information about someone who was intending to open to me and share their energy channel in the first place. I was simply the receiver of a radio signal.

My husband was planning his exit from the army, getting ready to put his new qualifications to good use and to keep his promise to me that we would settle down before our children were high school age as that was when I felt they would need consistency and stability in their education the most. Meanwhile my expanding psychic knowledge had started to bring problems as well as gifts.

My premonitions, still received mainly in dreams, became increasingly detailed and more difficult to deal with. I very infrequently had a good night's sleep. Instead of continuing to open to more of the psychic world, I sought out every piece of information that I could on closing down and protecting the self that I could lay my hands on. I applied both old and newfound knowledge quite fervently. Nothing worked. I had taught many of the techniques in class and knew that they worked as the feedback had been wonderful. Most of them had once worked for me but didn't anymore. I exercised. I meditated. I even altered my diet but got no relief. Almost every night I would dream with prophetic accuracy. Some of it was important and some trivial. It made not a scrap of difference what it was, I simply couldn't stop it happening.

Then, on 29th March 1996, I sat in our lounge room reading to my youngest daughter while the eldest watched television. A newsflash preceding the 6pm news blared suddenly, and there was Princess Diana's face before us. My blood turned to ice, and I felt violently ill as a strong premonition came to me. For a moment I thought I would vomit as a huge wave of nausea rushed through my body. Diana was going to die, shockingly. In my mind I searched for the words to explain what I felt in my body. It was like a suicide. Sudden. Totally unexpected. People would be just as shocked as if she had killed herself. I knew beyond all doubt what I was experiencing was a premonition as the still alive princess was shown carrying out her duties and the news item came to an end. Later that evening I recorded the event in a dream journal that I had recently started. Perhaps I thought that if I wrote it down it wouldn't occur. Perhaps I just wanted to shake off the awful feeling that clung to me. Was I hoping to be proven wrong about what I had seen as well, or was I recording it because I knew that if it happened, I myself would be unable to believe that I had foreseen the event? I thought back to her wedding day and how I had felt then that she was making the biggest mistake of her life, and I shuddered. 'Please God, don't let this happen to her.'

A couple of weeks later, again seated in my lounge room, a friend picked up a magazine. It had a picture of Princess Diana on the cover. 'I wouldn't mind swapping places with her,' she commented.

'You wouldn't have long to live then, would you?' I snapped at her. Since the premonition, I felt dreadful whenever anyone mentioned Diana's name. Startled, my friend looked at me oddly and quickly changed the subject. My outburst worried me greatly. Until now I had kept my premonitions largely private. I only shared them with my husband, and it was completely out of character for me to be so forthright, and about something so important too. I didn't want to turn into some kind of kook that blurted things out and scared people. Although it would take some time to put the incident and the premonition to the back of my mind, it would not be my last outburst on the subject.

In the middle of the following year, my daughter's godmother arrived. We were going out for a pleasant day to look at craft shops together. She had nothing to do with the psychic side of my life, and I was looking forward to a day of complete normality browsing craft shops and having a leisurely lunch. When she arrived, I wasn't quite ready to leave, and she stood in the kitchen waiting as I stacked the last of the breakfast dishes away. On the kitchen table Diana's face peered up at us from yet another magazine.

'Oh, wouldn't you love to be her? Not to have her life but to have her money and her clothes,' my friend drooled.

Again, I snapped, 'No, you wouldn't. She's going to die young, you know!' My voice was both forceful and loud, and I shocked both of us with my outburst.

My friend's mouth dropped open. Ever down to earth, she composed herself quickly and looking at me curiously, she asked, 'What do you mean by young?'

Flustered and distressed by my behaviour I floundered, 'I don't know. I don't even know how old she is now, but if she's thirty-three then she won't see thirty-four; if she's thirty-four, she won't see thirty-five. Drop it will you!' I was so distressed by the words coming out of my mouth as I realised from them that this really meant soon. Too soon.

My friend picked up her handbag. 'Well, on that sombre note, I think we had better go, don't you?' she said quietly.

When Princess Diana was killed in a car accident on August 31st,1997, I had moved interstate. My friend's first words as I picked up the phone to her were, 'Tell me that you didn't say that. Tell me that that day in your kitchen didn't happen.'

I cried. I cried a lot. I wasn't particularly a Diana fan; in fact, I didn't really follow royalty at all as they had never interested me, but I cried for Diana, and I cried for myself. By the time she died, I had faced and struggled to accept the full responsibility of knowing. I had struggled to accept that this sense I had was never going to go away, and I wouldn't always like what it showed me. By this time there had already been two other horrendous world events which I had dreamed of, in detail, and over which I had no control. Diana's death was the third. They say that things come in threes, and in my case this was certainly true.

The first of these horrendous premonitions was so vividly awful that my screams woke my whole family. My husband informed me later that it took several minutes to calm me to a sobbing state wherein I babbled hysterically about the mad man with the gun and repeated over and over, 'It's Port...Port something. A man's name. Port something. Oh God. It's all green, like in England. There's an old church. Oh God, Oh God, he mustn't, he can't! He's killing them! Oh God, it's Port SOME-THING! Why can't I remember? It's a boy's name, a man's name! It's there. I can see the signpost, but I can't read the name!' I sobbed hysterically, babbling and clinging to him as if my life depended on it. Given what I was seeing, I might have thought it did. I was trapped for some time in the psychic world inside my head. I was so terrified I was oblivious to the fact that I'd woken my children who had come running to the bedroom and were now severely distressed by my behaviour. My husband tells me it took a good ten minutes before I calmed down enough to even become aware of them.

Slowly though, too slowly, the mother in me came to the

fore. Battling the pictures that were repeating themselves in my head, I moved carefully out of my nightmare and went through all the right soothing motions for my girls. 'Mummy just had a nightmare about a crazy man killing people, but it was just a nightmare. It wasn't real. It isn't going to happen. It was just a nasty nightmare, like you have when you get ill. Mummy has a virus.' I calmed and reassured them and with my husband's help I got them back to bed. The whole time I shook violently and wave after wave of sickening nausea crashed down on me as scenes replayed over and over inside my head even while I comforted them.

My husband and I returned to bed where I clung to him tearfully. Quietly continuing to cry I described the carnage that I'd seen. 'It was so real, so awful,' I gulped.

'Perhaps it's a movie?' he suggested hopefully, 'you've dreamt whole movies before.'

'I never watch horror movies,' I sniffed, 'I don't even read scary books. Why would I dream something that I would never watch or read?' I was utterly terrified by what I had seen. 'What if it really happens?' I asked him. 'Oh God, why can't I remember the rest of the name? It was Port something. I should tell the police. What would I tell them though? I can't tell them where exactly it was. Oh God. I must remember.'

I clung to him seeking comfort and safety from the awful broken visions that played on repeat in my head. Together, each lost in our own thoughts, we watched the sun come up, and as it did, I turned to him and said, 'It's a boy's name, Port "boys name". It looks like England, and it has old stone buildings. Why can't I remember the name?'

My husband, still worried, tried guessing the names of ports that he knew, but I shook my head. The trauma of my visions of death had been too much, and the name was gone. We discussed what good it would do to go to the police with the information if I remembered the name and realised that of course I'd not be taken seriously. I'd just be another nut job on the loose to them. I had no name, no dates, couldn't identify the location. I was useless. By now, I was convinced that what I had seen would happen, and I was struggling mentally and emotionally.

I crawled through the day like someone who had received a severe shock and when night came I prayed for an uninterrupted sleep. I did not want a repeat of the previous night's events. I was not so lucky. This time there were different details of the carnage that I had seen the previous night, but now it was like I was watching a news report. The shock and horror were still there, but I felt in this dream as if I was an onlooker rather than the participant I had seemed to be the previous night. I woke sobbing quietly. It was too awful to contemplate that it could be true, but it would be on the news. The knowing was in full force.

The following evening, when my students arrived, they thought I was unwell.

'Are you sick?' questioned one.

'You look rough!' greeted another.

'I am unwell.' I spoke hesitantly. 'I've had really bad dreams the last couple of nights.'

'Ooh, what have you been seeing?'

'Nothing. No need to talk about it now,' I mumbled, feeling sick to the stomach. I couldn't talk about this; best it stayed within my family. I got on with class. It was early April 1997.

My older brother was getting married, so later that month we travelled up to Queensland for his wedding and a well-deserved holiday.

Our girls were especially excited as it was unusual for them to have a holiday that didn't include moving house! Like them, I was light-hearted and carefree, chasing them through the maze at the butterfly house we stopped at along the way, squirting cold water on each other in the carpark as, sundrenched and hot by mid-morning, we headed for the cool of the café.

By the time we reached the Gold Coast, my mood had completely changed. All I wanted to do was go into hiding. I had the weight of the world on my shoulders, and no-one could do anything to please me. I felt like my body was dead. My husband, used to my frequent bouts of pain and tiredness, put my behaviour down to the trip.

'It's not that,' I told him, 'something feels truly awful. It's like...,' I searched for the right words, 'it's like something is about to go terribly wrong. I feel like I'm not part of my body. I feel like I'm about to be pushed over a cliff. I don't know! I just want to be alone!'

I tried very hard to snap out of it, searching for reasons for this unwanted and unwelcome change of behaviour. The sun had literally disappeared, and it was now pouring with rain. I momentarily concluded that perhaps it was the lack of sunshine that had me depressed. Not that I'd ever been like this before when it rained, but I was desperate to find a reason. I really didn't want to spoil our holiday, but, when I refused to go and play in the pool with the children, my husband looked at me strangely.

They all knew that I loved to swim in the rain. The most I could do was make myself lean over the balcony and wave as my children cavorted with their dad. As I forced myself to smile, huge waves of tears engulfed me. I went to lie down. What on earth was wrong with me? I had been so happy all the way up. Where did yesterday's fun go? I thought back to the laughter and jokes we'd had as we tried to find our way out of the maze the day before. When had I started to feel that something bad was going to happen? I couldn't pinpoint it. I vowed to shake it off, and by the time the family returned to the room I was acting with at least some semblance of normalcy even if I couldn't find the excitement of the previous day.

I felt heavily drugged and filled with dread, and I repeatedly had to remind myself to act like I wasn't dying. The rain poured down, and I felt literally like I was slowly drowning. I had no idea what was wrong with me and, not having felt this way before, assumed it must be a virus.

The following day as we prepared for the wedding itself, my false act of happy mum was breaking down, and I was openly snapping at everyone. I was so awful that I almost ruined our girls' excitement at attending the wedding. This was a huge deal for them, and I had to keep apologising to both them and my husband as he tried desperately to maintain some sort of harmonious balance within our small family. He had an uphill job; the whole time he kept looking at me with concern etched on his face. He knew this wasn't me and something was seriously wrong. He took my words from the previous day about something bad happening very seriously. On the way to the wedding, I warned my him to be extra careful.

'I know that you think something is going to happen, but do you know if it is going to happen to us?' he queried quietly.

'I'm almost certain it's got nothing to do with us, and it has nothing to do with the wedding either. I just want you to be careful in case I'm wrong,' I replied. I was looking forward to the wedding, but part of me was emotionally displaced and incredibly edgy. It was a sense of impending doom and yet not for me. I couldn't find the words to adequately explain, and I had no idea what the event was. It messed with me mentally and emotionally to a great degree.

My personal glum feelings aside, the wedding itself was beautiful, the torrential rain even stopped for the occasion, but sadly, only a part of me was there.

The next day I was like a tightly coiled spring and every

muscle in my body ached with the tension. It seemed vitally important to me now that at least the children have a good time as I was obviously stressing my husband out with my behaviour. He was worried that I was too ill to go out and wanted to cancel our plans, but I insisted that we follow our original plan and take them to Sea World. I needed to be in the fresh air. I needed my family to enjoy themselves. It was a compulsion, the complete opposite of what I was actually capable of myself. I felt that if I was to stay indoors, I might start screaming and never stop. When we told them where we were going, the fog and tension in my brain didn't abate at all, and I watched their excitement as if from a distance. I was an outsider looking on. Spaced out. Separated from real life.

The rain that had abated for the wedding returned with a vengeance. It simply poured down, but the weather had an advantage for us as it kept most of the tourists away from the theme park. The children thought having the rides almost entirely to themselves was an absolute blast, and I went through the motions of smiling and replying to their delighted chatter feeling like I was moving further and further away from them.

Eventually it became too much for me and, making excuses for me yet again, my husband took them off on their own while I settled into a chair in the cafeteria area. As they walked away, my body screamed at them not to leave me while my mind berated me for behaving this way. I wondered if I was going completely mad. I was deeply and deathly tired. I registered that the only time I had ever come close to this awful feeling was when I became unwell prior to my near-death experience but, at the same time, I recognised that this time there was extraordinary fear and a never before felt depth to the feeling of disaster and death inside me. Even today I cannot find adequate words to express what my mind and body were living through, but I felt like danger was everywhere. I was literally drowning in it, even while nothing was actually wrong with any of us and my children were happy. It made no sense. I made no sense. I just wanted it to stop.

Later that evening when we finally bundled our tired family back into our holiday apartment, my husband switched on the TV hoping to catch the news. My edginess had been replaced by a very deep and inexplicable depression and instead of snapping everyone's heads off, I simply wanted to cry. Every kiss and cuddle from the girls found me holding them too tight, trying to keep them as safe as possible.

'What's wrong, Mummy?' my little one asked several times. Each time I told her that I really didn't know but that I just needed cuddles today. For the first time ever, I didn't want to let them go. I just wanted to hold them and keep them close. It was such a strong feeling that even a room's width apart felt too far away and knowing this was unhealthy, I was fighting to let them go and behave normally.

'News is starting,' my husband called out, and I forced myself to join him at the kitchen table. The girls set themselves up there with their journals and pencils and started to write about their holiday.

Within minutes I was in deep shock. A massacre had occurred at Port Arthur in Tasmania. There before me was my dream of a few weeks previously, every detail, every event. It had not been a nightmare, not even a movie as I had still hoped. It was real. My husband said absolutely nothing; he just came and held me as the news reporter continued to talk.

My eldest daughter looked at the television and then, with a strange look on her face, looked at me. 'It's your dream, Mummy,' she stated in a quiet and shocked voice.

I sat stunned hearing more and more of the details I had related to my husband only weeks before. Suddenly I couldn't breathe. I had to escape. I had to run. Breaking free of my husband's comforting arms I ran to the bedroom slamming the door shut behind me. I was going to vomit. I needed the bathroom.

After vomiting, I gasped, panicking like a hunted animal. I splashed cold water on my face and looked into the mirror. It reflected the pain in my eyes, and the pain triggered the movie screen of my dream all over again. A completely unplanned primal howl escaped from my mouth, and I launched myself back to the bedroom, threw myself on the bed, curled up in a tight ball and sobbed as if my own world had fallen apart.

Thoughts raced through my head. Enormous, over-whelming guilt poured through my body. I should have done something. I knew what the killer looked like. I remembered half of the name of the place. I should have done something. I should have tried! The thoughts raced as I melted down in mental and emotional turmoil.

Only later would I understand that even had I remembered all the information I had foreseen, I had not known when the event would take place; nor is ours a society which readily accepts such information. As my husband had said the night of my dream, 'Even if you went to the police and knew where the place was, they wouldn't take you seriously. They'd dismiss you as a kook.'

I felt like a kook. I had no coping skills to deal with this and for a long time afterwards I carried an inordinate amount of guilt on my shoulders for not preventing the incident. I did not deal with life at all for many weeks afterwards. I didn't feel fully connected to reality and just felt ill and dazed. The more details of the event that were released, the worse I felt. I did not want this ability that had fascinated me up to this point. I wanted it to go away. I was utterly drained.

Slowly, I returned. I was changed in ways that I still find too hard to describe, but life dragged me back into it. Life doesn't recognise that you are grieving or broken. It doesn't provide you with answers about how the brain performs in ways that science claims it can't. It just goes on. Recognising that this phenomenon that I had experienced was related to and yet different to what I did in the readings that I gave and the courses that I taught, I continued to work, but that too was different.

The energy around me had intensified. The information that I wrote prior to each reading usually formed a comprehensive reading in itself. The cards, which I had always recognised as a tool, were laid out but almost fully disregarded. I had suddenly become more mediumistic and highly auditory. My client base changed too. Now I attracted people who were grieving the deaths of loved ones. Sometimes the questioner wouldn't be able to verify the information that I passed to them, and this worried me. I would always ask them to check with someone else and get back to me. I openly explained that I didn't want to pass on information that wasn't verifiable. I felt strongly that there were enough frauds working in the psychic field, and I feared that dealing with this 'other world' could easily make me one of them. It was sometimes several months before the client would call back to tell me the information given had been correct, but I was always relieved to hear from them. If I was wrong, then my conscience wouldn't let me continue to work.

I remember telling one lady whose mum had recently passed away that she had three spirits come into the room with her and that one of them was holding the mother's son. Throughout the session they kept insisting that I give her this information, but I held back, feeling that I couldn't pass it on. The session continued a little longer than normal, and she verified everything that I'd told her as correct. I had established that there were two living children in her family. I finally plucked up the courage and hesitatingly asked if her mum had lost a son. The woman looked startled and replied in the negative. In my sight, on the television screen in my head, an elderly male figure stepped forward from his spiritual group. He showed me that he was holding a young boy's hand. He insisted that I tell her that her mum was to be reunited with her son, and that another elderly male who was still alive could give the girl the information that she needed to know. 'Tell her to ask the man,' he insisted.

I passed on the information, but she remained perplexed, so much so that at the end of the session she informed me that she was pleased with the reading but that she felt the part about the little boy was incorrect. Fair play to her, she then said that she would ask her uncle. She thought that he would probably think she was silly, but she would explain why she asked and felt that he would be honest with her. She felt that asking her dad, the only other living male close to her mum would be the wrong thing to do.

This event concerned me. I didn't want to have given her the wrong information. There again, if it was correct, it could unlock some family secret that might cause problems. I recognised that I demanded perfection from myself. I realised that I thought that if I was to help people then the messages had to be one hundred percent accurate and useful, or I had failed them. I now worried constantly and was thinking of giving up my occupation. However, every time I reached the stage of convincing myself that I just couldn't do this work anymore, I would receive a phone call or a letter thanking me for my help and confirming and clarifying the information I had passed on. This was exactly what happened regarding this incident.

A couple of weeks later the lady returned with more questions and cheerfully informed me that her uncle had confirmed that she'd had a brother born some years before her. This first child had died of unknown causes, and her parents had been naturally devastated. The loss made them wait several years before being brave enough to try for another child.

'I was shocked,' she told me. 'We never knew anything about him. I went to my dad and he admitted that the story was true, and that I did have an older brother that I never knew. He told me that Mum insisted they never spoke of him to us children. He said she also took down his pictures and hid them away. He didn't agree with her, apparently; he thought they should have been open about him with us. Very sad.

'Still, it's nice to think that she is reunited with him, and you might like to know that bringing all this out into the open has somehow healed an issue I've had with my parents for as long as I can ever remember. My dad has confided in me and is warm and showing he cares, which he never did. I always thought I wasn't good enough for him, for them. It turns out, I was. I am!' The young lady beamed at me. My faith in the information I was passing on was renewed.

No-one can be 100 percent accurate. No matter how hard you try, you're going to fail sometime.

A lady came to see me after losing a pair of expensive earrings. She believed they were somewhere inside her home but couldn't find them. I began to get pictures. Mentally I travelled slowly through her house to her bedroom. After some moments. I told her that there was a pair of earrings on the floor beneath the bottom drawer of her dressing table.

'I'm not sure they are the right ones though. Something about this picture doesn't feel spot on,' I told her.

Off she went to search. After removing the dresser drawer, she found a pair of earrings alright. They were even the same colour as the pair that had gone missing. The only problem was that they were a cheap pair of dress earrings she'd forgotten she'd even owned. For the life of me, I couldn't tell her what had happened to the ones she really wanted back. Sadly, this is not something you ever gain total control over. Fortunately for me the woman had a good sense of humour.

By contrast there was the woman who had lost a beautiful, and precious to her, watch. It was a sentimental gift, and she hadn't owned it long before it disappeared off her arm. Both she and her husband had searched their home from top to bottom. She had also checked her workplace and together they had searched both their cars to no avail. I told her that it was in the boot of a white car but that it was certainly not obvious to the eye. It was well hidden underneath a dark cover, very low down where it was very dark.

She did own a white vehicle, but she insisted that it had been checked thoroughly. 'Please check it again, I'm absolutely sure that you will find it,' I almost begged her.

She did, with no result. Her husband thought that seeing a psychic was a load of mumbo jumbo, but he must have loved her because he offered to check her car for her one more time, himself. He emptied the boot. Nothing. He took up the carpet and checked the spare tyre and the various lumps and bumps of metal around the area. Nothing. Then, as a last resort, he undid the spare tyre and lifted it out. There was her missing watch. How it got there was anybody's guess. They certainly couldn't work it out. However she was still elated when she telephoned me with the good news.

Only once did I have a complete disaster. I agreed to do a reading for a gentleman and the closer it got to his arrival, the stranger I felt. His visit had been hastily arranged and was not on my scheduled working day. I tried to contact him to cancel, but I couldn't get through on his mobile. My head eventually felt about five times its normal size. Since the visit had been hastily arranged, I was unable to sit and do my usual pre-reading writing session before his arrival. If I had I would have realised that something was seriously wrong. Not with him, with me! The poor man came for advice and got the opposite of everything that was correct out of my mouth. Fortunately, he was no fool, and he spoke up, pointing out every mistake I made. Throughout the reading I was aware of what was happening and yet unable to stop it. It was a disaster! When I finally completed the session, he insisted on paying for my time. I apologised and told him he was not required to pay me a cent as this was not my normal reading. He threw his money down on the table and marched out. The problem was me although I didn't know what it was. A few hours later I was ill. From that time on, I immediately cancelled a session if I felt at all unusual. I doubt that I helped the poor man with anything at all, but he certainly helped me to learn about myself. I gave his money to charity.

On another day, a lady turned up with information on a veteran whom she claimed lived in another country and said that husband wanted details such as if the man was still alive and where he lived. From the moment I sat down to get details before her arrival, something told me that this client was coming to do something sly. I couldn't get past a wall that was there. It may not have been a bad thing, but she wasn't being honest about her motives. When the lady finally arrived I had almost no information that wasn't about her life and nothing at all about her question. I had to explain that as she had no right to know details of this lost male, it was unlikely that I'd be able to provide her with the information anyway. She didn't like it at all when I told her that we have no right to pry into the lives of others and that I could read for her and what affected her directly but nothing beyond that. I offered to get the phone number of the correct authorities who could help her husband track down veterans, and the look that passed over her face gave her away. She didn't want authorities involved, and she certainly wasn't going to use the normal military channels for veterans. This was not a genuine person. I told her quite bluntly at that point that I don't use tarot to spy on others, we don't have the right to do that, and that she would have to go through the correct authorities if she wanted to renew contact with the man, whoever he was to her. I suspected that she was looking for a past love.

It was the lighter side of my work that kept me going through the times when everyone who walked through the door seemed to be a victim of a bad marriage, sexual abuse, childhood abuse, or severe injury inflicted either by others or by car accidents. These were people who really needed help to get their lives back on track. The cards would always show the steps and give positive help. Slowly, I realised that this was my place. I was to be the catalyst, the go between. I passed information on as it came. Sometimes it came with a firm telling off for the questioner; at other times, it was a gentle hand holding sympathy and showing the direction in which they could step forward. The person always responded, and they were always given guidance that lifted their spirits and gave them hope. I was humbled by the interactions with them. A tough day for me was often followed by good news: the missing dog was found in the location I pinpointed; the much-loved grandfather had survived his heart operation just as I'd predicted; a ring was found; and a job was offered. Every time I came close to walking away, the phone would ring announcing someone who wanted to express their gratitude for my help.

People asked me a few times what brings me the most joy in my work? This was hard to put into words, but one of the loveliest experiences I had was opening my letterbox to find a thank you note and a cheque, payment for a past reading. A year or so before this I had done a reading for a woman and discovered that she was a victim of domestic violence and had just escaped with her children. She was almost penniless but had decided to pay for this reading looking for guidance and hope. She was a proud lady and when I refused to take payment from her, asking her instead to put the money towards the necessities for her family, she was mortified. After chatting for a little while, we reached an agreement; when she was set up and comfortable with her budget again, she would pay me, not before. She needed the money more than I did as she was struggling to put food on the table. Tearfully she agreed. I didn't care if I she paid me. People have been good to me at times in my life, and I was now able to pass it on, so I did.

The day I opened the letterbox and took out that envelope, with no return address, and read her note of thanks, I cried. She was safe. She and her children were safe. It doesn't get better than that.

Chapter 22

Saving My Family

Meanwhile my life continued to change, and I continued to grow. Interacting with people and their problems puts you in a constant place of development. While I taught them, they were also teaching me by sharing their stories. I analysed myself and my progress yet again. As a child I had wanted to teach, but this wasn't the type of teaching I had planned. I spent many hours mulling this over. Was this ability that I held the reason I had always felt different from others as a child? Was this a good or a bad thing? Was it really a weight to carry all this responsibility for guiding others or was it a blessing? Was I messing with people's heads, or was it possible they were messing with mine?

By now I felt that my abilities were positive, and I could put them to good use, but I wasn't sure that I was strong enough for the weight of responsibility that entailed. I was giving my all to everybody, clients and family included, and it was taking a toll. I recognised a real need to pull back from the constant giving. I realised the world held a bottomless pit of people in pain searching for help with their issues, and I was only one person.

I needed to find my balance again. I had stopped doing party readings by now, so slowly I started to say no to requests for help and to stick to boundaries about my time and commitment. My husband had completed his studies but was now busy seeking employment interstate, so we had effectively swapped one pressure for another. It was definitely time to take care of our personal stressors.

A new source of stress had arisen for me as I started to see things in my own cards that I really didn't want to see. Hints of bad stuff to come. As my husband had opportunities for employment in Canberra where we were happier than anywhere else, we had lived, he wanted to stay put, enjoy our established group of friends and continue, initially at least, to rent the house we were living in. I opposed this, strongly convinced by nothing more than a gut feeling and a pack of picture cards that we had to leave. For me this was really a hard thing to contemplate as I was happy with life in Canberra, but my intuition was driving me. Something was going to go wrong, and we could not be here when it did.

After consulting and reconsulting my cards many times over, I insisted that we move back to Queensland where we now knew almost no-one and had no friends at all. My husband loved Queensland, so that wasn't an issue for him, but he felt that there was very little work for him there. He had far greater chances of employment in Canberra and a much easier transition from military to civilian life if we stayed where we were. As my intuition spoke more strongly to me with each passing week, I forced myself to find the words to tell him why we had to move and what I was seeing. If we stayed where we were then a member of our family was going to get cancer. I believed it was one of our children. Simple. Blunt. Sickening words. He was shocked. After discussing my feelings, the hospital and treatment requirements, which would likely mean time in

Sydney and how hard that would be for us physically, financially and emotionally, we decided we would move.

From that day on I was running away. We talked about it often. My husband insisted that it was most likely to be me who fell ill because of my poor medical history, and I was happy to agree with him, but I knew what I had seen, and it was not me. Could I put it into words? No. Even now, I recall my shock when I first picked up the message and how that was followed by a complete blankness. Disbelief followed by an intense nausea, shaking, and an overwhelming primal need to escape. The information was simply too awful to absorb, and mentally I kept pushing it away. I could tell my husband only that it was maybe a couple of years down the track, but beyond that I truly couldn't see the details because I couldn't bring myself to look more closely.

One evening I sat in my study, cards spread before me, and looked up at the wooden panelled ceiling. I had told lots of people by now, including my husband, that he would get a new job in August, 1997, which was fast approaching. I felt that we would not be living here by the start of September. As I continued looking at the ceiling, I asked for support for me and for my family. I knew that I could not continue giving to others through my readings and have the energy to hold my family together through what I knew would be a huge emotional upheaval. We would be both leaving people we cared for and heading towards an emotionally devastating illness in our family.

'I need to know,' I spoke aloud, 'that I can use this psychic talent to protect and help my family. I've given just about all I can give. Now I want you to show me that I can help my family too!' What was the point of my talent if I couldn't help my loved ones and myself?

I soon received my answer in a very unexpected and most

unpleasant way. Two weeks after I had implored my roof for help, my daughter asked to watch the old Canberra Hospital being imploded. The event was being publicly feted. We had watched overseas implosions on television and had all been fascinated by them, so I understood why she wanted to be there.

About a year before I had dreamt of an implosion where pieces of the building had gone in all directions. I couldn't properly remember the dream when I awoke but recalled enough to ask my husband if that could happen to a building. 'Only if someone got it wrong,' was his answer. He wanted to know where this building was situated, but all I could tell him then was that it seemed a long way away and not immediate.

'I guess we will see it on the news eventually,' I'd said and thought no more about it.

When my daughter asked to attend the hospital implosion, I did not consciously recall my dream, but I immediately felt nauseous. 'Maybe', I told her, and she went off to see if her dad was interested in going. I knew by now that the strange feeling of sickness meant that something was not right about this situation. My husband, however, decided that we should all go to watch this unusual event; he thought it was a great idea. I told him that I was worried and felt uncomfortable about it, but I couldn't tell him why. I felt I knew something in the back of my mind about it, but hard as I tried, I couldn't bring it forward.

He tried to reassure me: 'I've been to lots of explosions with my work. If we go where we are allowed and nowhere else, then it won't be a problem. This is possibly the only time that the girls will get to see one for real. Cheer up!'

Cheer up! Did he have any idea of how I really felt? Obviously not. I definitely did not want to go.

On the day of the event, I became very edgy. The world took on a different hue. As at the time of my brother's wedding,

I became impossible to be around. Several times I suggested that we stay home and watch the implosion on the evening news. No go. They all wanted to be there.

After about our fifth argument that morning, my husband finally exploded: 'YOU don't have to come, you know!'

I froze. I couldn't send them along without me. I had to be there! It was important that I be there. I recognised in this my basic instinct to protect my family, which was overwhelming and compelling. Then, while trying to contemplate staying home and letting them go in their father's safe care, an unknown male voice spoke loudly in my head: 'NO!' I shook my head trying to dispel the noise he'd made. I didn't question who he was; I simply obeyed. 'If you're going, then I have to,' I stated, but I couldn't bring myself to be nice about it.

When we arrived at the viewing site there were hundreds of people everywhere along the lakeside. By now I felt like I was going to break into a zillion little pieces and splinter into the grass, and I was suffering a severe tension headache. I remonstrated with myself for spoiling what should be a fun family outing, but it did no good. I continued to behave like a bad witch.

'We'll park here,' my husband said, as he pulled onto the grass island opposite the hospital. My stomach did back flips and instant dread fill my gut. I tried to make him move the vehicle to another spot, about six spaces from where he had stopped. I verbally bit his head off, insisting that we needed to be further up. My behaviour was shameful. I was making no sense to anyone except myself at this point, and when he laughed at me and refused, I amped up, knowing beyond all doubt that this spot was dangerous.

'If you don't move the car, I will move it myself!' I insisted.

I could see his face. He was thinking, 'Anything for peace,' as he moved the car. I am still unsure about whether he is just very tolerant of me when I am like this or just smart enough to realise that I am more stubborn and determined than he is.

We stopped. Everyone but me got out. I couldn't. The girls bounced around to the side of the car. 'Come on, Mum!' They were excited and wanted to find a place to sit.

My husband came around and opened my door. 'You look awful,' he commented. 'Will you be alright to come for a walk?' He indicated the foreshore of the lake.

'We won't stay down there, will we?' I whispered, also gesturing to the foreshore.

'Not if you don't want to, but it will be nice to go for a walk while we wait. We can come back here if you like.' He watched my face closely.

Slowly I got out. My legs felt like lead. 'Okay,' I muttered, 'let's go.' We called the girls and told them to hold our hands to cross the busy road where police were busy directing traffic.

As we reached the kerb, I looked down towards the right and my mind churned out pictures like a sea of blood. All I could see was red, blood-red. My daughter put one foot off the edge of the kerb, and I yanked her back forcefully. 'No!' I yelled, 'we can't go down there.' I turned to my husband. 'We mustn't go down there!'

My feet were frozen to the spot. He had now had more than enough of my strange behaviour, and his face lit with anger. I tried to explain, to get my words out. Suddenly, as I spluttered incomprehensibly, panicked and unable to find words, understanding dawned. 'Something is really wrong, isn't it.' It was a statement not a question. 'We need to go home.'

I pointed to the crowd on the foreshore. 'They all need to go home, they're in danger,' I whispered. My eldest daughter's face crumpled as she heard the words 'go home'. I turned slowly and saw the bridge behind us.

'Can we go somewhere else to see it? Is there somewhere

safe?' my husband queried gently. He obviously didn't want to leave either.

My eyes swivelled around and then went back to the bridge. 'Up there.' I pointed towards the end of the bridge. 'We will be safe up there.'

He explained to the children that we were now going to go and stand on the bridge. 'Has Mummy had one of her feelings?' one of them asked. 'What's going to happen?'

My eldest came to my side and looked up at me. I heard myself reply soothingly, 'You need to be in a safer spot. I want you to be safe.' Grudgingly she accepted that I wasn't going to tell her. She had picked up on my anxiety and knew this was how it was going to be.

My legs were heavy, and my feet dragged as we walked slowly across the grass and up onto the bridge. At this stage it was half empty. My girls pointed to some children rolling down the grassy bank to one side.

'Can we go and play too?'

I felt mean. I had spoilt their outing. 'I guess so,' I said, and the eldest took off. I watched for a minute, and my panic grew. 'Please make her come back here to us,' I begged my husband. I needed to keep them close, to touch and protect them, but from what? The children were returned to my side but, eventually, our eldest got bored and once again begged to be allowed to go and play. Receiving a stern no from me, she turned to her dad, and once again asked him what was wrong with me?

'Mum's pretty sure that something is going to go wrong, and she wants to make sure that you are safe,' he told her.

She looked at me, her face serious. Moving very close to me she whispered, aware of other people around us, 'Is it like your dream of the shooting.'

'Yes, only this time I can't quite recall what happens,' I told her honestly. From that time on she stood as patiently as an angel, close to my side for over an hour. As time progressed, even with my babies close by, my agitation increased.

Someone moved next to us. My husband knew them and introduced us, but I saw them through a fog. I felt moronic and had difficulty uttering polite monosyllables let alone sentences in reply to their chatter. My sense of danger was at an all-time high. When my husband suggested walking the length of the bridge 'to stretch our legs while we waited,' I froze yet again.

'No.' We had to stay exactly where we were.

'Are we safe here?' he probed gently.

'Yes.' I was sure that if we stayed exactly where we were until the whole event was finished, we would be okay. We weren't to move. We couldn't go down to the grass. We couldn't stand anywhere else along the bridge. We had to stay put. We should have stayed home!

When the first attempt at imploding the hospital failed, there was a delay of about twenty minutes, maybe half an hour. As word passed around the crowd that the implosion had failed, I felt like celebrating. I wanted to leave immediately. It hadn't worked, and we could, should, go home. I could take the children away, and it wouldn't be my fault that they hadn't seen the implosion. My relief was immense.

We couldn't leave though. Traffic had been stopped and from where we stood, we could easily see that there was no way that we would ever have been able to get our car out. A murmur passed through the crowd. There was going to be another attempt to bring the building down. The murmur reached us, and I thought I was going to be sick. My legs weakened, and my husband grabbed me as my knees buckled. He held me tightly until I recovered.

It was time. Our daughter and my husband held their cameras at the ready. I clung to the little one. 'Oh God!' I heard myself implore as the building before us exploded rather than imploded.

The crowd's initially loud cheer dulled and silenced as large pieces of the building flew up into the air and across the lake. Chunks of concrete and iron rained down onto the boats in the designated 'safe' area in the water and bricks fired into the crowd below us. *Déjà vu.* I had seen it all before. I turned my head in time to see concrete pieces flying over the centre of the bridge where my husband had wanted to walk half an hour before. This is what I had been blocking out and why I had needed to keep my family safe by my side. This was what I feared. I had known.

Devastatingly, one young girl lost her life that day; many more on the foreshore and on boats in the water were injured. When we returned to our vehicle it was undamaged, but six spaces away, where we had initially parked, another vehicle had a huge chunk of concrete in its bonnet. In what seemed like ages, but must have only been minutes, ambulances were every-where. For some time afterwards, their sirens were the only noise. The crowd moved almost silently. People stood in groups hugging each other, crying, shocked.

I had protected my family. I could not alter what had happened, but I had protected my family. Later that evening, after crying over the news that a young girl had died and seeing the area where she had been sitting at the lakeside, my husband gently reminded me of a morning a year or so before, when I had woken from a dream and described an implosion that had gone wrong. I still had not expected this vision to be part of my own life. I had expected that it would happen overseas, perhaps because at that point the only implosions I had ever viewed on television were overseas. Who knows? However, thinking this had allowed me to put the dream completely out of my mind. I had filed it, knowing at some point I would see it on television or in a movie but not feeling any danger to my own family. Yet, when the time came, subconsciously I still reacted.

It took me several weeks to come to terms with my memories and the reality of the event. Once again, I felt a heavy sense of responsibility mingled with guilt and fear. I had learned I could protect my family, but I could not prevent these events from occurring. I wanted and needed time out. Mentally and emotionally the toll of knowing was adding up. It was too big a burden, and I wanted to turn the visions off.

Precognition, I decided, was both useful and useless. It was great to protect me and my family; however, it was of little good if I couldn't prevent such horrible events from happening to others. Every time I recalled the feeling inside me at the lake, where I had wanted to run up and down the foreshore yelling at people to get out of there even while the logical side of me knew that they would think I was insane, and I'd be dragged off by the police, I felt sick, overwhelmed, and greatly responsible for the outcome. The mental and emotional impact was huge.

In retrospect, I recognised that it had been a tough but rewarding year, and for the latter I was grateful, but now I needed to recuperate. I talked about needing a year off and finding a way to stop the premonitions of these ongoing disaster dreams.

I thought my prayers were answered when my husband accepted a job offer in Queensland. If I wanted to continue doing tarot readings, I would have to start from scratch in the future, but for now there was an ending, and it could last as long as I wanted it to. It was August 1997, and, as I'd predicted, we were gone before the end of the month. We were leaving behind us some of the best friendships we had ever made as a family, so emotionally we knew the next twelve months were likely to be tough for all of us. A new state, a new job, new schools.

It would not be easy but, we had a lot of experience under our belts of starting afresh, and no matter how tough it might prove, we knew we would survive it. Before we left though, I made a pact with myself: no more psychic work until I was well enough to cope. My mental health was suffering as I didn't understand where the information came from, and I was obviously struggling with the outcomes I was living through. It needed to stop. It didn't.

When Princess Diana died, we were in a motel in Queensland, in the middle of our house move. The following day we were to move into a rental property, intending to spend our time there until we decided which part of Brisbane we wanted to settle in. Just as had happened previously when premonitions were about to become a reality, I became edgy and jittery. Just as before, as the day progressed into evening, I ended up becoming downright nasty. My poor family knew something was obviously wrong with me but not what. Well, we all shared that issue. Initially I had no idea.

Eventually my children and then my husband went to sleep, but I couldn't sleep at all. I tried for an hour or so, then gave up and prowled the small room like a caged lion.

Being more experienced with these feelings now, I knew what they meant, and I searched my mind for specifics. Something bad was about to occur but what? Diana's face appeared before me in that little space on the inside of my forehead that I called my psychic viewing screen. I recalled my awful prediction. Surely it couldn't be that? It seemed too awful to contemplate and so unlikely that I pushed it away. She was so young. Her children were so young. Surely not? It would be something closer to home, surely?

Her face appeared again and again on my internal screen. Instead of going with the flow, I became crosser and crosser with myself. Why wouldn't my mind just let me relax and get some sleep? What was it that was making me feel so awful, so terrible? Why did her face keep appearing? What on earth was going to happen this time? The thoughts kept churning until in the end all I could think about was her. Diana, Diana, Diana.

The morning news delivered the shock to the world. Still awake at dawn, I was the first in the family to hear it. I was upset. 'Why?' I asked myself. 'Why her? Why me? Why did I need to know in advance? How could I know in advance? Why did I know at all? What good did it do? It certainly didn't help at all to save her! What the hell is the point of this ability?!'

For days afterwards I tormented myself. We moved into our new home, and as we did so. her death and my knowing were always there at the back of my mind, eating away at me. Finally, about a week or so after the move, and by now suffering nervous exhaustion, I found the time to sit down and meditate.

During the meditation I asked that I be given a year to rest. No premonitions. No *deja vue*. No mysterious spiritual visitors. 'If you have a job for me to do,' I told the spiritual world, 'then I can't do it unless I recharge my batteries. This stuff is destroying me. I need to find out who I am and come to terms with all of this. There has been too much, too fast. It must stop! There must be time for me. I'm just one human being, and I'm breaking.'

Even in my damaged state, I was aware that I had promised to do something, had returned to fulfil some type of mission. I never seemed to fully forget, but at this point, my main concern was me. If my life really did have a purpose, even if this type of work was involved, I needed it to stop. I needed a rest, and I truly hoped I would get it.

To my surprise the dreams continued, but now they came in symbols. There were no more horrific premonitions. Those dreams that did come were mildly interesting, newsworthy items that let me know that my psychic abilities were still functioning. Ever so slowly, I recovered from my ordeal, and as I did, I began to question.

Had I gone off track? Was I doing, or had I done, what I had promised my 'God' when I died? Should I study again? For years I had lived with the idea that if I didn't 'become somebody' in a professional sense, then I would be a failure. I had after all promised that I would do something, something that had seemed terribly important at the time. Since I didn't seem to have achieved any professional status, I felt that I must have failed to fulfil that promise. I was very unhappy with this deduction, but no matter how I tried, I failed to reach any other conclusion

If I expected my time out to be easy, I was wrong. I spent most of 1998 searching through the huge number of incidences and coincidences in my mind. I opened filing cabinets in there that I had not looked at for many years, and the more I opened, the more I found. Every single one brought forth things to analyse, think about, process, question and, sometimes, to discard. Without ever having planned to, I spent much of that year searching through my mind in the hope that I would find the answer about what I had promised.

The personal questioning seemed endless. I wore myself down constantly going around in mental circles. Why did these things happen? Were there any real answers? Should I have the answers? Did I really want them? Why had all this weird stuff happened to me in the first place? Why did I still think it weird after all this time?

Slowly, very slowly, I worked a few things out. Of course, there were no answers; there were only ideas and opinions. Of course, I was going to have trouble accepting these things. I was brought up to explain my every action in a logical way. Why did my brain still argue with itself over which side of it was right? Did there even have to be a right or a wrong value in an argument? Why was I even arguing with myself? Could logical thinking and psychic sensing have their own individual value in my life? Every time I arrived at this point, my mind would counter with, 'Yes they could, but...,' and the mental circles would start another loop.

My biggest problem was that I worried about fulfilling my promise when I still had no idea what that was. Contemplating this failure I considered my next move. What direction should I head in now? I felt like I was running out of time. The feeling grew stronger the closer I got to forty years of age. If I was going to retrain for anything substantial, I needed to get on with it, but how do you plan a life around something that you can't remember? The mental pressure I placed on myself was intense.

Since my mental circles were getting me nowhere, I decided to put pen to paper and try to make sense of my thoughts that way. My tarot cards kept telling me that the answers were back in my past, so I decided that that was where I'd best begin. It seemed too obvious an answer; after all, the past was where I'd both made and forgotten my promise, but back I went anyway. My childhood memories go almost back to my beginning, so this was not a simple task. I soon found that a dots and dashes approach, making abbreviated notes about my memories, was just as confusing as going around in circles in my head. There had to be a better way.

One morning as I stared at the confused notes on early thinking, I decided it might be easier if I wrote my memories out in chronological order, story style, and I hesitantly started to do this. Of course, as anyone who has already done it knows, this too has its headaches. Anyone with memories also has the associated feelings that go with them. I found myself crying all over again for my little white bunny on its green-jelly grass hill! Reliving was wonderful, traumatic, tiring. I persevered for a few weeks, but progress was slow, and confusion still reigned. Where was my answer in all this? I consulted my cards again and received the same message. I tossed them aside, disgruntled with the lot of them.

Shortly after this I required major surgery and during my weeks of recovery, I decided to take a different approach to discovering my promise. Perhaps writing down all the strange events that I'd lived through, including my near-death experience, would be the therapy I needed to unlock the memory of my forgotten promise. I became a woman on a mission! I have incredible drive and determination once I set my mind to something, and, having reached the conclusion that the sooner I got my past weirdness on paper, the sooner I would have my answer, I set myself a rigid timetable.

Initially I was driven just by strong motivation, but I also resumed my old habit of reading my tarot cards daily, and they were showing me yet again that something both life changing and shocking was heading towards our family. I felt the urgency to get my answer before this new challenge arrived. Hopefully it would help me to avoid whatever disaster was looming. A feeling of impending doom grew stronger in my chest over the coming weeks. As it did, I wrote faster, worked harder, pushed myself. I had to stop this unknown thing from hitting us. It became a feeling I couldn't seem to escape.

It was after I had completed writing about my death experience at eighteen that I again turned to the sky to ask for help. I found that although I had talked of my experience to a few people over the past years, the act of committing it to paper was more emotionally draining than anything I had imagined. With every word I wrote, I was back in that hospital bed reliving the pain. Writing released emotions that I thought were already healed. I was completely unprepared for their reappearance, especially with such force. That night, still not recalling my promise, I retired to bed with the weight of the world on my shoulders. 'Please,' I begged the heavens, 'if you want me to know, then you're just going to have to tell me.' My forgotten promise was haunting me.

I awoke the next day with that it's-a-wonderful-day sensation we all experience occasionally. I had been dreaming; the details were unclear seconds after I awoke, but the message was brilliantly clear. I had received an answer.

I was almost as surprised at the swiftness with which the answer came as I was at its simplicity. Did it come immediately because I was genuinely seeking help or because my mind had put so much mental effort into trying to dissemble the puzzle? I didn't know, and I didn't really care right then. The simple discovery of what I now believed to be the truth made me feel like a young child looking at her filled Christmas stocking. Happy, just doesn't describe it. I had been chasing my tail when the answer was right there in front of me the whole time. I was a victim of my own overthinking, complicating things as humans tend to do.

From the time I'd died, I believed that I'd made a promise to my 'God', one which meant I would fulfill something deep and all encompassing. When I awoke that morning, I realised that I'd not promised my God anything and that my God had no expectations of me whatsoever. He had put out his hand to help me cross the stream. It was not God who stood in judgement of me. If I had wanted to die and go to God, then I was welcome. He had held out his hand to let me. It was my choice. No, it was not to God but to myself that I had made the promise, the commitment that I had fought so hard to identify.

I was born with a life path and the talents and abilities to complete it in my own way, but I had never accepted who and what I was. Maybe I couldn't find a label or a category, a file name even, for myself, but that was okay. I was who I was. My promise therefore was surely simple; to be here, to live. To live whatever years I was given using the natural abilities and talents I was born with and rise to the challenges of everyday life.

I needed to accept myself. I had searched for years for personal success, reaching out to grasp the next tool that I thought would bring me somehow closer to my indefinable goal. Now the pressure was gone. There was nothing to strive for. I just had to let life happen.

I recognised I was my own harshest judge. No-one else was responsible for my feelings or behaviours. Finally, I viewed myself in a different way and saw that I could be kind to myself as well as to others. I too deserved kindness. I could look at my life, warts and all, and recognise my achievements, whereas once I had seen only the perceived failures. I recognised that I had already become The Teacher and The Healer, and in doing so, I had helped people. If there had ever been a debt to pay, then surely I had repaid it? I acknowledged I'd been a dedicated mum, a good wife and friend. For the very first time in my forty years, I took some pleasure from my view of myself. I freed myself from my own chains.

Had I though? Although I was hugely relieved at the recognition of being where I needed to be, I still had, deep inside, a niggling doubt, a slight feeling of hollowness. I'd spent forty years focussing on what I lacked and my failures, and my logical mind wasn't going to change on a pin no matter how good the conclusion I'd reached while asleep. I was the daughter of a narcissistic mother. I was trained to condemn myself first and foremost. Transiently it crossed my mind to question why this exhilarating sense of newfound freedom didn't touch that hollow space inside. What was hidden in there? What did it contain? For now, though, I was happy, and I wasn't going to do further probing. Didn't I deserve some peace of mind? It all seemed so simple in the light of day. Why had it taken me so long to work it out?

This different take on what had happened to me brought me a sense of peace. I realised that I didn't have to choose to operate completely from my psychic side nor from my logical. I was free to operate from either, any given time. If they clashed when I thought too hard, I needed to simply accept that there were no answers for what occurred in my brain and body, for what didn't make logical sense. My inner struggle to conform to society's idea of normal and to understand that which didn't fit was unnecessary. I realised that I could continue with my inner fight for the rest of my life, but if I did, I would die battling. Why not just accept it? Understand that the logical and the seemingly illogical that turned into reality were both a part of myself and accept them. Could I do that? Simple in hindsight, but why not? After all, I couldn't cope in the world without logic, but if my psychic senses were to disappear, I knew I would seriously miss them. They were an integral part of who I was and acknowledging this brought me strength.

Acceptance was merely another step along the pathway to completion of my promise although I wouldn't realise this for quite some time. I still had to live through the vision of running away from the screen they had shown me and being overcome with grief. I had written about it, but now, possibly as a survival mechanism in the present, I concluded it had been one challenge too many. If I accepted that my life was just going to run its course, and that I couldn't avoid the inevitable challenge, then I would meet it the way I was meant to. That meant owning all my abilities. Surely, I could do that?

Deep down, a part of me truly hoped that owning my abilities and my personality would lead me to ultimately avoid the oncoming crisis in my life. Perhaps it would allow me to change course?

I was naïve, human and wrong. I am no hero.

Chapter 23

My Child Has Cancer

I f I thought I had experienced pain, I was wrong. If I thought that I had experienced worry, I was wrong. If I thought that I had experienced grief, then I was a naïve child dipping her toes in a cold stream. If I had ever thought that I controlled any of my life, I was about to discover the opposite.

Just as I had seen in my tarot cards my youngest fell ill. Viruses. Colds. Sore throats. Tummy upsets. They came more and more frequently, and I became more and more certain something was seriously wrong with her. By now I was living a relatively normal life, taking time out from the stresses of working with my psychic senses and the wealth of problems that people had brought to my door. I now rarely touched my cards. Since they almost constantly showed me impending disasters, I was eventually unable to cope, and for my own sanity, I had packed them away. I did no more daily card reads. Premonitions, when they came, were usually in the form of symbols, and these were both less confronting and easier to ignore.

The past couple of years had been wearing. My children had not adjusted well to their interstate move and emotions ran high for a year or so. I suffered with frozen shoulders and was officially diagnosed by a rheumatologist, for the second time in my life, with fibromyalgia.

I was run down after a major operation on top of everything else, and I had lost a lot of interest in life. With no friends and no interest in making any, I lived in a mundane kind of fog.

Slowly though, reality pushed its way through, and my intuitive side emerged from the cloudiness. The message was clear. My daughter was ill. Seriously ill. One day I knew it, and the next I knew it beyond all doubt. Intuition is like that; you can only ignore it or subdue it for so long before it becomes loud, and the sound fills your whole head and body until it's all you can think about.

There was nothing visibly wrong with my daughter. She was as cheerful and happy and outgoing as she had always been. She was healthy looking, but was she? Everyone else thought she was, but I was her mum, and I thought differently. We had endless trips to doctors, endless minor illnesses. My worry increased. To me, her joyful, cheerful face had lost something. At first, I couldn't quite put my finger on what the change was, and unable to explain it, I became consumed with worry for her. Something was wrong, and I knew I wasn't imagining it.

Christmas 1999 arrived. I looked at her in an even more serious light. Instinct told me that something was badly wrong with her. Her GP insisted nothing was wrong with her, that her white count was slightly raised due to a mild virus, but I didn't believe him. Further examinations and tests proved fruitless. I had learnt by now that the feeling inside of me which I had nicknamed The Knowing was always correct. It had never let me down, and it was loudly letting me know that I was right; something was seriously wrong with my child.

In a rather desperate attempt to find answers, some fact with which I could confront a doctor, I tentatively unpacked my cards and spread them before me. Suddenly I flashed back to my tarot room in Canberra. Cancer! Emotions rushed through my body with a ferocity and intensity that instantly reduced me to a shaking wreck.

'No, surely not? That's not what they mean!' I spoke aloud even although I was totally alone. I pulled myself together. The cards were almost identical to the ones that I had laid out in Canberra not long before our move. 'Rubbish! I've lost my touch,' I exclaimed, again to no-one. The emotions were too hard to process silently. I was in denial. This could not be right! Angrily I shoved the cards away in a box. I tried desperately to push my fear away.

On New Year's Eve, on the stroke of midnight, as my little one jumped jubilantly into our surprisingly cool swimming pool and whooped with laughter, I turned away in tears and rushed indoors to collect myself before she saw me. The sight of her had filled me instantly with a deep dread. Later, when she was safely tucked up in bed, I confessed my fears to my husband.

With tears trickling down my cheeks, I told him, 'There's something seriously wrong with her, and I don't think that the doctors are going to pick it up until the very last minute. They may be too late.'

I felt physically sick saying this out loud. He was stunned. He knew me well enough to know that I wouldn't be in this state, and I certainly wouldn't be telling him about it, unless I was certain that I was correct. Busy as always with his work, he hadn't realised that all her minor illnesses were abnormal, but now he was listening. 'Keep dragging her back to the doctors.

It's got to manifest into something they will recognise eventually,' was his only advice.

Even then I couldn't bring myself to voice the word cancer nor tell him what I had seen in the cards. How do you speak that word aloud as a parent? You are in denial until you have to face it; until someone tells you it is the truth. Even knowing what it was, I couldn't speak it because I didn't think I could hold myself together if it was spoken aloud. Saying it would make it true, and I wanted to hang on to that tiny shred of hope that I was wrong even while knowing I wasn't. It was a very sobering start to what was to be the very worst year of our parental lives.

By mid-January our little girl had diabetes-like symptoms, sometimes appearing as if she had low blood sugar. Being a type 1 diabetic myself, I was easily able to check her blood sugar. It was always normal. Diabetes was not the issue. Bouts of shaking and weakness appeared more and more frequently, as did mild bouts of nausea. 'Viral infection,' said her doctor.

Chatting on the phone to an interstate friend I told her that I feared something was seriously wrong with our child and again told her that I didn't think it would be picked up until last minute.

'What do you think it is? Diabetes?' she asked.

Silence. I struggled with the word cancer. You just don't say that to people without a diagnosis, and, as I mentioned previously, to say it aloud was like owning that it was true. No parent wants that. 'I...I don't know. Worse I think.' More silence. We moved on with our conversation.

By March our daughter had developed tachycardia, bouts of rapid heartbeat which occurred for no apparent reason. At first these were irregular and infrequent. Again, we had to trust our doctor when he put them down to a viral infection. He examined her thoroughly, did blood tests. With only a slightly raised white blood cell count, they showed nothing of importance. Another virus was a fair explanation.

The bouts of tachycardia became more frequent, more debilitating. We arranged for her to see a heart specialist. This man assured us that this condition occurred occasionally during puberty and that we shouldn't be concerned. Palpating her bowel area as part of her examination he commented on her full bowel.

I spoke up. 'That can't be right. I know she isn't constipated. She used her bowels this morning.'

The specialist stared at me. 'Well, she's pretty full up now', he answered, obviously irritated by my outspoken answer.

Frissons of fear pulsed through me. His attitude to my comments made me feel both foolish and overly protective. I wasn't, was I? Angrily I battled to sort out my feelings.

The specialist handed me a letter to give to our GP. I had taken on board his attitude towards me and opened the barely closed envelope when I got home. Was I the problem? It would seem so in his opinion. 'The child has no problems, but the mother needs to be reassured,' I read. I dissolved. How could the intuition I had learned to trust be so wrong? Was I really the problem? Loudly, from somewhere deep inside me, came a need to continue fighting. A sense of rightness, a sense of utter conviction. My daughter needed help, and something was being overlooked. Sure enough, I was soon to find both his diagnosis and his attitude towards me unforgiveable.

My 'baby' rapidly became just that. She ate less. She moved less. Once an active participant in any weekend activity her father could roll out for her, now she lolled around reading and watching TV. She was too tired to ride her bike and in fact her last bike ride had seen her bedridden for the rest of the weekend. She certainly wasn't going to repeat the process. 'Viral fatigue,' our doctor told us. 'Give her time.'

By the time Mother's Day arrived in May she was missing a lot of school, and I was secretly a wreck. She felt nauseous most of the time and now ate almost nothing. She tried to eat, mainly to keep me happy, but food had lost any appeal. More tests. Still viral was the prognosis. By now though, our doctor was also shaking his head, concern written across his face. I was not surprised. She was still bright in herself and still shone for an audience, and the test results still showed only a slightly elevated white count. Surprisingly she even appeared to have put on a little weight in the past few months despite her poor eating. No one other than me was unduly concerned. I realised that our doctor's concerned face was likely more about the mother than the patient.

I felt like I was carrying the weight of the world on my shoulders. Why did no-one else think there was anything wrong with our daughter? It was at this time that the nightmares started. This time, my husband suffered them as well. My husband's dreams involved rescuing his family from floods, drownings, and horrendous storms. He who normally didn't recall a dream to save his life would wake up yelling, shaking and bathed in perspiration. Vivid memories would fill his mind for hours afterwards. My dreams were more symbolic. Huge ships would be heading straight towards me; my boat would capsize. Long corridors trapped me with no way to escape from the unseen enemy hiding within. Our dreams were all disturbing and worrying and not at all like my psychic visions.

Then one night I dreamt that our youngest had died. I was at her funeral. I sat at the front of the church and watched as strangers stood up and talked about her. I couldn't hear what they were saying. I looked to the side of the alter. There was a table with things on it and a picture of a girl. I couldn't focus on the picture. I was crying too much, getting too distressed. Then shock. What was that slouch hat doing there? Our daughter didn't have a hat like that. What was it doing at her funeral?

I jolted awake, bathed in perspiration, my pillow soaked. Sobbing. 'She's dying,' I sobbed to my husband. 'I dreamt I was at her funeral.' The dream was one of my premonitions. I knew because they have an atmosphere and clarity like nothing else. I was utterly devastated as you can imagine. We were both very frightened.

Still the GP could find nothing. She vomited for three weeks. She ate only rice. More blood tests. "Viral," said the doctor. She was now sleeping on a beanbag as lying in a bed hurt too much.

The vomiting increased in frequency. Ignoring the doctor's surgery, we took her to the hospital. They took bloods, did urine tests. They came back fine, again with a slightly elevated white count. 'Viral' they said. They rehydrated her and asked if her back pain had eased.

'A little,' she replied bravely. They ignored my comments about her changing abdominal and stomach shape entirely.

'You can take her home,' they said. My heart sank.

'This cannot be happening,' I said to my husband. 'She should be kept in. Why can't they see how sick she is?'

I questioned them. I repeated how bad the pain in her back was and that she could no longer lie flat. 'Probably strained a muscle with all the vomiting,' was their answer.

Her medical history didn't matter. My voice didn't matter. They sent her home. They said to give her a week, keep her hydrated, and then bring her back if there was no improvement. I'd been doing that for weeks already, so their words just made me feel like I was going crazy. What was wrong with these people? Couldn't they see that my child was critically ill? I was not imagining this! I wasn't!

For a few days, thanks to the rehydration, the vomiting

ceased. She ate a little rice but nothing else. Inevitably the vomiting returned. Once a day, three times a day. Then, the day arrived when she could no longer keep anything in her stomach. My husband went to work. I drove her straight to the local hospital, a smaller version of the one she'd been to a week or so before.

She couldn't stand up straight by now and even with my help she struggled to walk inside. We waited for hours only to receive the same treatment but no blood tests this time as they'd only been taken one week before! *No sense in repeating them!*

We got the same answer. 'Viral. Take her home.' I nearly broke down then. This time I was to give her Phenergan for the vomiting and to keep giving her Panadol for the pain. I was utterly devastated. By this stage, it seemed so obvious that she needed help desperately that I couldn't understand why they kept throwing us out because that's what it felt like. I left with her that day believing that my child was going to die at home because of medical neglect. I looked straight-faced and stony as I half carried her to the car, but I was bordering on hysteria.

By ten am the following day we were back at the hospital, and I was determined that I wasn't taking her home until they gave me a more accurate diagnosis. As she could no longer sit in a chair she lay on the floor in Emergency and received a bed within twenty minutes. The doctor came and again asked if blood tests had been taken at the previous hospital, and I answered in the affirmative. We waited. I phoned my husband, following my intuition. I felt that this was it. Today we would get an answer, and he needed to be here. Our child was dying. I knew it.

It would take him an hour to get to us. I couldn't wait an hour to eat due to my diabetes, so, unwillingly, promising to be as quick as I could, I left her side to find a café where I bought a drink and a sandwich which I wolfed down on my way back to her side. Inside I was bawling. Outside I remained stony faced. I was wound as tight as I could get.

When I returned to her bedside, I was utterly shocked to see her looking like a stroke victim. One side of her face had totally collapsed. I took a deep breath and asked her if her face was alright. She said that it was fine and moved for me to get a better look at it. Half of her mouth had not moved as she spoke. It took all my strength to show no fear in front of her as I went to call a staff member.

Now they paid her attention. Finally, I was taken seriously. Now she was examined thoroughly. The examination was followed by an ultrasound where the rudest, most obnoxious woman I have ever met in my life proceeded to tell off both my daughter and me because my daughter couldn't lie flat on the table, and I couldn't make her! I was very angry and shocked by her behaviour. The child was obviously seriously unwell, and this staff member was abusing us.

For the sake of my child, I kept myself calm and tried to speak soothingly to her as I tried to hold her in a suitable position for the ultrasound. Her skin turned porcelain with pain. I was aware that every word I spoke to the woman herself sounded like icicles dropping into a glass, but I held myself together. The woman, realising at last that the child was genuine, took her rudeness out on the nurse, abusing her for not arranging pain medication for the child. The whole thing was a horror show. I vowed never to set foot in that hospital again.

The woman's manner changed abruptly when she saw the images on the screen in front of her. My daughter's gut was filled with massive tumours. The screen showed what looked like a large silhouette of Micky Mouse's head aside other lumps. She then proceeded to berate me for not asking the staff to take pictures much sooner! To my daughter, though, she never said another unkind word.

I wanted to vomit. Violently. My worst fears were confirmed. I didn't need a doctor to tell me. I just wanted to hold my baby, fix her, make her better. Reality isn't like that though. I knew I couldn't fix this.

'What's wrong with me, Mummy?' she asked weakly.

'Oh, we don't know yet, sweetheart. There's something in your tummy, but we'll have to wait until the doctor reads the scans.' Was that really me answering her? Was I really saying these words? Was any of this really happening?

No bed. They made her curl into a wheelchair this time. I honestly don't know how she managed it. The pain was etched into her porcelain-white, distorted features. An ambulance was ordered for a short trip to have more scans taken elsewhere. I watched on as one by one every medical person in the private clinic they had taken us to went in the room to look at the scans as I talked quietly to the nurse that had escorted us there. We chatted about the problems she was having with her son, I remember that, although I don't recall what they were. I was operating on two levels; the public face side was on show, the one that wouldn't allow them to see my fear and my pain, and the mother who was already shattered. The staff had no idea that I knew what was wrong with my daughter. I knew. They kept acting like nothing was wrong. That this was normal procedure. I maintained my iron self-control with difficulty. Until someone said the words, to my face, told me that my child was going to die, I was determined to maintain a strong façade.

They said them. The words no parent should ever have to hear spoken. Hours later, someone with the authority to do so, took me and my husband aside in a room with only glass separating us from the other staff who already knew what he was going to say, and who watched us throughout the whole conversation, He told us that our daughter was now palliative with stage 4 leukaemia and that we should gather our family.

Without saying the words death or dying, he placed great emphasis on 'gathering our family'. He then told us that an ambulance would transport her to another hospital, the one she had been sent home from twice, as they would take care of her from this point as the hospital we were currently in didn't provide palliative care for children.

I wanted him to be quiet. I wanted the staff outside the window to stop staring at us. I wanted to get back to my daughter. My iron control was slipping. It was out in the open. We had our diagnosis. Instead of breaking down, I turned to ice. I wasn't angry, just completely cold. This should never have occurred. I had had plenty of warning and had tried so hard to prevent it. It should never have reached this stage. We certainly shouldn't be stared at by strangers while being given this news. All of this was wrong.

We went with him and listened while he told our child. He was kind, gentle, asking her if she knew what cancer was, telling her that she had leukaemia, and then quietly, respectfully, leaving us all together.

Our daughter's eyes filled with tears. Briefly she looked down at the floor and then up, and our eyes met. Mine were filled with tears; hers were now clear. 'Don't worry, Mum,' she whispered, 'I'm going to be fine.'

We hugged. We all hugged. My eldest daughter rarely cried in front of anyone and even more rarely hugged her sister, but her eyes spilled over, and she cuddled her close. My husband hugged all of us. Before my eyes, they all transformed. They became stoical, strong. At the same time my husband aged. Shock was written on his face, etched deeply into newly arrived grooves. I watched them as if from a great distance. Inside I was falling apart, splintering, shattering, destroyed by a pain that had no boundaries, no limits.

Our beautiful girl sat there, hunched, broken, pale, fragile and yet brave. I looked at her face and prayed that she would be correct, that despite the diagnosis she would be fine. Grasping at straws? Who knew? My pain was too intense to tell.

We were so lucky. Like much they had already gotten wrong, the doctors' diagnosis was incorrect. Our daughter did not have end stage leukaemia. She did have cancer. She had stage 4 Burkett's lymphoma. It is a very fast-growing cancer, not detectable in blood tests until the very final stages when the white blood cell count that has been slightly raised for months suddenly escalates massively in numbers.

At the time of her diagnosis, she could have already died. Had one of her tumours burst for any reason, the toxins flooding her system would have rapidly killed her. She underwent ten months of often crippling chemotherapy, but the braveness that she exhibited from the start remained with her, and mentally she remained strong throughout the treatment. The difference between the two cancers is remarkable; with Burkett's she still had a chance.

When she lost her hair, she covered her head in butterfly tattoos and carried herself as proudly as her fragile body would allow. Whenever she was well enough, she found time to comfort and play with the 'babies' in the ward. She was determined, brave, mostly cheerful and utterly certain of where she was heading. The doctors had the chemicals, and we had love and humour, and we used them all to the max in the next few months.

Our daughter had no doubt that she was going to survive. The battle for her had been in getting a diagnosis to start treatment. As far as she was concerned that was sorted now. I had brought our girls up to listen to their intuition, and that's what she focused on. Later she would tell me, 'When they told me I had cancer, I was a little bit upset. I think I already knew though. Then a voice in my head told me that I would be alright, and I knew I would be.' Her faith was simply amazing.

I can't say that I was as stoical or as brave as our daughter. There were no voices in my head, only pain. As a mum, the delivery of the diagnosis was my worst nightmare coming true. I responded to my daughter's needs with as much love as I could muster, more than I knew I possessed, but outside of that my world was just pain. Repeatedly I caught myself silently begging, 'Please God, don't take my baby!'

Over the coming months, one of us was always at her bedside. Being alone was now her fear rather than cancer. So we pulled out all stops to ensure that one of us was always there. We nursed her, loved her, cheered her on, and even pushed her when she needed it. We worked in shifts with over-lapping hours, but one of us with always with her.

Going home was another matter. As soon as I walked out the door of the hospital, my tears flowed. I would howl all the way home but pull myself together to greet my elder daughter, still so young herself, at the other end of the journey. Once she was in bed, I would cry quietly again. I slept very little and always woke to the feeling of my heart splitting open afresh, my mind continuously repeating the mantra, 'Please God, don't take my baby.'

One of my students had once had a vision of me wearing a blue cardigan, wind blowing a gale around me, my head thrown back, in a garden that fitted the description of where we currently lived. It had perturbed her as she had picked up that I was in pain. An image of her telling the class about this returned to me as one night I literally howled at the moon during a storm as I tried to release my internal pain to the wild.

Later, when her treatment had finished, my husband confessed that he too had cried on his way back and forth from the hospital. We both knew that the other struggled, but once our daughter came out of intensive care after her initial treatment, we had no private time together to discuss our feelings and emotions, and so we had kept up a front, remaining strong for each other with all our energies focussed entirely on our little family. Both girls needed special but different types of care. Making time for them both was never going to be balanced, such is the nature of life when one young child is seriously unwell, but we did the best we could for our eldest, as we had no family in town to support her.

It was near the end of our daughter's third cycle of chemotherapy that I made a conscious decision to reconnect with the spirit world. Since before her initial trip to intensive care she couldn't bear to be touched. Even light touch was unbearably painful to her. She really had a dreadful time of it all. One night I watched as the chemotherapy dripped down the tube into her arm, and she tossed and turned restlessly, drugged but still obviously in discomfort even as she slept. I longed to cuddle her, to give her the physical love and healing touch that she had always treasured so much. I knew she needed this healing touch almost as much as she needed the chemicals going into her veins as prior to treatment, she was a frequent cuddler. I felt helpless at not being able to provide that one simple act that had always helped her.

Sitting at the end of her bed, I wondered if perhaps I should try to heal her without touch. I felt sure that that could be done, and I was desperate to do more to help her. When I say, 'heal her', I am not talking about healing her cancer but healing the emotional effects and the side effects caused by being in constant pain. I figured that whatever the outcome, energy healing could only help, and if it didn't, then it at least wasn't going to hurt her.

In my mind I threw out a challenge to whatever was out there, or whoever was possibly around me in spirit at the time.

Did I believe there was anyone there? I didn't have a clue if any of this could possibly help, I was just a mother in a desperate, emotional, and highly fatigued moment, grasping at straws. I just wanted to be able to do something to help her.

I immersed myself in a visual mediation, imagining all the cancer cells being wiped out by filling her body with the same bright, white, cleansing light, that I'd tried to cover our house with back in the UK when attempting to practice white lighting. I soon felt my body humming with the strange buzz that it hadn't experienced for a long time. I held the picture in my mind, my eyes open, for as long as my exhausted state would allow.

During this process I left no room for my own doubts. I was completely focused on helping my daughter. This was coming from pure love. it was all that I had left to give.

The white light soon filled the space behind the curtains which formed a little cubicle. I extended the light from ceiling to floor without difficulty. A white mist descended and then thickened and brightened. I soon realised that that this light was far brighter than the white I had initially imagined, and instead of participating in creating it, I simply watched it develop and shine lighter and brighter. I was in awe.

As the human mind naturally does, I eventually drifted out of meditation and back to full awareness. I sat there stunned by what I'd experienced, stunned by the sheer luminosity of the light and the incredible peace that had been brought with it. I did not imagine it. My intention started the process, but it continued independently, and hours passed with both of us completely immersed in it. I hadn't slept a wink. I had simply watched in fascination.

I slowly realised that it was dawn and that my daughter was in a deep and comfortable sleep. Her breathing, now hard to detect, was very slow and heavy. Feeling happier that she was finally getting a decent rest, I moved my chair closer to her side. Dwelling on what I'd just experienced, feeling ridiculously like I'd been given a holiday and had something to celebrate, I soon dozed off.

When she woke up, she was chirpy, and soon after she asked me if I would get into bed with her for a cuddle! Choked up and completely surprised, I said that I might hurt her if I did that.

'No, no, it's better now. That awful pain has gone away.'

This was brilliant news, and yet at the same time, it seemed so amazing. I didn't care about the why or even the how. I was just grateful. With the chemotherapy still dripping slowly into her veins, I climbed carefully into her bed and cuddled her, and that's how the nurse found us an hour later when she came and opened the curtains.

Our child survived. We were incredibly lucky. Devastatingly, many others passed away during her treatment time.

There were funerals. I couldn't deal with them, but my husband attended several. One particular child touched me from the start, and together we attended hers. To the side of the altar was a table displaying mementos of her life, including a framed picture of the child and an Aussie slouch hat. I dreamt her death before I even met her. I had been in her mum's body feeling her mum's pain that night. The worst pain there was. She was not our child but that made no difference. We grieved for her, for all the children who did not survive. Life can be utterly cruel.

My intuition had kept my own daughter safe. I had fought with my husband first about not settling in Canberra for fear of losing a daughter, and then about where we would live when we arrived in Brisbane. We moved to the south side of the river which we didn't know at all, having previously only lived on the north side. As it turned out, on the south side we fell into the hospital catchment area containing one of only two paediatric oncologists in Australia who also held pharmacology degrees. One lived in Brisbane, the other in Melbourne. The two places I had said were safe for us to move to without knowing why.

It was this man's ability and willingness to not only perform his normal day's work but also to spend his night in the hospital laboratory producing a patient-specific chemotherapy concoction which he created after interacting with the original protocol's designer in France and many other specialists that gave our daughter her chance at life. Given the advanced stage of her disease, the normal chemical protocol would have killed her.

Chapter 24

Revelations

O ur daughter completed her chemotherapy and her health improved. In March 2001 she returned to school. She would have several more trips to the operating theatre for lumbar punctures, but for now we were playing the waiting game, and she was well. We had seen too many deaths, too much grief and all harboured enormous pain, but our family was seeking a new normality: a way of living that allowed the different people we had become to get on with life outside of the hospital system once again.

After months of intensive parenting and trauma, having her back at school left me in lost space. The house was suddenly empty again, and in true mum fashion, I worried about how she would cope with her still low but improving energy levels. I busied myself with chores and wrestled over my own fears about how a child who was just starting to regrow her immune system, who was still very fatigued and emotionally wrung out, would get through the day. What would it bring for her? How long until she picked up an infection? All normal mothering thoughts considering what she had been through.

In addition, with the pressure off, I was ready to have my own exhausted breakdown, and there was room for that to seep into my consciousness while I worked. I had almost finished the vacuuming and had just glanced at my watch and wondered to myself if indeed my daughter was going to manage to stay at school for the whole morning when, without warning, I was plummeted back into my near-death experience, back to being eighteen....

'They' were taking me back to look at the screen. I was sobbing hysterically. I didn't want to go. I couldn't do this. It was too hard. How could they take her away from me, this precious joy that I loved so absolutely? How could they put me through the struggles that they showed were ahead of me and then take away the 'love', shatter this wonderful family, destroy me? I saw no point in going on. They manoeuvred me back to look at the screen once again. Soundless reassurance, gentle pressure, awareness. Like a child I was led and shown more while the tears continued to stream, and the knife wound that their pictures had inflicted continued to rip me apart. I felt only pain and grief. In my mind it was over. Hopeless. There was no point. I would never be happy.

The pictures continued, and through a blur of tears and murmurs of reassurance I was shown that my child would live. It would be awful. I would both feel and live through the pain, but she would be alright in the end. They went on to show me the next few years, quickly, briefly. Life was to change. My child's illness was the turning point. There would be a few years of challenge but then life would improve. I gasped in amazement as they showed my husband's future. He would change so much. Then the screen went blank.

They were talking to me wordlessly. Mind to mind. More reassurance. Choices. I didn't have to do this. I could stay. A male spoke. Serious. Stern. I had chosen this path, this challenge. I didn't have to complete it. I could repeat it later. It would be harder. Circumstances would change. Each time it would be made more difficult. They showed me my child and the outcome, mental pictures this time. I could not do it. I chose to die. There was the stream, my God holding out his hand to me. There was my foot moving towards the water. I had a flashback to what they told would happen. I couldn't go forward.

Then suddenly I had to do it! I could not walk away, give up, fail. Much as I wanted, I could not die. Somewhere inside me, in an instant, I made my choice. I promised. 'I'll do it,' I cried. Great heart wrenching sobs. 'I promise. I promise. I'll do it, I promise!'

I wanted to cross that stream so much, but it would have been so wrong. I couldn't. Then, I experienced one brief glimpse of the hospital room I had woken up in back then. One moment reliving the intensity of the physical and emotional pain of that moment and slap! With no warning I was back in the present again, twenty-four years later, standing stock still in my lounge room and hanging onto the vacuum cleaner pipe for dear life.

I was shaken, shocked. What followed was an ecstatic realisation that this was what I had really promised! I had promised to return to the life that I did not want. I had promised to come back and live through the challenges it would constantly throw at me, including, eventually, to nurse a much-loved child through a journey with cancer. I was here to learn simply by living. Through this journey I would learn about the depths of pain and love that that involved. I would learn to make an absolute commitment to someone other than myself, to put their needs before my own. In an instant the memories of being moved back to the screen after moving away in my initial distress returned; the memories of my child surviving, of not having to suffer her ultimate loss.

I realised that my child would live. She wouldn't come out of remission. I didn't have to wait another year to find out if her life would ultimately be lost despite her recent win. My child was going to live! I was doing what I had promised! I had needed to accept my abilities to be of use to her in her hour of need. I had learned what pure love was; the genuine willingness to offer up my life for hers if necessary, that readiness to sacrifice completely for her life to continue. It was my personal challenge, and I had experienced exactly that moment during her journey.

I had cried to God, whoever and whatever that was, to take me and spare her and had meant it in the depths of my soul. Did I question what God was during that moment? No. Did I need to? No. I reached out to the whole of the universe seeking help and where it came from was of no concern. Your God, my God, a God. I just needed help, and I asked for it.

As my brain processed this, I felt a sense of euphoria. I was now walking on air, over the moon, excited, happy, humbled. My child was going to live! I was grateful. I was free. I felt the chains that had burdened me for years fall away. I was used to my still young body feeling old and tired, that was simply how I lived with fibromyalgia, but what I hadn't realised was the sheer weight of the self-imposed burden I had carried for the past twenty-four years. I thought that I had lost that weight when I finally accepted my self, but this turned out to be so much more. I was utterly certain that this was exactly what I was supposed to do: live my allocated life and meet the challenges it presented. That's all any of us must do. This time I had no niggles, no untouched spaces in my mind and no other questions to be answered. For the next hour or so I walked on air.

As the initial euphoria subsided, my mind travelled its usual pathways, and I thought deeply about what had just unlocked in my head. It made sense to me now that I couldn't recall what I had promised. It wasn't special. It wasn't a thing, per se. It was indeed just to come back and live the life I had been assigned. 'Complete the mission and you get what?' I wondered. It didn't matter. My job was to keep living. To survive whatever life threw at me. To climb over the challenges and hurdles and take the learning along the way and carry it with me, hopefully to make good use of it at some point along the route. This is what I was here to do. Maybe I was paying back karma, I thought. Did I even believe in Karma? If I had remembered the promise, I could have lived avoiding the cancer challenge. I doubted that I would have risked having a child if I had recalled this potential event. I know I couldn't have. I don't have that in me.

The euphoric state was a healing in itself, but as it subsided over the next few days, my mind began to complicate things as it has always done. My child had just finished chemotherapy, and 'they' said she would live. Would she though? I really wanted to believe but the acceptance of my initial euphoria developed logical holes. My mind had shown me what I wanted the most. 'They' had shown me what I wanted the most. Why couldn't I believe them? I did initially. One hundred percent.

Logic now spoke up loud and clear. There were no guarantees. Coming out of remission happened. This was after all cancer! I bargained with myself. 'If she makes it through the first year then, then I might believe absolutely.' I was annoying myself, bringing my mood down. Any other parent would have taken the huge dose of comfort offered and run with it, but not me.

The releasing of my promise and the recognition that I had fulfilled it also brought tears over the next few weeks. A large parcel of grief, from deep inside me, surfaced slowly and was released. The trauma of my original and genuinely horrific experience, never dealt with and carried for the past twenty-four years, emerged and was gently washed away. Tears of relief followed. I cried for the young girl lying naked on a bed, stared at by passing strangers and doctors alike. I cried for the pain she went through, the lack of self-worth she'd felt realising that they'd shoved her in a cupboard. The trauma she'd suffered when punched by the night nurse right after her near-death experience. I cried for the little girl inside her who just wanted to have her dad by her side throughout the ordeal and who'd thought he wouldn't come.

After a lot more thinking about the events, a lot more processing and consideration, I recognised that I needed to believe, more than anything else, that our daughter would be alright and that my so-called logic was really an outlet for my deepest fear that she might not be. Once I'd sorted this out in my mind, I was able to better control my thought processes. At eighteen years of age they had told me in detail that I would have a child who had cancer and survived. The events had occurred exactly as they'd told me up to this point. There was no reason to live in fear of the outcome. I wouldn't.

Two years later my daughter was considered completely cured. As parents we felt we had won Lotto. We still do. I admit I felt a little foolish for ever having had any doubt that she would make it. My mind was my biggest problem.

In my mid-thirties, I was asked if I would mind having my near-death story included in another person's book. I heard myself answer strongly but politely, 'No, I'm sorry. This is my story, and it doesn't yet have an ending. When it does, I will write about it myself.'

I recall being distinctly surprised by my answer. I had wondered then what the ending would be and if indeed I would ever make the time to write it all down. It was certainly not a well thought out reply. Had I known on some level that I would reach this point? Was that a part of what I had been shown on the screen? Was it one of the things I didn't retain in my conscious mind?

Why did I return from my near-death experience to face all of this? I recall being so overwhelmed by what they showed me on that screen, but the answer is clear. I came back because of love. First and foremost, the deep love that I felt for my younger brother who had already helped me survive for as long as I had. During my near-death experience seeing his distress over my ultimate death made the option of not returning unfathomable to me.

Secondly, 'they' had shown me the family that I would one day have and all the love that was within it. In my heart my world was complete. This was my wish and my goal. This kind of love was what I craved.

Then they showed me my daughter's awful illness, and I recognised that the price of love was to face intolerable pain, so I ran away. As a teenager, already in emotional pain and physically suffering, I couldn't face more of the same let alone the loss of a much-loved child.

'They' had then convinced me to return by showing me that while I could remain with them, wherever we were, I would have to return to a different life at some point. The different lives I would have to choose between appeared far harder through my eyes. At least one included sexual abuse and another parental alcoholism and violence. I didn't want to go through childhood again, let alone live a tougher one. It would be easier to complete the remains of this life in which I was about to escape into adulthood anyway. I had the feeling of love for my younger brother, and the promise of more to come with my own husband and children. Choosing to stay was the better option.

I don't think I was expected to react the way I did to the sight of my future child getting cancer. I think I was supposed to watch the whole journey unfold. I don't think that the hurt and trauma, that focus I put on potentially losing her, was ever supposed to occur. I was supposed to have retained the part about her survival. It's likely my own life experience of losing relatives to cancer, with no survivors, accounted for my unexpected reaction. I had returned with clear memories, retaining everything up until the nurse hit me. What if this was all a plan gone wrong?

This thought led me to question whether spirit controls everything and whether it makes mistakes. Perhaps the nurse hitting me wasn't a mistake but a deliberate way to make me forget. On the other hand, maybe I was supposed to remember, and the nurse's random behaviour was the mistake in the plan? There I was, once again asking questions from every angle!

What I learned from my near-death experience and my child's cancer journey was that love really is all that matters. Your whole life centres around your sick child and family at these times. Your world is all about the love you feel for them. Life itself is given value by the love you feel for others, and the bonds that you form with them while you are here.

I learned from life that we all have abilities that science can't yet fully explain. I believe they are all a natural part of being the human animal that we are, and I would like to ask, assuming you don't have a diagnosed mental illness, that you listen to your intuition, always.

If the voices in your ear or in your head give you accurate information, please don't waste your life feeling weird, kooky, or whatever term society uses to describe those who exhibit different abilities. You are merely using skills that a certain percentage of people aren't. We all possess these abilities, every one of us. We can all stimulate and strengthen these senses and grow these pathways in our brain. All we need to do is trust that they are there, somewhere, even if they are weak or seem entirely hidden. Sadly, we live in a society that operates largely from a scientific and logical perspective, but, if you can trust that there is more to your amazing brain than we yet understand, you can develop these other senses and abilities and use them to help you live your life and to help your family and friends live safer lives. It's worth it.

Chapter 25

Dreams and 'Seeing'

I have used my abilities many times, sometimes even when they can't do any good. Before the tsunami and earthquake hit Japan in 2011 causing mass devastation, I went to walk out my front door accompanied by my children. As I opened it, I noticed that the sky was the wrong colour. To me it was an eerie deep green instead of the sky-blue usually displayed. My children looked at me strangely, telling me that the sky was a normal colour. I hesitated to go shopping and insisted that we get what we needed and come home as soon as we could. By the afternoon I could no longer hear birds and the intensity of the green in the sky had doubled. I felt danger everywhere. I wouldn't allow any of my family to leave the house. They listened and stayed put.

By the following morning the sky was back to normal for me, and I could once again hear the birds chirping. My sense of danger had disappeared. The earthquake and the following tsunami had already hit. At no point during this was my family ever in danger. We were safe and sound in Australia. It was a major disaster, and the location didn't seem to matter. It, or the energy of it, affected me.

When the World Trade Centre was hit on 9/11, a long-standing dream of mine became real. This was one where I knew I wasn't involved in any personal way, but I'd had recurring and worrying dreams that had started with two planes flying towards two towers standing side by side for several years. The towers had always been far away, and I was always at a school, standing on a veranda and looking outwards towards the horizon when the first plane appeared. The dreams had started in my twenties, and I'd thought that perhaps they indicated a coming war. The first time, I was alone watching a plane appear from my right and fly towards a very distant tower. In the second one, several years later, I was calling my husband, telling him to come as I felt danger from a plane heading towards the city towers. Same visuals: two towers, one plane. Always the sense of danger.

The next one had me collecting our children ostensibly from their classrooms and keeping them close to me, and my husband rushing from work to be with us. We stood together as planes approached the tall buildings. By this time I was certain that it meant a war was going to happen, and buildings were going to be bombed. I was also certain that it wasn't in Australia but in America. My fears intensified with the final dream which occurred approximately fourteen months before 9/11; we once again stood together, but this time we watched huge volumes of smoke rise from one of the towers. I never dreamed the dream again. The next time I saw my dream, it was on the news. It was real. I went into shock. I have never had the dream since.

Premonitions are certainly not all awful. They don't have terrible outcomes all the time. Sometimes they are much closer to home and highly useful. I call the following story my 'third time lucky' event.

When she was attending university one of our daughters had a good friend who sometimes slept over at our home. She was interested in my psychic abilities, and we spent several hours discussing them over the course of the friendship. The girls eventually went their own way, taking different courses and only occasionally catching up, so I hadn't seen this young lady for quite some time when I woke up one morning and just knew that I had to see her. It was such an unusual thought, and I had no reason to feel that way, so I brushed it to one side and got on with my day.

By the following morning, the need to see her had trebled. Over breakfast I asked my daughter if she'd seen her lately and was told that she hadn't and that she was hard to catch up with as they were both busy. I let it slide.

Two days later the feeling was overwhelming, so I bluntly told my daughter that I needed to see her friend ASAP and asked her to organise a coffee catch up urgently. She looked at me strangely, obviously wondering why her friend was suddenly so important to me, and asked me why? I told her that I really didn't know, but it was important.

The following day she told me that they'd been in touch but hadn't made a date to catch up. I went cold. I said to her that if she couldn't get us together then to please give me her number to arrange a meeting myself. Now, I never asked her for friends' numbers. They were not my friends, and I wouldn't overstep boundaries. My daughter was obviously shocked by this and my forthright talk. I was going to catch up with her friend come hell or high water and it had to be soon. My instructions to her were, 'Make it happen.' Unwillingly, she set a date. It wasn't convenient for her, and it wasn't convenient for her friend, but 'Mum said she needs to speak with you!' holds a bit of a punch when Mum is a psychic. I still didn't know what I wanted to talk to the girl about, which made my request seem much stranger.

The following day I woke up from dreams about a car accident on the motorway. There were either three or four women in the car, something fell from under the bonnet and the car flipped at speed. There were severe injuries and at least one death. I never saw the driver, but I did recall that someone in the vehicle was wearing a dark suit of the type that one would wear only for work. I deduced that the ladies were on their way to work based on that and the colour of the light in the dream. I did not associate it with my daughter's friend. It was just another awful dream. By this stage of my life I was able to block out much of the gore of accidents and only retained glimpses that I needed to interpret.

Mid-morning, we headed to the café where I was to meet my daughter's friend. I had the most awful stomach-ache, and my head felt woozy and giddy. I needed to be home in bed, but I knew that this was something I had to get through. I still didn't know why. I didn't know what I was there for. I didn't know what I was going to say. I'd brought my tarot cards. They were the only thing I could think of which might be useful. My only driver was intuition. I had to see this girl. I had to talk with her. I could only trust that the words I needed to tell her would appear. This was one of those times when a part of my mind questioned my sanity, but I have learned to override that logical voice and let intuition win out.

We were drinking our coffee, and the friend was talking about a strange 'mentor' that she was now working for when I felt the need to pull out my cards and read for her. Using the mentor situation as a segue, I pulled them out and for the next ten minutes or so we discussed the cards, and she asked questions about the situation.

I was starting to wonder what I was doing when my energy shifted. There was the fizzle down my spine; I was about to deliver the information I needed to give her even though I didn't know what I was about to say. I interrupted her chatter and heard myself telling her about her car. I know very little about cars. I'm the girl who was shown how to top up her oil and water and change a tyre by her father, but apart from topping up with petrol, never learnt another thing about them.

I heard myself telling the young lady that she was to drive her car to her home that night, and she was then allowed to drive it to the nearest garage the following day, but she must not under any circumstances drive it anywhere else at all, not even to the corner shop. It needed a mechanical inspection urgently. Worried by my words, she asked if she would be safe driving home, and I immediately said yes.

She told me part of her journey included a motorway. I sat and thought hard about it, but again the answer was a definite yes. When she asked what was wrong with it, I saw a large object on the right-hand side under the bonnet and four bracket-like pieces. Only one of these brackets had what I would describe as a pin or a screw in it, and it was rusting through.

I explained what I saw. I gave her strict instructions to go to the mechanic at the garage and ask him to check the right-hand side under the bonnet and look for four broken and rusted parts that were causing a rattle. She said that there was no rattle. I told her I didn't care, but he would take her seriously if she said that. I didn't know what car she had, so I didn't know what was where under the bonnet, but I said that it seemed to have something to do with the engine. I could be wrong, but it was dangerous. I made her promise that she wouldn't drive the car other than to go straight home. I don't know why I knew she was safe to go home, as it was quite a drive, but I was certain that she was.

Bless her, she drove her car straight home and booked the car into the local garage around the corner from her to be looked at the following morning. Because he'd known her for years, the mechanic said he'd look at it for her that day and wouldn't make her wait longer.

Mid-afternoon she got a call to say that her car was undriveable. Three of the four pins that held the engine in place were missing and the remaining pin was almost completely rusted through. Her engine could have dropped out of the car at any moment. She rang me in shock. I felt sick and relieved at the same time. My dream of the women in the car who were driving down the motorway when something fell out from underneath came straight to mind. She had listened!

She's probably not the only person who has taken my advice, but she was the third life I'd knowingly tried to save, and the only one that I knew who had listened. I cried with relief.

About two years ago as I write this, I dreamt about a young male who committed suicide by throwing himself in front of a train. This man had no intention of dying. Right up until that very last second when his brain misfired and he jumped, he was contemplating life not death. I won't share this story in any detail because it's not mine to tell, but the way I heard about his life demonstrates the complexity of my own and how the world works its mysteries around and through me.

I awoke from a horrific dream in which I watched a young man speak to his female housemate who was until recently his girlfriend. I watched him, highly distressed, leave the house carrying a backpack/bag over one shoulder and attempting to ride a pushbike to the train station as he usually did. Finding himself too distressed by his recent conversation with her to ride, he got off the bike and hid it under a bush, concealing it from the road and intending to collect it that evening on his way home from work. He continued towards the station becoming more distressed over her recent conversation with him and ended up sitting on a bench in a green space or small park for some time. He then proceeded to the platform recognising that he would be late for work if he didn't hurry up. He was still upset, dragging his feet but intentionally on his way to work. He didn't make it. I will leave the story there other than to say that I woke up with tears streaming down my face and remained shaken for the rest of the day.

Fast forward two years. I signed up for a short book writing course run from the USA. I put my name down to be paired up with a writing buddy in the same country I lived in, Australia. The idea was to help each other stay on track with writing our individual books, and obviously being in the same time zone would help. The following week we met up via Zoom as we lived in different states. We chatted about our intended manuscripts which both of us had already started writing. My writing buddy turned out to be the mum of the young man whose death I'd previously dreamt of. At that point, it was approximately eighteen months since he'd passed away. I was able to fill her in on some of the details of his last moments. I had seen a baby stroller. I had seen the green space. I talked of the bench. She had not yet found the strength to visit the site of his death, perhaps she never would, but his brother had recently visited, and he confirmed that there was a green space with a bench by the railway station. When he went to stand where his brother would have last stood, jammed in the fence on the other side of the tracks was a broken baby stroller. The world is a very complex place.

While most of the stories included in this book are from the first half of my life, there have of course been many others. I have dreamed of murders and suicides and disasters. I have dreamed important details alongside the useless information that forms part of an everyday life. What use is it to foresee that you are going to forget to buy bread for lunch the next day if, no matter how many reminders you give yourself, you still come home without that loaf of bread?

I have learned that I can only offer information. I am not the one responsible for what the recipient does with it. We are all entirely responsible for our own choices. This was a very hard lesson for me to learn. It took a while. I have always wanted to fix things, prevent people from getting hurt, divert them from pain. I had to learn that that was not my job, not my responsibility. My job is just to deliver the information that comes, and I have little enough control over even that.

Chapter 26

If This Is You

I hope that one day all of us will acknowledge and own the wonderful sense of Intuition that we all have but which as a society we tend to dismiss. It is designed to keep us safe, is perhaps one of our most primitive instincts to save us from danger. It is not odd or unusual to have these feelings. At some point every single one of us has experienced an event that we found unusual or unexpected. Try not to dismiss your feelings regarding it. Don't call yourself weird or kooky. Stop. Listen. Learn. This is a basic instinct. It's helping you. Give it the space in your mind to do just that.

You MAY NOT BE a visual person like me; you may be more an auditory person and hear messages, or you may smell or sense danger. Pay attention to it. Don't walk through life dumbed down and blind to the skills that you were born with. Give them the space to grow. You won't be sorry. At no point do you have to develop them as widely as I developed mine. Today it is quite easy to learn how to use these skills, how to develop them from the start, and of course how to control them. The information is readily accessible. Use it.

If I was to start this journey all over again, I would still dive in as deeply as I did despite all the sadness, horror and fears that I have encountered, but I don't advise it for others. In my quest for knowledge and understanding, I pushed myself to my limits, and there is no need to go that far. Just dabble, splash around in the edges of the pool. Learn how to keep yourself and your family safe. Be excited by your skills. That is enough. That is useful.

As I drift into my retirement years, I am, in my mind, and probably always will be, still just that ordinary little girl from Wales who felt different and knew nothing about psychic or spiritual abilities, who accidentally grew up retaining her spiritual links, battling her own mind as she lived her life on the cusp, one foot in this world and one in another. I met my own idea of God, and, in order to return and enjoy what life had to offer, I made him a promise, a promise that I had no choice but to fulfil. A promise I complicated. I just had to live.

Along the way I discovered that I had more depth of character, more love, more courage and more failings than I ever would have believed. I learned about my weaknesses and my faults and came to own them. I became the teacher of my early ambitions and the healer I was told I would be. Finally, I have found acceptance of who and what I am. In our society I will always be considered strange. I'm good with that now. I'm not strange to me. I'm just myself. I'm all I know, and that's all that matters.

No doubt life will continue to challenge me. It's meant to. We are, I believe, here to learn. For now, I find myself remarkably at peace. I hope that if you too are struggling with your journey that one day you can say the same. When we all lived in villages, there was always someone like me that the villagers sought out for help and hope; if not in their own village, then in the next one over. These skills have been with us for thousands of years. Don't reject them just because today there's little respect for them. It's not meant to be an easy journey, but you have been born with all the tools you need to manoeuvre your way through it. Don't ignore them. Don't forget them. If you have them, then use them. Learn to trust your inner voice and know that with it, anything is possible.

End Note

If you enjoyed this book, please consider leaving a review online at the retailer where you bought it or on review sites like GoodReads.

You can correspond with Lynne on Facebook: https://www.facebook.com/Lynne65writes/